A

CIVIL WAR

ROUND TABLE

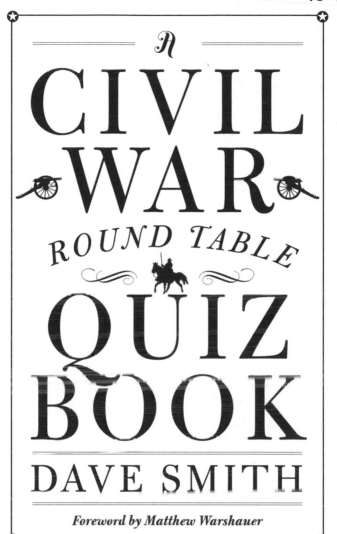

QUIZ BOOK

DAVE SMITH

Foreword by Matthew Warshauer

Potomac Books
Washington, D.C.

Potomac Books is an imprint of the University of Nebraska Press

Library of Congress Cataloging-in-Publication Data
Smith, Dave, 1932–
  A Civil War Round Table quiz book / Dave Smith.
    pages cm.
  ISBN 978-1-61234-580-2 (pbk. : alk. paper)
  ISBN 978-1-61234-581-9 (electronic)
  1. United States—History—Civil War, 1861–1865—Miscellanea. I. Title.
  E468.S635 2013
  973.7—dc23

          2013008125

Printed in the United States of America on acid-free paper that meets the American National Standards Institute Z39-48 Standard.

Potomac Books
22841 Quicksilver Drive
Dulles, Virginia 20166

First Edition

10 9 8 7 6 5 4 3 2 1

For Frank Smith of the Fifth Maine Infantry, my grandfather,
and for Sgt. Jacob Henry Garrigus of the
Eighth Connecticut Infantry, my great-grandfather,
who lived it.

For Albert and Isabel Garrigus Smith, my parents,
who inspired my love of history.

For Joan, my wife and best friend, who has endured the
countless museums, lectures, forts, and battlefields,
yet remains my greatest fan.

For Michael and Susan, my children, who may have learned
more history than they really wanted.

For Adrian, Emily, Heather, Sara, Avery, Alyssa, and Andy,
my grandchildren,
who have been a great inspiration to me
and who all did well in history.

"No great work is ever done alone."

CONTENTS

CONTENTS

CONTENTS

FOREWORD

The Civil War remains a part of America's consciousness. Its enormity demands it. Never before, or since, has the nation experienced bloodletting on such a massive scale. With some 620,000 dead and many more wounded, both the North and South reeled from the war's duration and intensity. One merely needs to drive through towns in virtually any part of what then made up the United States to find Civil War monuments erected to those who fought. These memorials were created to make sense of the loss and to instill lasting lessons for future generations.

As with the monuments that dot the landscape, books on the Civil War fill library shelves. One can find every conceivable topic from the politics of secession and slavery to Abraham Lincoln to war tactics and many more. The diversity reveals the enormity of the subject and, very important, the continual quest to know more about this war that has so captivated people from all walks of life.

Academic historians are most thoroughly invested in this mass of publishing, to the extent that historian David Herbert Donald once remarked, "There must be more historians of the Civil War than there were generals fighting in it, and of the two groups, the historians are the more belligerent." But scholars by no means represent the majority of those Americans who are devoted to the subject. For many decades enthusiasts and buffs have taken part in Civil War Round Tables and in doing so explored the war from a vast array of perspectives. These are the people, I often joke, who can recite the name of every colonel's horse. They also help to maintain the history and legacy of the war. They are the ones who visit the battlefields and museums each year, who donate to the battlefield preservation funds, and who often join the reenactors who faithfully don the uniforms of another age so that our present generation can gain a better understanding of the horrific war that challenged the nation. I never cease to be amazed at the depth of understanding and consideration that these often self-taught "buffs" bring to the table. If the professional historians are the generals of the struggle, these private scholars are the foot soldiers.

It is with such truths in mind that I heartily recommend Dave Smith's wonderful book, *A Civil War Round Table Quiz Book*. Further, I offer a challenge to academic historians: take the quizzes and see how you do! The extent and range of Dave's knowledge will amaze and befuddle even the most stalwart Civil War aficionado. In this sense, the book is a wonderful learning tool. Answering the questions requires research in a broad variety of subjects and will inevitably lead to a deeper knowledge and understanding of the war. The best part is that it's fun. My forage cap is off to Dave for his commitment and interest in creating a book that will surely be a hit.

Matthew Warshauer, PhD
Professor of History,
Southern Connecticut State University
Cochair, Connecticut Civil War Commemoration Commission
Author, *Connecticut in the American Civil War*

PREFACE

Shortly after joining the Hartford Civil War Round Table I began to look for ways that I might help the organization. It had an established leadership, a long history of presenting quality programs, and a fairly stable membership, a number of whom were very knowledgeable. It seemed to me that the best way to help was to find a way to increase the sophistication and interest of all the members. For most of us, the more we learn about the exciting period, the better we understand it and the greater our fascination.

The Civil War is a huge subject. To gain a full understanding of it, one must have a thorough grounding in U.S. history from the nation's founding to the outbreak of the war and beyond through Reconstruction. The war was fought on land and sea and even in waters thousands of miles away. It was a political and diplomatic war. Further, it influenced literature and news reporting and sparked rapid gains in technology. In one way or another, the war probably touched virtually every home in America. In a nation of 31.5 million people, it took the lives of an estimated 618,000, but that number does not include civilian deaths. Nor does it address the many soldiers who survived as cripples or in broken health or the displacements and property destruction.

With a subject so broad and deep, the average Civil War Round Table member can't even scratch the surface by attending eight or nine lectures a year and, perhaps, reading a half dozen books on the topic a year. What tool could we use to expand and broaden the knowledge of all members to include the lesser-known but nonetheless important aspects of the conflict?

I approached Round Table president Robert Dow Wolff and offered to produce a monthly quiz. The quiz would fit on one side of one sheet of paper and go out with the meeting bulletin. Answers would be discussed at the next meeting. Mr. Wolff pondered the idea and decided to give it a try. Almost immediately, it became a popular feature of the meetings. It also served the purpose of settling the group down and focusing members before the featured talk.

Topics have run a broad range. Quiz 1 concerned nicknames and was titled "Everyone knows Stonewall, but how about Old Blinky?" Old Blinky, by the way, was Union Gen. William H. French. The men noticed his habit of blinking rapidly when he spoke. Of course, that moniker was one of those behind-the-back nicknames.

I've devoted less attention to the best-known events and figures of the war. Most students, even casual students of the war, already know something of Lee, Longstreet, Grant, and Sherman. They have read of or visited Gettysburg, Antietam, Fredericksburg, and Chancellorsville. Lincoln and Jeff Davis are also familiar topics. Instead, I have tried to introduce the Round Table members to actions at such places as Wilson's Creek, Port Royal, Stones River, Corinth, Island Number 10, and the Salisbury Prison. We have explored such topics as pontoon bridges, the use of railroads, wagon trains, and field artillery. We looked at such lesser-known figures as Gideon Pillow, Capt. Tom Custer, Dr. Hunter McGuire, Stephen Dodson Ramseur, Jedediah Hotchkiss, and Benjamin Grierson.

Despite the thousands of books written on the war, many important aspects have been largely ignored or neglected. The war in Virginia, Maryland, and Pennsylvania where the South enjoyed its greatest successes continues to receive disproportional attention. Meanwhile, the war in the West and the navy's role in the blockade and river wars, where, arguably, the war was won, are much lesser known. We attempted to expose our members to more of the neglected war.

As we used the tool we came to understand that most of these quizzes were not so much a test of knowledge but new doors to open with more exciting events and interesting people behind them. The answers are more important than the questions because they allow us to bring in additional interesting facts and stories. Initially, those who had the answers at meetings were a small group of the most knowledgeable members. In time, answers began to come from others, showing us that they were doing some research in preparation for the meeting. Many of the younger members were using Internet sources.

Numerous times, friends and associates urged me to put the quizzes into book form and publish them. Finally, in early 2011 after about a hundred quizzes had been produced, I wrote a proposal and submitted it to Potomac Books. I am thankful that the publisher agreed with my friends. I can only hope that each of you reading the book will find it a useful and fascinating trip though the war that finally made us "one nation, indivisible."

SECTION I

AN END TO COMPROMISE

I n the early days of the republic, it seemed that slavery might fade away on its own and not be a divisive issue. That was not to be. After Yankee Eli Whitney invented the cotton gin, cotton boomed and, with it, slavery. The Missouri Compromise gave hope of a permanent resolution, but new issues surfaced and produced new tensions. The United States annexed Texas, and that action led directly to a war with Mexico. The huge new territory that the United States acquired led to greater battles over the extension of slavery. The Compromise of 1850 pleased no one. In the decade that followed, the Southern states spun toward secession and the nation toward sectional war.

The coming fury would center on the lawyer and politician who lived in this house in Springfield, Illinois. Abraham Lincoln, a state legislator and one-term Whig congressman, would be propelled to the national spotlight by his famed senatorial campaign debates with Stephen A. Douglas. His election to the presidency was the spark that ignited secession and led to war. *Photo by the author*

John Brown pledged to dedicate his life to the eradication of slavery. Those efforts climaxed in this fire engine house on the grounds of the U.S. Armory at Harpers Ferry, Virginia (now West Virginia). His attempt to seize the facility and spark a slave revolt and exodus was a dismal failure. However, while the battle ended in Brown's capture, his bold revolutionary act and his personal martyrdom were an important part of the chain of events that would bring freedom for the nation's nearly four million slaves. *Photo by the author*

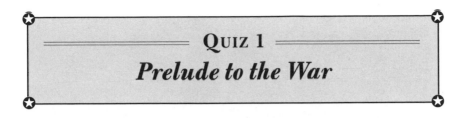

QUIZ 1
Prelude to the War

The American Civil War didn't happen simply because Abraham Lincoln was elected president. Many events over many years led the South to secession and the North to armed resistance. Let's see if you know the details of some of them.

1. When did the first slaves land in the colonies? (A) 1619. (B) 1634. (C) 1687. (D) 1701.
2. When Missouri was admitted to the Union as a slave state, what state was admitted as a free state?
3. The greatest voice of abolitionism was that of William Lloyd Garrison. What was the name of his newspaper?
4. When the Charleston, South Carolina, postmaster found abolitionist material in the mail in 1836, what did he do?
5. Also in 1836, the South demanded a gag rule that would prohibit Congress from receiving petitions on or discussing what aspect of slavery?
6. What did David Wilmot of Pennsylvania demand in his famous "proviso"?
7. What former president was the presidential candidate on the Free Soil ticket in 1848?
8. By what margin was Dred Scott's case defeated in the Supreme Court?
9. Why didn't anyone stop Preston "Bully" Brooks in his sneak attack on Charles Sumner?
10. What weapon did John Brown have in quantity and planned to arm the slaves with for their rebellion?

QUIZ 2
Bleeding Kansas

For the rest of the country, the Civil War began in 1861 and ended in 1865, but not in Kansas and Missouri. Unrest there started much sooner and didn't end with the Surrender at Appomattox. Let's see what you know of that bloody border war.

1. What piece of congressional legislation was the spark that ignited the border war in Kansas?
2. The legislation was based on a concept called popular sovereignty. What prominent national politician embraced the concept and was considered the father of the bill?
3. In what year did Kansas begin to bleed?
4. Who coined the term "Bleeding Kansas"?
5. What did the "Border Ruffians" do to upset the balance of power?
6. What nickname did Connecticut native John Brown receive for leading antislavery forces in Kansas?
7. Eastern antislavery societies shipped many "Beecher Bibles" to the Free Soilers in Kansas. What were they and for whom were they named?
8. This former Indiana congressman voted for the bill that sparked the border war, but he moved to Kansas and became a leader of the antislavery forces. He later was elected to the Senate from Kansas. Who was he?
9. The pro-slavery people in Kansas adopted a pro-slavery constitution, which President James Buchanan tried to force on Congress. The pro-slavery constitution was named for the town where it was enacted. Name the town.
10. A Mexican war hero who had been San Francisco's first mayor was named territorial governor of Kansas. He resigned when the pro-slavery forces made their power play. He was?

QUIZ 3
Scott and Brown

In the 1850s, a slave seeking his freedom and a rabid abolitionist pledging to end slavery, even by violent methods, became symbols of a nation on a sectional collision course. Dred Scott's case reached the Supreme Court, and its decision would cause outrage in the North. John Brown's attempt to launch a slave rebellion set Southern passions ablaze. Let's look at these two cases.

1. An army surgeon took Scott, his slave, with him to two new posts. Where did they go?
2. Who was Scott's lawyer?
3. Before the decision came down, an important national figure improperly discussed it with two or more Supreme Court justices. Who was the national figure?
4. How did the court line up on the case?
5. What major piece of legislation was overturned in the *Dred Scott* decision?
6. The case would have been less controversial if the court had ruled more narrowly on one initial issue. What issue was that?
7. For a time John Brown was engaged in the family business. What was it?
8. He studied to become a clergyman but was forced to abandon that goal. Why?
9. After his first wife died, Brown married for a second time. How many children did he father from the two marriages?
10. Brown became notorious for an incident on Pottawatomie Creek in Kansas. What happened there?

11. Brown enlisted the aid of the "Secret Six" in launching his Harper's Ferry attack, but another famous abolitionist withdrew his support and distanced himself from the events. Name him.

12. When a supporter talked of freeing Brown, what was his response?

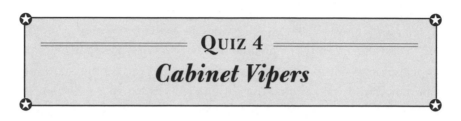

QUIZ 4
Cabinet Vipers

On their way to Lincoln's inauguration, James Buchanan told the president-elect that, if he was half as happy to become president as Buchanan was to leave the office, then he must be the happiest man ever to take the job. Buchanan's administration was embattled, both from without and within. Three Southern cabinet members tried to manipulate Buchanan into recognizing secession.

1. Buchanan and one member of his cabinet were considered "doughfaces." What does the term mean?

2. A Connecticut politician in the Buchanan cabinet was a doughface. Name him.

3. One Southerner, the leader of the secessionists in the cabinet, tried to push Buchanan into pro-secession policies. He later left the cabinet under indictment for conspiracy and fraud. Who was he?

4. Another cabinet member from the South would later try to burn down New York City. He was?

5. One of the Northern cabinet members was called General. Name him.

6. A Northern cabinet member would later be severely criticized for having a woman hanged. He was?

7. Buchanan brought a talented and high-strung lawyer into the cabinet, and he immediately began reporting everything back to the Republicans. Name him.

8. This Southern cabinet member became the first presiding officer of the Confederacy. He was?

9. He wrote the opinion for Buchanan that while the slave states lacked the power to secede, the North had no authority to stop them by force. Name him.

10. Who was the veteran soldier and politician brought in to fill an important post in the closing days of the administration?

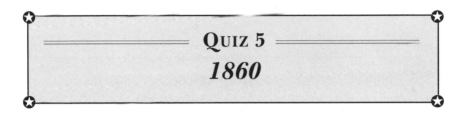

QUIZ 5
1860

The United States was out of compromises. John Brown's body had hardly begun moldering in his grave. Abraham Lincoln was nominated and elected, and South Carolina made good on its threat to secede. Kentucky senator John Crittenden tried desperately to find neutral ground but failed. Meanwhile, other important events occurred in that turbulent year. Let's look at some of them.

1. An innovative method was designed to deliver the mail. What was it?

2. Americans were optimistic as a popular European reformer tried to establish a unified democratic government in his homeland. His name was?

3. Publishing in the United States received a huge boost with the introduction of a new and popular series. It was?

4. The Prince of Wales visited the White House and lured the president's niece into an adventure. Where did they go?

5. A songwriter from Pittsburgh wrote the last of his "plantation songs." Name it.

6. The 1860 census was completed. What was the population of the United States, and how many people were slaves?

7. A book published in England the previous year set off a public debate between two prominent Harvard professors. What was the book?

8. Two ships collided on Lake Michigan with many lives lost. Name the ships.

9. A prominent Asian nation established its first foreign embassy in Washington. Name it.

10. A young woman broke the gender barrier when she was admitted as a divinity student at St. Lawrence University in New York. Name her.

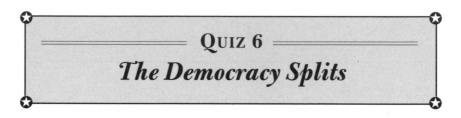

Quiz 6
The Democracy Splits

The nation would be torn asunder in 1861, but first the nation's only national political party, the Democrats—commonly called The Democracy—had to be split. Southern disunionists achieved their objective at the 1860 national convention. That split led directly to the election of Republican Abraham Lincoln, to secession, and to Civil War.

1. Stephen A. Douglas was the frontrunner for the Democrats' 1860 nomination, but he was unacceptable to many Southerners because of a doctrine he expressed during his Senate debates with Lincoln. What was that doctrine?

2. An Alabama delegate serving on the platform committee precipitated a crisis by demanding a promise for the protection of slavery in the territories. He was?

3. What two states bolted from the convention when delegates chose the "Northern" platform?

4. What Yankee voted fifty-seven times for Jefferson Davis and later walked out with the Southerners?

5. Where did the dissident delegations go?

8

6. What ruling by the chair caused a fifty-seven-ballot gridlock?

7. In Baltimore, a credentials fight led to yet another walkout. Where did they go?

8. Senator Douglas finally received the nomination. What rule had to be broken to achieve it?

9. The Southerners called their convention the true one. Who did they nominate?

10. Why did the Southerners stop off in Richmond before going home?

QUIZ 7
Spinning toward Secession

The party conventions and presidential election of 1860 spawned a series of events that would rapidly move the country toward disunion and civil war. Test your knowledge of the people, places, and events that immediately preceded the nation's second revolution.

1. The Democratic National Convention would fail when the Southern delegates walked out because Northern delegates would not give in to their demand for a strongly pro-slavery platform. In what city did it meet?

2. The Republicans met up the road in Chicago, but in the spirit of the times, Lincoln remained in Springfield and let others handle his candidacy. Who led that effort on his behalf?

3. Chicago built a huge building for the convention. Was it called (A) the Corn Palace, (B) the Illinois Pavilion, (C) the Wigwam, or (D) the Lincoln Dome?

4. Who was Lincoln's primary rival for the nomination?

5. Lincoln's nomination was assured when this "favorite son" shifted his delegates to Lincoln. He was?

6. After the failure of the first national convention, Northern Democrats and Southern Democrats met separately and named sectional tickets headed by Stephen Douglas and John Cabell Breckenridge. In what city or cities did they meet?

7. In an attempt to find a compromise ticket to defeat Lincoln, the border states nominated John Bell as a fourth candidate. Under what party label did he run?

8. Match the vice-presidential candidates with the presidential candidates. For president: Lincoln, Douglas, Breckenridge, and Bell. For vice president: Edward Everett, Hannibal Hamlin, Herschel Johnson, and Joseph Lane.

9. True or false: Abraham Lincoln received more electoral votes than did the other three candidates combined.

10. About what percent of the popular vote did Lincoln receive?

11. One of the losing candidates finished second in the popular vote but received the fewest electoral votes. He was?

12. A pro-Lincoln marching society called the Wide Awakes originated in what Northern city?

13. When the electoral votes were cast and counted, who had the responsibility of declaring Abraham Lincoln the president-elect?

QUIZ 8
Mr. Lincoln of Springfield

Abraham Lincoln arrived in Springfield, Illinois, as an ambitious young man with little formal education, no money, and seemingly little prospect of greatness. He left twenty-four years later as president-elect of the United States and headed for immortality. Let's look at how his Springfield years changed and shaped him.

1. Who was Lincoln's first law partner?

2. Lincoln was first elected to the legislature from New Salem. Where did the Illinois legislature meet then?

3. Lincoln met Mary Todd of Kentucky when she came to Springfield to stay with her sister. What was the name of her sister's husband?

4. Lincoln had a previous relationship with another local woman and proposed marriage, but she turned him down. Who was she?

5. While out riding the judicial circuit, Lincoln frequently shared a bed with the judge who was something of a mentor to him. Name the judge.

6. After his single term in Congress, Lincoln was offered the governorship of a territory. Which one?

7. Lincoln almost fought a duel with a local politician who later became a Civil War general. Name him.

8. When Lincoln married Mary Todd, they moved into a place of lodging where their son Robert was born. What was its name?

9. Everyone knows about the Lincoln-Douglas debates, but earlier Lincoln had lost out on a Senate seat to another Democrat. Who was he?

10. Lincoln's last law partner was a fellow Whig who wrote nasty things about Mary after Abraham's death. Name him.

11. In 1856, Lincoln came close to being nominated for an important office. What was it?

12. In his most famous criminal case, what did Lincoln put into evidence to prove his client's innocence?

ANSWERS

1. Prelude to the War

1. **(A) The first slaves landed at Jamestown, Virginia, in 1619.** They
    probably came off a Dutch ship. For those with Mayflower roots,
    please note: your African American neighbors' ancestors may have
    arrived here slightly earlier than yours did. Slavery was still legal in
    England then, and it seemed a perfect solution to fulfilling the
    great need for workers to plant and harvest crops and maximize the
    value of the new colony. In some Spanish colonies, native "Indian"
    populations were enslaved, but they tended to die off quickly under
    the harsh conditions. By contrast, African slaves in British North
    America tended to multiply.

2. **Maine was admitted with Missouri in 1820.** It was formerly a part
    of Massachusetts and admitted as a free state. That compromise
    preserved the balance between slave and free states and kept the
    Senate evenly divided, but larger populations in free states meant
    growing Northern power in the House of Representatives. The
    Missouri Compromise also established a geographic northern
    boundary for slavery that kept the lid on sectional differences until
    the question of land taken from Mexico surfaced in the late 1840s.

3. **The newspaper's name was *The Liberator*.** Published in Boston,
    Garrison's paper was not universally popular in Massachusetts,
    where many saw no problem with slavery and some saw Garrison as
    a troublemaker. Despite confronting mobs and death threats, he
    held his ground and eventually convinced many that he was right.

4. **The Charleston postmaster impounded the abolitionist materials.**
    Then he asked his boss, Postmaster General Amos Kendall, what he
    should do. While he was waiting, a mob of slave owners broke into
    the office and burned the offending materials. The postmaster was
    told that, in the future, he should hold such literature and give it to
    anyone who asked for it. He should then record the requester's
    name and make it public as someone advocating slave rebellion.

5. **The gag rule was applied to slavery in the District of Columbia.**
   The initial issue of the gag rule covered debate over slavery in the
   District of Columbia, but it eventually included debate over slavery
   in the new territories. As both the Democrats and the Whigs
   belonged to national parties, they wished to suppress the slavery
   debate because it might result in the parties' splitting. When the
   Whig Party died after the 1852 elections, many Northern Whigs
   joined the new Republican Party, which was opposed to any
   expansion of slavery.

6. **Wilmot demanded that slavery be barred from the territory taken
   from Mexico.** He attached a rider to an appropriations bill stating
   that no territory taken from Mexico in the war then being waged
   could ever become a slave state. Mexico had abolished slavery, so
   territory taken from Mexico would already be free territory. The
   South, however, demanded its share of the new lands. This conflict
   created a split in the Democratic Party as some Northern
   Democrats became Free Soilers.

7. **Martin Van Buren headed the Free Soil Ticket.** He failed to
   capture a single electoral vote, but he took enough Northern
   Democrats' votes—291,263—to tip the 1848 election from Democrat
   Lewis Cass to Whig Zachary Taylor.

8. **The vote stood 7–2 against Dred Scott.** He gained his freedom
   anyway when a family member bought him and freed him.
   However, the strong pro-Southern decision convinced many in the
   North that there would be no compromising with the
   "slaveocracy." Chief Justice Roger B. Taney (pronounced TAW-nee)
   went well beyond the basic issue in the case when he wrote that
   Negroes were an inferior race, that they were not and could never
   be citizens, that the Missouri Compromise was unconstitutional,
   and that slave property could be taken anywhere legally.

9. **Bully Brooks had armed men backing him when he attacked
   Sumner.** A delegation of fellow Southern representatives
   accompanied Preston Brooks to the Senate chamber. Lawrence
   Keitt of South Carolina, who later served as a Confederate colonel

and was killed at Cold Harbor, carried a pistol and prevented anyone from coming to Sumner's aid. And you thought politics are rough and tumble now!

10. **John Brown had a large supply of pikes.** He reasoned slaves could use them with little or no training. A pike is a sharp spear point mounted on a long pole. Interestingly, the ones he had were manufactured in Connecticut.

2. Bleeding Kansas

1. **The Kansas-Nebraska Act of 1854 ignited Bleeding Kansas.** This law, which established the two territories, nullified the Missouri Compromise and allowed the residents of the territories to decide the issue of slavery.

2. **Stephen A. Douglas was father of the plan.** The Vermont-born Douglas was a senator from Illinois and saw popular sovereignty as a way to avoid a confrontation with the South and save the Democratic Party and the Union. He was wrong.

3. **Kansas hostilities began in 1854.** As soon as the Kansas-Nebraska Act was adopted, pro-slavery and Free Soil organizations began pumping in settlers and arms. Armed conflict was the inevitable result.

4. **Horace Greeley coined the term.** The owner and editor of the *New York Tribune* was strongly against slavery, and his influence went far beyond New York City. With newspapers reporting the ugly details, violence in Kansas alarmed many in the North.

5. **Border Ruffians illegally voted in Kansas.** They were men from the Missouri black belt who rode into Kansas by the hundreds on Election Day to vote for pro-slavery candidates. Kansas had but fifteen hundred registered voters, but six thousand votes were cast. In one town with twenty registered voters, six hundred votes were cast. This process was repeated later during the territorial legislature's elections and put the power into the hands of the pro-slavery faction.

6. **John Brown became known as Osawatomie Brown.** Unlike some Free Soil settlers, Brown was determined to fight against the pro-slavery forces. He led like-minded men in the Battle of Black Jack and at Osawatomie and was a hero in the eyes of the abolitionists. However, his cold-blooded murder of five pro-slavery men at Pottawatomie Creek, Kansas, marked him as a fanatic and a dangerous man.

7. **Beecher Bibles were Sharps rifles.** Antislavery societies in the East shipped cases marked "bibles" to Kansas. Often they contained Sharps rifles. They were named for the Reverend Henry Ward Beecher of Brooklyn, New York, brother of writer Harriet Beecher Stowe.

8. **James "Jim" Lane.** A redhead, he led the Jayhawker forces against the pro-slavery Border Ruffians and served the territory and later the new state of Kansas in the Senate. After one unsuccessful suicide attempt, he killed himself in July 1866.

9. **The Kansas Constitution was adopted in Lecompton.** It was President Buchanan's support of the proposed Lecompton Constitution, despite the fact that a majority of Kansans opposed it, that made Stephen Douglas break with Buchanan.

10. **The territorial governor was John White Geary.** He was named territorial governor of Kansas and tried to walk an impartial line between pro- and antislavery elements. He resigned when the administration backed the pro-slavery elements and their Lecompton Constitution. Later he was a Civil War general and governor of Pennsylvania, where he was a champion of the forty-hour work week, mine safety, and Negro suffrage.

3. Scott and Brown

1. **Scott was taken to Fort Armstrong and Fort Snelling.** Armstrong was in the state of Illinois and Snelling in modern Minnesota, then a part of the Wisconsin Territory. Both locations were free territory under provisions of the Northwest Ordinance and the Missouri

Compromise. Because slavery was illegal there, Scott later argued that he should be a free man based on his residency there.

2. **Scott's lawyer was Montgomery Blair.** He was the son of the powerful Francis Preston Blair and a West Point graduate. During the Civil War he would serve as the postmaster general in Lincoln's cabinet. Brother Francis, formerly a congressman from Missouri, would become a major general and command a corps under Maj. Gen. William T. Sherman.

3. **The improper contact was by President-elect James Buchanan.** Initially, he wrote to Associate Justice John Catron of Tennessee to find out if the much-anticipated decision would be handed down before his inauguration. Then he contacted Associate Justice Robert Grier, a fellow Pennsylvanian, and convinced him to vote with the Southern majority so the vote would not be entirely on sectional lines. It was also rumored that Chief Justice Taney gave him a sneak preview of the decision because, before the decision was made public, Buchanan promised in his inaugural address that the Supreme Court would shortly put the slavery issue to rest.

4. **The court voted seven to two.** Associate Justices John McLean of Ohio and Benjamin Curtis of Massachusetts were in dissent. Those in the majority were Taney (Maryland), James Wayne (Georgia), Catron, Peter Daniel (Virginia), Grier, Samuel Nelson (New York), and John Campbell (Alabama). All nine wrote opinions.

5. **The Missouri Compromise was overturned.** The compromise prohibited slavery in the territories north of the southern border of Missouri. The *Dred Scott* decision allowed it into all territories, thereby upsetting the balance that had stood since 1820. The immediate effect was to open the door to slavery in the Kansas Territory and bring on the conflict that became known as Bleeding Kansas. It also ruled that blacks were not, and could not become, citizens and had no rights a white man was bound to respect. Rather than quiet the debate on slavery, it increased it.

6. **The court could have ruled on "standing" only.** The initial part of the ruling asked if Scott could legally bring suit—that is, whether he

had "standing" before the court. The justices ruled that he did not. Had they stopped there, the case would have ended. However, Taney and his Southern majority wanted to go beyond that point and settle the questions of the status of the slaves and the right to bring them into the territories. Taney declared that blacks, free or slave, were not and never could become U.S. citizens and that blacks had no rights a white man was obliged to respect. In throwing out the Missouri Compromise, the door was opened to warfare in the territories.

7. **The Brown family business was tanning and leather.** John Brown learned the business from his father as did a former apprentice named Jesse Grant, the father of future general Ulysses Simpson Grant. After leaving the army in 1854, Ulysses worked many jobs and ended up in his father's tannery and thoroughly hated it. Brown was a fairly successful businessman, but he had his ups and downs and was bankrupt at one point.

8. **Brown had eye problems and lacked money.** John Brown studied at Plainfield, Massachusetts, and Morris Academy in Litchfield, Connecticut. However, having developed eye problems and being short of funds, he had to give up his plans to become a clergyman. He was raised in the Congregational Church but later broke with it and never joined another church. He remained a very religious man, though, and saw himself as doing the work of God.

9. **He fathered twenty children.** His first wife, Dianthe Lusk, bore seven and Mary Ann Day, who was only sixteen years old when they married, bore the other thirteen. Only eleven children lived to become adults. Brown did not spare his sons, involving them in his dangerous work. Two were killed with him at Harpers Ferry while another managed to escape. Another son was killed in Kansas.

10. **The Pottawatomie massacre involved the killing of five Southern settlers.** Brown and about twenty followers took three men from one family from their home and killed them in cold blood. A distance away, they took two more men from their homes and killed them on the spot. It was said they were hacked to death using

broadswords. Brown probably came to believe that these men endangered his family. The other side called Brown a cold-blooded killer. The Kansas Territory had become a battleground.

11. **Abolitionist Frederick Douglass grew wary and withdrew.** Brown had financial support from the likes of Gerrit Smith and Samuel Gridley Howe, but black abolitionist Frederick Douglass tried to talk him out of it, believing it to be suicidal. When Brown refused, Douglass quietly passed the word to other black leaders to stay out of it. Douglass admired Brown but did not allow his friendship to cloud his judgment.

12. **He refused any escape attempt, preferring martyrdom.** A supporter, Silas Soule got into the jail at Charles Town, West Virginia, and offered to free Brown and carry him north. Brown said he was too old to spend his life on the run. He was also recovering from serious wounds. He voiced the opinion that he would aid his cause most by becoming a martyr for the abolitionist cause. Indeed, he was. When the war came, Union soldiers marched to battle while singing of John Brown's body lying in the grave while his soul was marching on.

4. Cabinet Vipers

1. **Doughfaces were Northern politicians who supported Southern demands.** Famously sharp-tongued Virginian John Randolph used the term during the Missouri Compromise debate to describe Northerners who sold out their principles. He sneered at them, calling them weak, timid, and half-baked. Masks made of actual dough were in use then.

2. **Isaac Toucey was a doughface.** He had an impressive résumé that included such jobs as governor of Connecticut, senator, attorney general for President James Polk, legislative point man for President Franklin Pierce, and secretary of the navy for Buchanan. Nonetheless, he was a Southern appeaser in New England, where antislavery sentiment was growing. He was also seen as a definite

second-rater. He would pass the job along to Gideon Welles, another Connecticut Yankee who was of a far different political stripe.

3. **John Buchanan Floyd urged a pro-Southern policy.** The former Virginia governor did everything in his power to aid secession in his post as secretary of war, including shipping 115,000 rifles and muskets to Southern armories in 1859 alone. He also attempted to ship heavy ordnance to Galveston, Texas, and Ship Island, Mississippi. In 1861, he was indicted for fraud in a case that involved stolen Indian bonds, but he could not be prosecuted because he had testified before a congressional committee on the matter. As a Confederate general he is best remembered for escaping from Fort Donelson, Tennessee, and leaving Simon Buckner to surrender.

4. **The future Manhattan arsonist was Jacob Thompson.** He was born and educated in North Carolina, practiced law in Mississippi, and represented that state in Congress. As secretary of the interior, he was a part of the Southern cabal. After his resignation, he became inspector general of the Confederate army and later was a "confidential agent" to Canada. The unsuccessful plot to burn New York City was under his direction. Later, he fled to England, taking all the money under his control along with him. After the war, he lived large, returned to Tennessee, and died rich.

5. **The General was Lewis Cass.** New Hampshire–born and educated, he was a brigadier general in the War of 1812, governor of the Michigan Territory, and served as President Andrew Jackson's secretary of war and later as his minister to France. In 1848 he was candidate for president, but a Free Soil split among Democrats led to Whig Zachary Taylor's election. After service in the Senate, he was Buchanan's secretary of state and pushed the president hard to hold federal property and suppress secession. He resigned in protest over Buchanan's failure to do so.

6. **The cabinet member involved with the hanging was Joseph Holt.** A late arriver in the cabinet, he served first as postmaster general, then as secretary of war when Floyd resigned, and was involved

with attempts to resupply the forts. During the war, he was judge advocate general of the U.S. Army and prosecuted Maj. Gen. Fitz John Porter. He helped prosecute the Lincoln assassination conspirators and used underhanded tactics including the suppression of John Wilkes Booth's diary. The hanging of Mary Surratt was especially unpopular, and it was later learned that the jury that had found her guilty wrote an appeal for clemency. Holt made sure President Andrew Johnson never saw it.

7. **The Republican informant was Edwin McMasters Stanton.** The man had a gift for intrigue. Later, he would sneer at Lincoln and refer to him as the "original Gorilla" before serving in his cabinet as secretary of war. In Andrew Johnson's cabinet he would work with the Radical Republicans to undermine the president. But he also was a gifted administrator and came to admire Lincoln.

8. **The future Confederate leader was Howell Cobb.** Buchanan's secretary of the treasury had been governor of Georgia and Speaker of the House. He played a key role in establishing the new Confederacy and presided over it until Jeff Davis arrived to take the reins. Disappointed at not getting the top job, he joined the army but did not play a major role. Under his order, the infamous Andersonville Prison was built in Georgia.

9. **The author of a "Catch-22" opinion was Jeremiah Sullivan Black.** He was a distinguished jurist and a member of the Pennsylvania Supreme Court. His nomination to the U.S. Supreme Court failed by only one vote. While he saw the federal government did not have the power to stop secession, he did support the resupply and reinforcement of the forts. Later, he was an attorney for Andrew Johnson at his impeachment trial, for Secretary of War William Belknap in his, and for Samuel Tilden in his disputed election with Rutherford Birchard Hayes.

10. **The late arriver to the cabinet was John Adams Dix.** His public service dated to the War of 1812 and included terms as governor of New York and as U.S. senator. As secretary of the treasury, he ordered his New Orleans office to shoot on the spot anyone who

tried to haul down the national flag. Confederates intercepted the message and howled, but it made him famous in the North. He joined the army as the highest-ranking major general of volunteers. Because of his age he was primarily a desk general, but he put down the draft riots in New York. Other achievements of his long career included postmaster of New York City, ambassador to France, and president of a couple of railroads.

5. 1860

1. **The mail was delivered by the Pony Express.** On April 3, the first relay left St. Joseph, Missouri. The mail sacks were delivered in Sacramento ten days later. The route was almost two thousand miles long. Riders hopped on a new horse every ten or fifteen miles, and new riders took over every seventy-five to a hundred miles. It cost $5.00 to send a half-ounce letter. The service would not last long. As telegraph lines extended across the country, the colorful service was discontinued in October 1861. The Pony Express helped hold California—and its gold—for the Union at the start of the Civil War. It has been said that the Pony Express rode more miles for Hollywood than for the original owners: William Russell, Alexander Majors, and William Waddell.

2. **The European leader was Giuseppe Garibaldi.** The sword bearer of Italian national unification was seen in the United States as a sort of Italian George Washington. He was so popular, in fact, that when the Civil War broke out he was invited to fight for the North. Garibaldi put two conditions on his service—that slavery would end and that he would command all Northern armies. Of course, his prerequisites killed the deal.

3. **Publication began of the dime novel.** The first Beadle & Company novel was published in 1860, and by 1865, four million had been sold. Initially, they struck a high moral tone and featured heroes such as Deadwood Dick, Martha Jane "Calamity Jane" Canary, and Christopher "Kit" Carson, although the stories often had little basis

in fact. Hundreds of titles were published, and many a Civil War soldier had a novel or two in his pack.

4. **The prince and the first niece went bowling.** The future Edward VII and Harriet Lane slipped off to Mrs. Smith's Institute for Young Ladies where they played tenpins. (At least that's what they claimed!) This story is rather ironic because Edward had the reputation as a playboy. Harriet Lane was the official White House hostess for her uncle, bachelor president James Buchanan.

5. **The last of the plantation songs was "Old Black Joe."** Stephen Collins Foster was the top American songwriter of the nineteenth century and captured the legend and myth of Southern plantation life better than anyone. Ironically, he was a Northerner who made only one trip to the Deep South, traveling from Cincinnati to New Orleans by riverboat. By 1860, his life was falling apart. His wife had left him and so had his talent. Gripped by alcoholism, the thirty-seven-year-old died from a fall in a New York fleabag hotel. He had only thirty-eight cents in his pocket.

6. **The 1860 census reported the U.S. population was 31.5 million people with a little less than 4 million slaves.** The population of the eleven states that would secede was about 9.5 million people, including most of the slaves. Given the questionable loyalty of the slaves, the North enjoyed a huge population advantage as war neared.

7. **Charles Darwin's *Origin of the Species* sparked the debate.** Swiss-born professor Louis Agassiz declared Darwin's theories to be pure bunk. American-born professor Asa Gray, who had corresponded with Darwin, rushed to the author's defense. The nub, of course, was how to square evolution with the Bible. That debate rages to this day.

8. **The ill-fated ships were the *Lady Elgin* and the *Augusta*.** On the night of September 8 in a gale wind, the schooner *Augusta* with a load of lumber was in trouble and tried to come alongside the side-wheel passenger steamer *Lady Elgin*. Instead, the *Augusta* rammed it. The schooner went off into the night and eventually made it to

port. The *Lady Elgin* broke up and sank. About four hundred of its passengers and crew died. Edward Spencer, a young student at Northwestern University, went into the water sixteen times and rescued seventeen people. A monument to his heroism is on the school's campus.

9. **The new embassy was opened by Japan.** Japan preferred to remain isolated, but in 1854 President Millard Fillmore sent Cdre. Matthew C. Perry to Japan to negotiate a treaty that called for peace and friendship, opened two Japanese ports to trade, allowed the United States to buy coal and supplies in Japan, and asked them, politely, to stop killing shipwrecked sailors washed up on their shores. Before Perry's visit, the Japanese had never seen steam vessels, and when Perry's black-hulled ships arrived in Tokyo Bay spouting smoke, the locals thought they were some form of dragon. Eighty-one years later, America came to regret not allowing Japan to continue sleeping.

10. **The gender barrier breaker was Olympia Brown.** She was the first woman admitted to study religion on the same full footing as men. She graduated and was ordained a Universalist minister, the first woman ordained in a major denomination. She preached in Vermont, Massachusetts, Connecticut, and Wisconsin and was an early and active suffragette. She was one of a few early leaders who lived to see the Nineteenth Amendment ratified in 1920.

6. The Democracy Splits

1. **Some disliked Douglas because of his Freeport Doctrine.** During one of the Lincoln-Douglas debates at Freeport, Illinois, Lincoln pressed Douglas about protecting slavery in the territories under his popular sovereignty law. Douglas replied that a territorial legislature would not need to take any action to eliminate slaves. Territorial legislatures would have to enact fugitive slave laws or no slaveholder would risk taking his slaves into a territory. This answer, given on free soil, was not well received in the South and made Douglas unacceptable to many Southern Democrats.

2. **William Lowndes Yancey demanded platform protections for slavery.** He borrowed language from Jefferson Davis so that his demand would seem moderate. The platform plank called for Congress to take action "when needed" to protect slave property in the territories. Northern delegates could not return home and run on such a pledge. Yancey must have understood that this proposal would split the party, and that action is probably what he wanted— to force Northern Democrats to give in or to separate. A split in the party likely would result in either the election of the Republican candidate or an election with no winner where the House of Representatives would choose the president. Either path could lead to disunion, and "Fire Eater" Yancey was a secessionist.

3. **The bolting states were Alabama and Louisiana.** It was prearranged. A smattering of other delegates—fifty in total—left as well. Their absence was enough to hamstring the convention. The delegations from the Deep South who stayed did so to prevent a change of rules that would allow a Douglas nomination.

4. **The Yankee collaborator was Benjamin Franklin Butler of Massachusetts.** It is one of history's ironies that Butler sided with the South here for later he would become one of the most hated Yankees in the South. Southerners put his likeness in the bottom of chamber pots and accused him of all manner of foul deeds. Jeff Davis, the man he had once supported, would order him hanged on the nearest tree if captured.

5. **The bolters marched off to Military Hall in Charleston.** There, they kept an eye on the main convention and waited to see if a return was in order. When the convention adjourned with plans to reassemble in Baltimore, the dissidents voted to do the same in Richmond.

6. **The chairman insisted that two-thirds of all delegates were still required.** Caleb Cushing was chairing the convention and ruled that, despite the defections, the same total number was required for nomination. The Douglas forces could not produce that number and found that it was almost impossible. Several compromise candidates were advanced, including James Guthrie of

Kentucky, Robert Mercer Taliaferro Hunter of Virginia, and Joseph Lane of Oregon, but none received more than the support of sixty-five and a half delegates. (Rules allowed split delegations and even split votes.) Believing a cooling-off period might help, the delegates took three weeks off and headed for Baltimore's Front Street Theater, where the weather and tempers might be cooler.

7. **The Baltimore bolters went to the nearby Maryland Institute in Baltimore.** The majority refused to reseat the Alabama and Louisiana delegates who had walked out in Charleston, so most of the other Southern delegates plus a smattering of others—110 men—left. About 195 delegates remained at the main convention.

8. **The two-thirds rule had to be broken.** By the end of the second ballot, most of his political enemies having left, Douglas had virtually all the delegates in the hall, but he still could not obtain two-thirds of the original delegate count. The delegates overrode Caleb Cushing's ruling, and Douglas was the nominee. They selected former Georgia senator Herschel Johnson as his running mate.

9. **The Southerners' wing of the Democrats picked Vice President John Breckinridge of Kentucky.** They selected Joseph Lane of Oregon as his vice-presidential candidate. Lane was born in North Carolina and had lived in Kentucky and Indiana. He had led Indiana troops in the Mexican War but was loyal to his slave state roots.

10. **The Southerners stopped in Richmond and joined with the Alabama and Louisiana delegations in support of Breckinridge.** Yancey's plan had worked. The Democrats were no longer a national party. Lincoln's election would give the Fire Eaters what they wanted, an excuse to demand immediate separation. The nation was sliding ever more rapidly toward war.

7. Spinning toward Secession

1. **The Democrats would convene in Charleston, South Carolina.** Southern ultras had home court advantage and put pressure on Northern delegates by demanding a national slave code. Northern

Democrats said that they could not go home and run on that platform. The Southerners knew that a party split at election time could not win, but they seemed to take the position that they would either have their demands met or leave.

2. **Lincoln's manager was Judge David Davis of Bloomington, Illinois.** A circuit judge, Davis was a longtime friend of Lincoln's who had ridden the circuit with him. Lincoln would later name him to the Supreme Court.

3. **(C) The Republicans convened in the Wigwam.** It's ironic that no sooner did the white settlers shoot, starve, or drive out the last native people than they developed a powerful nostalgia for them. Lincoln's supporters made good use of this home state advantage and packed the galleries with noisy Lincoln supporters.

4. **Lincoln's primary rival was William Henry Seward of New York.** Seward was the favorite and Lincoln a dark horse. Others with their eye on the nomination were Salmon Portland Chase of Ohio, Simon Cameron of Pennsylvania, Edward Bates of Missouri, and Supreme Court associate justice John McLean of Ohio. Most of them ended up in Lincoln's cabinet, where he could keep an eye on them. Seward, believing that Lincoln was not up to the job, offered to run the country for him after the election, but Lincoln politely declined.

5. **The favorite son was Simon Cameron of Pennsylvania.** Judge Davis would have to promise him a cabinet post, which led to trouble because of Cameron's dishonesty. Congressman Thaddeus Stevens would assure Lincoln that Cameron would not steal a red hot stove. Cameron did not last long as secretary of war and would be packed off to Russia as ambassador.

6. **The two wings of the divided Democrats would both reconvene in Baltimore, Maryland.** Both camps would meet there but remain divided, thus ensuring the election of Lincoln, secession, and the war. Baltimore seemed an appropriate place for this political battle because it was in a state with divided loyalties. It would remain in the Union but would supply troops to both the Union and the Confederacy.

7. **John Bell ran under the banner of the Constitutional Union Party.** Bell, a former Jacksonian Democrat, then a Whig and a Know-Nothing, was from Nashville. He would carry Virginia, Tennessee, and Kentucky. The nominating convention was held in Baltimore and attracted conservative Whigs, Know-Nothings, and a few unionist Democrats. Supporters hoped to provide a safe, middle-of-the-road haven for voters who wanted to avoid secession and war.

8. **The tickets were Lincoln and Hamlin, Douglas and Johnson, Breckenridge and Lane, and Bell and Everett.** Hamlin was a senator from Maine, Johnson a unionist from Georgia, Lane a pro-slavery senator from Oregon, and Everett a scholar and politician from Massachusetts.

9. **True: Lincoln did have more electoral votes than the other three combined.** Lincoln received 180 of the 303 votes, or about 59 percent. Breckenridge finished a distant second with 72 electoral votes.

10. **Lincoln only received 40 percent of the popular vote.** He received 1,866,452 of the almost 4.7 million votes cast. Of course, Lincoln was not even on the ballot in ten of the eleven states that would join the Confederacy. The lone exception was Virginia.

11. **Second in popular vote but last in electoral votes was Stephen Douglas.** He received almost 1.4 million votes but garnered only 12 electoral votes from Missouri and New Jersey.

12. **The Wide Awakes started in Hartford, Connecticut.** The organizations were more political than military in nature, but they were very popular and put on quite a show. Many participants wore paramilitary costumes made from colorful oilcloth that would sparkle and shine. Barrels of oil were placed along their line of march and, when lit, created quite a spectacle.

13. **The job of declaring Lincoln elected fell to Vice President John Breckenridge.** History is full of wonderful ironies. Because Breckenridge, as vice president, presided over the Senate, it fell to him—a man whom Lincoln had defeated in the election and would

defeat again when Breckenridge served as a Confederate general and secretary of war—to declare Lincoln the winner.

8. Mr. Lincoln of Springfield

1. **Lincoln's first law partner was John Todd Stuart.** Like Lincoln, he was a Kentucky-born Whig, but Stuart was formally educated, already established, and a militia major when he met Lincoln during the Black Hawk War. Stuart would be the first of Lincoln's three law partners.

2. **The Illinois legislature met at Vandalia.** During Lincoln's first term in the legislature, he worked hard to get the capital moved to Springfield. He never went back to New Salem, moving to Springfield himself to take advantage of the capitol's law library.

3. **Lincoln's future brother-in-law was Ninian Edwards.** He was the son of a former Illinois governor and served in the legislature with Lincoln as one of the "Long Nine," or nine Whigs from Sangamon County who were all six feet tall or taller. Edwards and his wife, Elizabeth, disapproved of Mary's marriage to Abraham. During the war, Lincoln appointed Edwards an army paymaster, but he had to resign after charges of corruption arose. Despite the strain, in the 1870s, Ninian and Elizabeth rescued Mary from an insane asylum and took her into their home.

4. **The previous lady friend was Mary Owens.** Tradition has it that Mary was no beauty, being on the hefty side and having bad teeth. Abe felt duty bound to propose to her. When she turned him down, she apparently made him the happiest man in Springfield or at least the most relieved.

5. **The judge and mentor was Judge David Davis.** Davis was a valuable mentor to Lincoln and treated him like a son. When Lincoln ran for president, Davis served as his campaign manager and brilliantly maneuvered the nomination in Chicago. Later, Lincoln appointed Davis to the Supreme Court.

6. **Lincoln was offered the governorship of Oregon.** It is well for history that he refused the job. He was really seeking the post of commissioner of the general land office, but it was spoken for. Disillusioned by the political process, Lincoln went home to Springfield and concentrated on the law. He would continue to do so until the passage of the Kansas-Nebraska Act began sliding the nation toward separation and war.

7. **Lincoln almost dueled with James Shields.** When anonymous letters lampooning him appeared in a local Springfield paper, Shields blamed Lincoln and challenged him to a duel. Shields was a short fellow, so Lincoln opted for cavalry sabers at three feet, relying on his long arms. Cooler heads prevailed, and they settled the dispute without bloodshed. In fact, Mary may have been the author of the insulting letters. After the near duel, she suddenly married Lincoln.

8. **The Lincolns lived at the Globe Tavern.** Apparently the couple hit it off right from the start. Son Robert was born there nine months later. The other three boys were born in the Lincoln's Springfield home, which they purchased from the clergyman who had married them.

9. **Lincoln was in contention for a Senate seat against Lyman Trumbull.** Lincoln had a majority of the votes but not enough for election. Trumbull and his Free Soil Democrat friends could not bring themselves to support a Whig. Rather than run the risk of destroying the fragile antislavery alliance and electing a Douglas Democrat, Lincoln threw his support to Trumbull. Later, with Trumbull in the Republican Party, Lincoln would profit from the magnanimous gesture.

10. **Lincoln's last law partner was William Herndon.** Another Kentucky-born lawyer, Billy Herndon was the third and last of Lincoln's law partners. He was more radical on slavery than Lincoln was and after the president's death claimed he had changed Lincoln's mind on the subject. He hated Mary and asserted that Ann Rutledge, not she, was the love of Lincoln's life.

His book *Herndon's Lincoln: The True Story of a Great Life* is filled with Herndon ego but still studied for details of Lincoln's life.

11. **Lincoln was seriously considered for vice president.** Lincoln came close to being the running mate of John Frémont. As the accepted head of the new Republican Party in Illinois, he was the favorite son and drew strong support; however, the honor went to William Dayton of New Jersey, a Princeton-educated jurist and senator. Lincoln later appointed Dayton ambassador to France, where he died in 1864.

12. **He put an almanac into evidence.** Lincoln was representing the son of an old friend. An eyewitness claimed to have clearly seen the defendant strike the fatal blow because there had been a full moon. The almanac entry convinced the jury that there was little or no moon at that hour. With the witness discredited, William "Duff" Armstrong was found not guilty.

AT WAR WITH OURSELVES

What was secession? Was it a rebellion or legal withdrawal? Would all the slave states leave or only some of them? Could a state remain neutral? What did the federal government have the right to do to counter this separation? What should it do? How would the new, untested president respond? Would the crisis end quickly? Many said it would. When President Lincoln called for troops to suppress

The Union strategy for winning the conflict was Gen. Winfield Scott's plan to blockade Southern ports and split the Confederacy with a campaign down the Mississippi River. Newspapers called it the Snake Plan or the Anaconda Plan. The tiny Union Navy, with ships like the USS *Constellation*, would be called upon to play a major role. The fully restored *Constellation*, pictured here, is now on display at Baltimore's Inner Harbor. *Photo by the author*

it, he asked for them for only three months. Both sides boasted that the other side was craven and cowardly. If the Union was not restored quickly, would it remain divided forever? Might it splinter into many pieces? Had the dream of our forefathers died? As the loyal states and the fledgling Confederacy took their first halting steps into the conflict, some of these questions would be answered.

Quiz 1
Old Fuss and Feathers

Winfield Scott: American hero, military visionary, presidential candidate, or vane popinjay? Or, perhaps, all of the above! When the Civil War came he was the commanding general of the U.S. Army but physically far past his prime. He could no longer mount a horse. Within a year he would be put aside for a younger man but not before designing the strategy that would win the war. Let's look at his long career.

1. Prior to joining the army he received a good education and launched a professional career. Where was he educated and in what profession was he engaged?
2. In what year did he enter the army and at what rank?
3. When the second war with Britain came, Scott emerged a hero after being captured in one battle and wounded in another. Name the battles.
4. At the conclusion of the War of 1812, Scott was offered a high-ranking post that he turned down; instead, he took a nice consolation prize. Name both the post and the prize.
5. When the nullification crisis came in South Carolina, Scott found himself in an especially hot spot. Where was he?
6. Scott became commanding general of the army in 1841. Whom did he succeed?
7. When the war with Mexico began, why did Scott not initially draw the most prominent role?
8. The Whigs nominated Scott for president in 1852, and while he gained 44 percent of the popular vote he carried only four states. Name them.
9. Taking on a quasi-diplomatic role, General Scott successfully settled a dispute over an international boundary. Where was it?

10. At the outbreak of the Civil War, some government officials were unsure if they could trust Scott. Why?
11. What protégé of the old general's greased the skids for his removal?
12. Where is Winfield Scott buried?

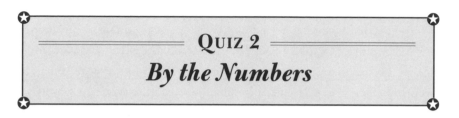

QUIZ 2
By the Numbers

When the Civil War began approximately 31.5 million people resided in the states and its territories. More than two-thirds of them lived in states that did not secede. Let's see what you know about the size and demographics of the United States in 1860.

1. Only two of the Confederate states ranked in the top ten in population. Which ones were they?
2. Which Southern state had the largest slave population?
3. Which Confederate state had the smallest slave population?
4. In two Southern states, slaves outnumbered whites. Which ones?
5. In five Southern states less than 1 percent of the black population was free. Which ones?
6. Conversely, which Confederate state had the largest percentage of free blacks?
7. What state (Union or Confederate) had the largest number of free blacks?
8. Only three Confederate states had a population greater than a million people. Name them.
9. In terms of white population only, the largest city in the South by a very large measure was?
10. The next seven were Charleston, Memphis, Mobile, Montgomery, Norfolk, Richmond, and Savannah. Rank them in order from second to eighth.

11. Among the slave states that did not secede, which had the largest slave population?

12. What slave state had the smallest number of slaves?

Quiz 3
Missouri Saved

After Fort Sumter, the border states teetered. Could the South drag them into the Confederacy? Could the U.S. government hold them in the Union? Missouri was a classic example. The state was pro-slavery in the Missouri River Valley west of Jefferson City and on the western side of the state, but it was diverse and more pro-Union elsewhere. Let's review the events that led to the initial Union victories in Missouri.

1. A congressman from a prominent family was the primary figure trying to keep Missouri from seceding. Name him.

2. The Missouri governor ran for office as a moderate but worked hard to take Missouri out of the Union. He was?

3. A small, redheaded army captain from Connecticut transferred in from Kansas and beat the Confederates to the punch at every turn. Name him.

4. An ethnic minority, many with military experience, was the Union's secret weapon. Where did they come from?

5. Who commanded the pro-Southern Missouri State Guard?

6. Over what St. Louis installation did those supporting the Confederates want to take control?

7. The Union Department commander supported the South and was a thorn in the side of Unionists. He was?

8. Unionists took the first overt military action. What did they do?

9. On the way back to their base, Union forces ran into a major problem. What was it?

10. Pro-Southern forces were forced to retreat. Where did they go?

11. Union troops followed and a skirmish was fought near what Missouri River town?

12. The Union commander split his army and sent a portion of it down the railroad to Rolla and hence to Springfield. Who commanded that wing?

13. A portion of that force under Col. Franz Sigel tangled with retreating state militiamen at what small town in southwestern Missouri?

14. The Union commander took another desperate gamble and attacked a larger, combined Confederate force southwest of Springfield. Name the place.

QUIZ 4
Wilson's Creek

One month after First Bull Run, aggressive Union actions in Missouri had all but eliminated Confederate troops from the state, but the situation was about to change. A Confederate force was moving on Springfield, and John Frémont, in command in St. Louis, refused to send reinforcements to his field commander. Rather than retreat, the Union Army moved forward and brought on the battle of Wilson's Creek. Let's see what you know about it.

1. Union troops were under the command of a little redheaded brigadier who had been a captain only a few months earlier. Name him.

2. A former Texas Ranger who once served under David "Davy" Crockett led the Confederates. Name him.

3. The Union commander split his forces and sent the smaller part of his command to the Confederate rear, where he attacked. Who led that force?

4. As the main Union force moved in, the Confederate Pulaski Battery slowed its advance. A force under Capt. Joseph Plummer was sent to capture or destroy it. In what field did this part of the battle take place?

5. The smaller Union command to the south won initial success until a tragic mistake allowed the Confederates to drive them off. What happened?

6. What former governor led the Confederate Missouri State Guard in the action?

7. What landmark was the site of the balance of the fighting during the battle?

8. What important but unfortunate distinction came to the Union commander when he was killed in the battle?

9. What future major general was functioning as chief of staff to the Union commander?

10. Name the Union officer who took command when the Union commander was killed.

11. After the battle, both sides took the same action. What was it?

12. The Union withdrawal from southern Missouri led to Gov. Claiborne Fox Jackson to declare Missouri out of the Union. In what town did this take place?

13. When the Union Army left Springfield, where did it go?

14. Why was that town selected?

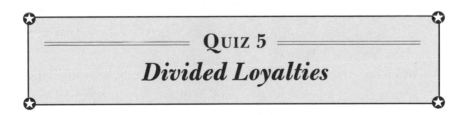

QUIZ 5
Divided Loyalties

Four slave states—Missouri, Kentucky, Maryland, and Delaware—remained in the Union, but many of their residents would have preferred secession. The Union forces occupied significant parts of the eleven states that seceded during the war, and those sections required some form of civilian government. The men who attempted to govern states of divided loyalties usually had their hands full. Let's see if you know some of them.

1. He became the only state governor killed during the war when he died at Shiloh. He was?
2. He worked openly with a New Yorker who commanded the state guard in an effort to take the state out of the Union. Name him.
3. He was the only U.S. senator from a seceded state to retain his seat. He was rewarded with the post of military governor and brigadier general. He was?
4. This military governor of an occupied state started the war as a colonel of the Twelfth Maine. Name him.
5. This state divided on geographic lines, and the mountainous western counties seceded from the "seceders." This man became head of the "restored government" in 1861. He was?
6. This native Virginian had lived in Pennsylvania before returning to Missouri during the secession crisis. When the elected governor fled, the state convention made him the provisional governor. Name him.
7. He tried to walk a middle path by declaring his state to be neutral, but when it didn't stick, he resigned. He was?
8. He was a pro-secession governor in a badly split state. When he was driven out of the state, he became a volunteer aide to several generals. Name him.
9. This border state governor followed a weak-kneed loyalist who vacillated a great deal. He, too, was a Unionist but no great friend of the black man. He was?
10. When eastern North Carolina fell into Union hands, he seemed the perfect choice for military governor. Within a year he resigned in a huff and headed for California. Name him.

QUIZ 6
The Confederate Cabinet

Critics of Confederate president Jeff Davis claim that his failure to surround himself with first-class advisers was one reason for the South's defeat. See if you can answer a few questions about the men Davis selected to support him.

1. Three of the original cabinet members were foreign born. Who were they and in what countries were they born?

2. One of the original cabinet members left the cabinet for a general's star and performed outstandingly at Antietam. Name him.

3. One cabinet officer held three different portfolios. Name him and the positions.

4. One cabinet member was captured with the fleeing President Davis in 1865 and held for a time at Fort Warren in Boston harbor. Who was he?

5. One cabinet member was the grandson of Thomas Jefferson. Name him and the office he filled.

6. Name the former U.S. senator from Virginia who served Davis as secretary of state.

7. Name the cabinet officer who had been vice president of the United States.

8. Name the three cabinet members who served throughout the war.

9. Which cabinet office had the most occupants? How many?

10. Six members of the Davis cabinet are listed below. Match them to their home states.

Cabinet Members	Home States
1. Judah P. Benjamin	A. Alabama
2. Stephen R. Mallory	B. Florida
3. Christopher G. Memminger	C. Georgia
4. John H. Regan	D. Louisiana
5. Robert Toombs	E. South Carolina
6. Leroy Pope Walker	F. Texas

QUIZ 7
The Union Cabinet

Abraham Lincoln surrounded himself with men of talent, but often they were, or had been, political foes. The president joked that it was better to have them close by where he could watch them. Let's see how you do with these questions about Lincoln's cabinet.

1. Which cabinet members did Lincoln call Mars and Father Neptune?

2. Which cabinet officer did Lincoln later name chief justice of the Supreme Court?

3. Which cabinet officer was seriously wounded the night Lincoln was assassinated?

4. When Simon Cameron was dumped as secretary of war, where was he sent?

5. Which cabinet officer served in Lincoln's cabinet and those of both his predecessor and his successor?

6. What longtime Lincoln friend became attorney general in 1864?

7. What prominent Maine senator became Lincoln's second secretary of the treasury?

8. What obscure historical figure served as attorney general for one week following the resignation of Edward Bates in 1863?

9. What cabinet member was the son of a member of Andrew Jackson's Kitchen Cabinet?

10. What member of the Lincoln cabinet had two sons who were Union generals?

Now, match the original cabinet members to their home states.

Cabinet Members	*Home States*
1. Edward Bates	A. Connecticut
2. Montgomery Blair	B. Indiana
3. Simon Cameron	C. Maryland
4. Salmon P. Chase	D. Missouri
5. William H. Seward	E. New York
6. Caleb B. Smith	F. Ohio
7. Gideon Welles	G. Pennsylvania

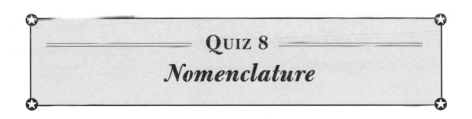

QUIZ 8
Nomenclature

Every war produces its own colorful language. Soldiers often gave pet names to objects that aptly describe the item and tell us something about the soldiers. We've selected twenty terms used in the American Civil War, some jocular in nature and some technical. Let's see how many you know.

1. Bohemian Brigade
2. Arkansas toothpick
3. Desecrated vegetables
4. Housewife
5. The Old Woman

6. Silent battle
7. Shinplasters
8. Shoddy
9. Sherman's neckties
10. Salt horse
11. Contraband of war
12. Havelock
13. Graybacks
14. Gabions
15. Zouaves
16. Dog robbers
17. Cracker line
18. Infernal machines
19. Spooning
20. Quaker guns

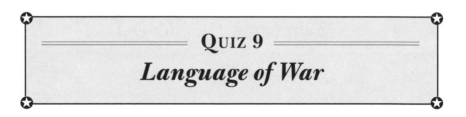

Quiz 9
Language of War

Every occupation or craft has its own language. West Pointers learned the army's jargon and taught it to the volunteers. Today, the historian and any others who turn to first-person material to research the Civil War need fair knowledge of the idioms. Let's see if you can define these military terms.

1. What was an "abatis"?
2. In building a fort or line, what was an "angle and return"?
3. What was the difference between a "Napoleon" and a "Parrott"?
4. What did a unit do when it was told to "demonstrate"?
5. How were troops attacking when they were moving in "echelon"?
6. What was meant by "enfilade" and why was it good?
7. When a plan to "envelop" was made, what was the plan?

8. What kind of position was a "lunette"?

9. What was a "redan" and who enjoyed its benefits?

10. If a line was "refused," what did it look like?

11. Where were soldiers going during a "retrograde" movement?

12. What part of a line or fortification was a "return"?

13. In what way was a "salient" different from the rest of the line?

14. What was a "screen" and who usually provided them?

15. When quartermasters listed "stands of arms," what were they counting?

16. What was happening when a unit "unlimbered" and what kind of unit was it?

17. What part of a moving army was the "van"?

18. What were Civil War generals talking about when they spoke of the "works"?

Quiz 10
Toehold at Port Royal

The Union Navy understood that blockading ports a thousand miles from the nearest navy yard was nearly impossible. They knew they must seize and hold harbors in the South. The first major harbor the navy captured was Port Royal, South Carolina, halfway between Charleston and Savannah. What do you know about that important operation?

1. Before settling on Port Royal, what point farther north was seriously considered?

2. Who commanded the army troops assigned to the operation?

3. As flag officer of the South Atlantic Blockading Squadron, he led the expedition. He was?

4. The first target was Fort Walker on the northern tip of Hilton Head Island. Who commanded the fort?

5. Why did the army troops not go ashore and attack the fort from the land side?

6. What was the name of the fort on Phillip's Island on the north side of the bay entrance?

7. Future operations were made easier when a Confederate general decided to defend positions farther inland. Who made that decision?

8. What was the first port in Georgia targeted from this base?

9. What was the first port in Florida attacked from this base?

10. A new army commander took over and issued an order that President Lincoln himself revoked. What was it?

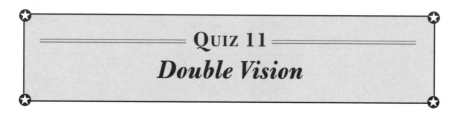

QUIZ 11
Double Vision

One thing you could count on from the Union's Maj. Gen. George McClellan was that he was always outnumbered. At least he thought so. This assertion flew in the face of the facts. The Southern white population was far smaller than that of the North. It would have been virtually impossible for the South to field larger armies, but that knowledge did not deter McClellan's claims. Was it faulty intelligence? This quiz looks at the Union's early attempts to obtain a realistic picture of Confederate strength and troop distribution.

1. Who was the first American Army general to establish an intelligence service?

2. When the Civil War began, the newly minted general in charge of the Washington defenses inherited the job of intelligence gathering and interpretation. He was?

3. When George McClellan arrived after First Bull Run, he brought in an experienced cloak-and-dagger man to run his intelligence operation. Who was he?

4. Winfield Scott's man was a shadowy character with a gift for self-aggrandizement. Name him.

5. As the number of detained citizens suspected of spying began to grow, this veteran military and political figure was given the job of sorting them out. Who was he?

6. Most Union efforts were aimed at counterespionage, or catching those who were disloyal and spying on the Union. However, one Union operative made several trips deep into the Confederacy and may have dined with Jeff Davis. Name him.

7. Gathering information was one thing, but interpreting it was quite another. The d'Orléans brothers had the job of analyzing it all. Who were they?

8. When McClellan's army reached the Virginia peninsula, the leaders discovered that a key river ran opposite of what their maps showed. What river?

9. A Chicago architect serving as a private soldier became the best scout and mapmaker in the Army of the Potomac. Name him.

10. A serious deficiency in one department of McClellan's army impaired his knowledge of the enemy and helped the enemy to know more about McClellan's army. What was the weak arm of McClellan's army?

11. What newfangled gadget did McClellan attempt to use to keep an eye on the Confederates?

12. In Northern Virginia, another Union general lost a battle when his intelligence sources dried up and he made some bad assumptions. Name him.

ANSWERS

1. Old Fuss and Feathers

1. **Scott attended the College of William & Mary and studied law.**
    For a short period he studied at the prestigious Virginia College,
    then moved to Richmond to read the law. He was admitted to the
    bar in 1806. While in Richmond, he observed the Aaron Burr trial
    for treason.

2. **He entered the army in 1808 as a captain of light artillery.** The
    army was expanding in anticipation of problems with the British.
    The following year he was court-martialed for remarks he made
    about his superior officer, Gen. James Wilkinson, and suspended
    for a year. He used the time to study tactics. Incidentally, Wilkinson
    was one of the great scoundrels of American history. While serving
    as commanding officer of the army he was also on the payroll of
    Spain as a spy.

3. **He was captured at Queenstown Heights at Ontario, Canada, and
    wounded at Lundy's Lane.** In the former action, his troops carried
    the field, but the British counterattacked and captured him in
    1812. Two years later at Lundy's Lane in Niagara Falls, Ontario, he
    had two horses shot from under him and was severely wounded
    twice. By war's end, he was one of America's top soldiers.

4. **He declined the post of secretary of war but received the Thanks
    of Congress and a gold medal.** Despite the honors heaped upon
    him, though, the honeymoon did not last. Scott quickly became a
    leading promoter of a strong professional army, something the
    majority Democrats both feared and loathed. Andrew Jackson
    disliked him intensely.

5. **During the nullification crisis, Scott served in Charleston Harbor,
    South Carolina.** As did Maj. Robert Anderson at the start of the
    Civil War, Scott commanded the Charleston defenses. His tact,
    discretion, and decisiveness were valuable in helping to calm and
    defuse a dangerous situation.

6. **Scott succeeded Maj. Gen. Alexander Macomb as army commander.** Macomb was another hero of the War of 1812 and had succeeded Maj. Gen. Jacob Brown in command of the army. Scott replaced Macomb at the time of his death. Scott would lead the army through the Mexican War and into the Civil War.

7. **Scott was bypassed early in the Mexican war because of his problems with President Polk.** Polk, an Andrew Jackson protégé, disliked Scott and had no desire to make a national hero out of a Whig general. Initially, Polk gave the plumb assignment to rough old Zachary Taylor, but Taylor was also a Whig and became bogged down in Monterey. Scott drew troops from Taylor and launched the brilliant Veracruz–Mexico City Campaign that won the war. Congress again voted him its thanks and another gold medal.

8. **As a presidential candidate, Scott carried Vermont, Massachusetts, Kentucky, and Tennessee.** The Whigs had won with Zachary Taylor in 1848 so they turned to a war hero again. However, Franklin Pierce, another Mexican War general, opposed Scott. He would be the last presidential candidate that the Whigs fielded.

9. **He settled the dispute over the Strait of Juan de Fuca between British Columbia and the state of Washington.** Over the years, Scott proved quite adept at handling similar touchy situations.

10. **Some distrusted him because he was a Virginian.** Although he had been born near Petersburg, he had long since become a citizen of the whole nation. After Lincoln's election he showed surprising vigor in keeping the peace and guaranteeing a peaceful transition of power. Southerners grumbled when they saw the army on Washington streets, but nobody tried to disrupt the Lincoln inaugural.

11. **He was eased out by George Brinton McClellan.** Scott recommended the younger man after First Bull Run, and he was brought in to build the Army of the Potomac. McClellan, meanwhile, did everything possible to undercut Scott and take his job. Eventually, he did.

12. **Scott is buried at West Point.** Though not a graduate of the school, the location was right because for so many years, he was the outspoken champion of a professional army. Scott was an imposing figure at six foot five and more than three hundred pounds late in life. His nickname of Old Fuss and Feathers referred to his love of military ceremony and ornate uniforms. Someone said of him that, walking down the street alone, he looked like a parade.

2. By the Numbers

1. **Virginia and Tennessee were the only seceding states in the top ten in population.** Virginia was the fifth-largest state with a population of 1.6 million. Tennessee ranked tenth with about 1.1 million. Of course, eight of the ten most populous states were in the North. New York had more than 3.8 million people, and Pennsylvania and Ohio both had more than 2.3 million. The population of Illinois was also greater than that of Virginia.

2. **Virginia had the largest slave population.** The Old Dominion had 491,000 enslaved blacks. The next four states with more than 400,000 slaves, in order, were Georgia, Mississippi, Alabama, and South Carolina.

3. **Florida had the fewest slaves of any seceding state.** It had a slave population of less than 63,000. By contrast, 57,000 free blacks lived in Pennsylvania.

4. **Slaves outnumbered whites in South Carolina and Mississippi.** Slaves were 57 percent of the population in South Carolina and 55 percent in Mississippi. Louisiana was close with 47 percent of its population enslaved.

5. **Less than 1 percent of the Negroes were free in Arkansas, Texas, Mississippi, Alabama, and Georgia.** Some states required freed blacks to leave the state or be re-enslaved.

6. **Virginia had the Confederacy's highest percentage of freed slaves.** Of the state's blacks, 10.6 percent were free. North Carolina ranked second with 8.3 percent.

7. **Maryland had the largest number of freed slaves.** By 1860, almost 84,000 Maryland blacks, or 49.1 percent of the total, were free.

8. **Virginia, Tennessee, and Georgia were the only Confederate states with a population of one million or more.** As previously indicated, Virginia was fifth, with 1.6 million people, and Tennessee was tenth, with 1.1 million. Georgia was the eleventh-largest state with a little more than a million people. North Carolina and Alabama were growing close to that number.

9. **New Orleans had the largest white population in the Confederacy.** The city had a white population of 168,675. By the same measurement, the next-largest Southern city was less than a quarter of its size.

10. **The next seven, in order, were Charleston, Richmond, Mobile, Memphis, Savannah, Norfolk, and Montgomery.** Charleston had a population of a little more than 40,000. Montgomery, the eighth-largest city in the Confederacy, had a white population of less than 9,000.

11. **Of the slave states not seceding, Kentucky had the most slaves.** The Bluegrass State had more than 225,000 slaves, even more than Texas, Arkansas, or Florida had. Missouri had 115,000 slaves.

12. **Fewest slaves were in Delaware.** It had only 1,798 slaves out of a total black population of almost 22,000.

3. Missouri Saved

1. **Francis Preston Blair Jr. played a key roll in keeping Missouri in the Union.** He was called Frank. His father was one of the great powers in the Democratic Party and his brother was in Lincoln's cabinet. He started as a Democrat, moved to the Free Soil movement, and hence to the Republicans. He was later a successful Union general.

2. **The secessionist governor was Claiborne Fox Jackson.** The Kentucky-born banker ran for governor as a Unionist but plotted from the start to take Missouri out of the Union. He later convened

a rump session of the legislature at Neosho that passed an ordinance of secession. Was Missouri out of the Union?

3. **Nathaniel Lyon of Connecticut played the key military role.** The West Pointer from the class of 1841 was a longtime Democrat, but he was sickened by what he saw in Bleeding Kansas and became strongly against secession. His boldness brought him early victories but also an early grave.

4. **The important ethnic minority was the Germans.** Many took part in the 1848 uprisings and had to flee their native land. They opposed authoritarian governments and abhorred slavery, so they sided with the Union and the Republicans.

5. **Sterling Price commanded the Missouri State Guard.** Known as Old Pap, he was a lawyer, farmer, and politician who served in Congress and as governor of Missouri. In the Mexican War he led the Second Missouri and was a brigadier general of volunteers. Though not a true professional, he enjoyed some successes and remained popular in his home state.

6. **The secessionist target was the St. Louis Arsenal.** Governor Jackson and General Price needed the contents to arm the militia and take Missouri out of the Union. Blair and Lyon wanted to put those arms into German hands and help preserve the state for the Union.

7. **The pro-Southern department commander was William S. Harney.** A native of Tennessee and married to a woman from St. Louis, Harney shared the Southerners' view, but he tried to walk a moderate line between Blair and Governor Jackson. Blair relieved him of duty, but he was later reinstated. When he obstructed Blair once again, his career ended.

8. **Unionists captured Camp Jackson and the Missouri State Guard.** After a carriage ride through the camp disguised as Frank Blair's mother-in-law, Lyon decided to act. He surrounded the camp and forced it to surrender, capturing and disarming the militia.

9. **Returning to camp, the Union forces ran into a riot.** Outside the armory a crowd gathered, and some of the people were angry.

Rocks flew, then shots. The German troops fired into the mob. When the smoke cleared, twenty-eight citizens including two children, two German Union soldiers, and three of the captured militia members were dead. Both sides blamed the other for starting it.

10. **Southern forces retreated to Jefferson City.** Unable to house his prisoners, Lyon forced them to take an oath of allegiance and released them. Most of them felt an oath given under duress was not binding, so they rejoined the pro-Southern forces and went upriver to join the governor at the capital.

11. **Troops clashed again at Boonville.** Lyon loaded his troops onto boats and went upriver. Finding Jefferson City abandoned, he moved on to Boonville, where he attacked the militia. Superior Union training and equipment made the difference, and the Union force routed the Southern troops.

12. **Union troops headed for Springfield were commanded by Brig. Gen. Thomas Sweeny.** Born in Ireland, Sweeny had lost an arm in Mexico before becoming a regular U.S. Army officer. Always willing to fight fellow officers and enemies alike, he resented volunteer officers and ran afoul of Grenville Dodge. He retired from the army in 1870 as a brigadier general.

13. **Forces under Colonel Sigel fought the state militia at Carthage.** With Lyon pushing them from behind and Colonel Sigel across their path, the Southern troops were in a tough spot, but they launched a determined series of attacks on Sigel and pushed him aside. They were able to continue south and joined forces with Benjamin "Ben" McCulloch coming north out of Arkansas.

14. **Troops under Nathaniel Lyon fought again at Wilson's Creek.** Price and McCulloch had combined to create a force larger than Lyon's. The Southern army was resting at Wilson's Creek. With no support from his superior, John Frémont, Lyon faced the prospect of losing much of the ground he had gained. He chose to attack, a decision that resulted in his own death and a lost battle; however,

his legacy was that Missouri remained largely in Union hands for the balance of the war.

4. Wilson's Creek

1. **Nathaniel Lyon was leader of the Union forces.** Once again, scrappy little General Lyon showed his willingness to fight, even under less than favorable conditions. At a time that President Lincoln was trying to find fighting generals, he had a very eager one in Missouri.

2. **The former Texas Ranger was Ben McCulloch.** He accompanied neighbor Davy Crockett to Texas but missed the Alamo because of illness. He distinguished himself at San Jacinto and was an Indian fighter and Texas Ranger. He was killed in the spring of 1862 at the Battle of Pea Ridge/Elkhorn Tavern, Arkansas.

3. **Franz Sigel led the attack from the rear.** A trained but slightly inept military officer, Sigel's main value to the Union was his ability to attract German Americans to the cause. Missouri had a large German population, and most of them were strong Unionists.

4. **The attack on the battery took place in the Ray cornfield.** Captain Plummer was a little slow in moving and a Confederate force under Col. James McIntosh drove him back across Wilson's Creek.

5. **The battle turned when Northern forces mistook enemy troops for friends.** Sigel mistook the advancing Third Louisiana for the gray-clad First Iowa and ordered his men to hold their fire. At forty yards, the Confederates fired and broke the Union line.

6. **The Missouri State Guard was led by Sterling Price.** The Virginia-born "Old Pap" Price was a somewhat effective general who had led troops in the Mexican War but otherwise had no military training. He led the Missouri Confederates throughout the war.

7. **The balance of the action took place on Bloody Hill.** It proved a strong position for the Union line, which held through three major attacks by the Confederates.

8. **Lyon was the first Union general to fall.** Sadly, Lyon would not be the last. Before the war ended, forty-six more Union generals and seventy-five Confederate generals would die in combat.

9. **Lyon's chief of staff was John Schofield.** The 1853 West Point graduate was on leave of absence from the army and teaching physics at Washington University in St. Louis. He later commanded the Department of Missouri before leading troops in Georgia, Tennessee, and the Carolinas. He defeated Gen. John Bell Hood at Franklin, Tennessee, and was a part of Maj. Gen. George Thomas's major victory at Nashville. Before he ended his forty-six-year career, he would become commanding general of the U.S. Army.

10. **When Lyon was killed, he was replaced by Sam Sturgis.** A West Pointer, class of 1846, he was a captain at the start of the war and a major at Wilson's Creek. He rose to division command but was shelved after being routed at Brice's Cross Roads.

11. **After the battle, both sides retreated.** With their general dead and low on ammunition, the Union troops went back to Springfield while McCulloch pulled his badly mauled force back into Arkansas.

12. **Governor Fox declared Missouri secession in Neosho.** This small town in southwestern Missouri was the capital of a government virtually in exile. Missouri and Kentucky were the only two states that both the North and the South claimed, but the North controlled the territories for most of the war.

13. **The Union force retreated to Rolla, Missouri.** The Union Army moved north and east to this central Missouri town.

14. **Rolla was chosen because it was on a railroad line.** It allowed the Union a secure supply line and quick contact with St. Louis.

5. Divided Loyalties

1. **The only state governer killed was George Johnson of Kentucky.** When Kentucky's neutrality policy failed, the Union quickly drove Confederate forces out of the state. The Confederates set up a shadow government with former legislator George Johnson as

governor; however, his governmental reach was limited to Confederate lines. Governor Johnson also functioned as an adviser to Gen. Albert Sidney Johnston and as a volunteer aide to John C. Breckenridge. After Johnson's horse was shot out from under him at Shiloh, he joined the First Kentucky as a private soldier and was mortally wounded in the second day's fighting.

2. **Claiborne Fox Jackson of Missouri tried to push his state out of the Union.** He conspired with Gen. Daniel Frost of the state guard to capture the St. Louis Arsenal and take the state into the Confederacy. Congressman Frank Blair and newly minted Gen. Nathaniel Lyon beat him to the punch and captured the state guard. Jackson fled with the Confederates and set up a government in Neosho that declared secession. Governor Jackson died of cancer in 1862.

3. **Andrew Johnson of Tennessee was the only senator from a seceded state to remain in the Senate.** The eastern counties of the Volunteer State had few slaves and remained loyal, as did Johnson. He was rewarded with the title of military governor and brigadier general. In an attempt to draw in as much support as possible from the Democrats, Lincoln ran for president in 1864 on the Union ticket with Democrat Johnson as his running mate. The choice proved tragic. After Lincoln's death the Johnson presidency devolved into an open political war with the Radical Republicans who wanted a harsher Reconstruction policy.

4. **The Maine Yankee ruling occupied Louisiana was Brig. Gen. George Shepley.** He was close to Ben Butler, who made him the military governor of occupied Louisiana for almost two years. Louisiana chaffed under Butler and Shepley, who lost no opportunity to rub salt into the Rebels' wounds and reward their friends at the same time. Shepley signed a blanket pardon that virtually emptied the state prison, turning dangerous criminals into the civilian population. When Michael Hahn was elected governor of the reconstructed state, Shepley moved to the Army of the James

in Virginia, where he served as Maj. Gen. Godfrey Weitzel's chief of staff.

5. **Francis Pierpont headed the restored government of Virginia.** After Virginia seceded, the loyalist convention at Wheeling declared a restored state government with Pierpont as governor. When West Virginia was admitted to the Union in 1863, Arthur Boreman became governor of the new state, and Pierpont moved to Alexandria, where he continued to function on behalf of the portions of Virginia in Union hands. He failed to push the Fourteenth Amendment through the state legislature and was displaced in 1868.

6. **Hamilton Rowan Gamble of Missouri was named provisional governor.** He was a successful lawyer who had lived forty years in Missouri before moving to Pennsylvania. When the secession crisis came, he returned home, and the Union-oriented state convention named him governor. He held the state in the Union and even ended slavery there. He died in office in early 1864.

7. **Beriah Magoffin of Kentucky failed to keep his state neutral.** He was pro-slavery but tried to reach a compromise and stay in the Union. He declared the state neutral and defied Lincoln's request for troops to put down the rebellion. After Confederate Maj. Gen. Leonidas Polk broke neutrality by seizing Columbus, and with the pro-Union legislature overriding his vetoes, Magoffin stepped down and returned home to his law practice and his farm. Later, he advocated the Thirteenth Amendment and urged civil rights for the freedmen.

8. **Isham Harris of Tennessee was driven out and became a volunteer aide.** A former congressman and a strong voice for secession, Harris lost his ability to govern when Nashville fell. He tried to move the government to Memphis but quickly found himself chased from the state by Union victories. He became a volunteer military aide and served Generals Albert Johnston, Pierre Gustave Toutant (P. G. T.) Beauregard, Braxton Bragg, John Hood, and Joseph E. Johnston. With a $5,000 price on his head, Harris

fled to England when the war ended. Returning home later that year to practice law, he became a Tennessee state senator from 1878 until his death in 1897.

9. **Maryland's second war governer was Augustus Bradford.** Following his predecessor, Tom Hicks, Bradford must have seemed like a rock of Unionism. One of his "rewards" for his service to the Union was to have the Confederates burn his house down. As governor he pardoned freedman Sam Green, who had been imprisoned since 1857, with the provision that he had to leave the state. Green's crime? Possessing a copy of *Uncle Tom's Cabin*.

10. **Edward Stanly of North Carolina did a short stint as war governor.** Stanly was a Norwich graduate and a lawyer who served in the U.S. Congress and in the state legislature, where he was Speaker of the House. He was considered North Carolina's greatest orator. He moved to San Francisco to practice law and was an unsuccessful gubernatorial candidate for the Republicans in 1857. Lincoln appointed Stanly military governor of North Carolina in 1862. Being from New Bern, a part of the territory seized in Maj. Gen. Ambrose Burnside's 1862 campaign, Stanly seemed a great choice, but the Emancipation Proclamation led to his resignation less than a year later and his return to California. He was the uncle of Confederate Brig. Gen. Lewis Armistead, who was killed in Pickett's Charge at Gettysburg.

6. The Confederate Cabinet

1. **Foreign-born cabinet members were Judah Benjamin, Stephen Mallory, and Christopher G. Memminger.** Attorney General Benjamin and Secretary of the Navy Mallory were born in the islands—St. Croix and Trinidad, respectively. Benjamin grew up in South Carolina and Mallory in Florida. Secretary of the Treasury Memminger was born in Germany and came to the United States as an infant. He was orphaned at age four but was rescued from an asylum by Thomas Bennett, the future governor of South Carolina.

2. **Robert Toombs quit and joined the army.** He was none too happy to be named secretary of state. He wanted to be president. At Antietam, his men delayed Burnside's attempts to cross the southern bridge. Toombs constantly clashed with the professional soldiers and said the Confederacy "died of West Point."

3. **Judah Benjamin held three portfolios: attorney general, secretary of war, and later secretary of state.** He was not popular with the public and had many political enemies, but Davis liked him and he was a faithful soldier for Davis. Some detractors may have disliked him because he was Jewish.

4. **John Reagan was captured with Jefferson Davis.** It's unclear why, but Postmaster General Reagan accompanied President Davis as he fled south. His chances of getting out of the country would have been better if he had gone alone.

5. **George Wythe Randolph was Thomas Jefferson's grandson.** What a pedigree the man had! Born at Monticello, he was the grandson of the great Jefferson and the son of a governor. He was an artillery general in Virginia and left the army to become secretary of war, but he stayed less than a year. He returned to the army, but when his health failed in 1864, he went to Europe.

6. **Robert Hunter was first Confederate Secretary of State.** The Virginian had been Speaker of the House before the war and a close ally of John C. Calhoun's. He was yet another talented statesman who did not excel in the Davis cabinet. Perhaps it was a matter of Davis's use of his cabinet rather than his secretaries' abilities.

7. **John Breckinridge had been vice president.** The Kentuckian was vice president in the Buchanan administration and the 1860 presidential candidate of the Southern Democrats. He was also an effective general who took the war portfolio in February 1865.

8. **The three cabinet members who served throughout the war were John Reagan as postmaster general, Stephen Mallory as secretary of the navy from start to finish, and Judah Benjamin.** Benjamin

also served throughout the war but, as noted previously, in three
different cabinet positions.

9. **Six men served as secretary of war.** It stood to reason that the War
    Department would be the hot seat for the Confederacy, but Jeff
    Davis, who was a West Pointer and had served as secretary of war
    under President Pierce, made the job more difficult. Davis
    micromanaged the department, effectively reducing the secretaries
    to high-level clerks. The six men who held the post were Leroy
    Pope Walker, Judah Benjamin, George Randolph, Gustavus
    Woodson Smith, James Seddon, and John Breckenridge.

10. **Match these cabinet members with their home states:**
    1. **Judah P. Benjamin, (D) Louisiana**
    2. **Stephen R. Mallory, (B) Florida**
    3. **Christopher G. Memminger, (E) South Carolina**
    4. **John H. Reagan, (F) Texas**
    5. **Robert Toombs, (C) Georgia**
    6. **Leroy Pope Walker, (A) Alabama**

7. The Union Cabinet

1. **Mars and Neptune were Edwin Stanton and Gideon Welles.**
    Lincoln called Secretary of War Stanton Mars after the Roman god
    of war and Secretary of the Navy Welles Father Neptune for the
    Roman god of the sea.

2. **The future supreme court chief justice was Salmon Chase.** On the
    death of Chief Justice Roger Taney, Lincoln named Salmon Chase
    to succeed him. Chase longed to be president, but failing that, the
    job of chief justice was a high priority. The move also relieved
    Lincoln of a talented but sometimes troublesome rival in the
    cabinet.

3. **Almost killed in the Lincoln plot was William Seward.** He was
    attacked in his home the night of Lincoln's assassination and
    slashed on the neck and face. He was nearly killed and badly

scarred. All photographs of him after that date were taken in full profile.

4. **Simon Cameron was sent off to Russia.** Cameron proved an inept and probably ethically challenged war secretary, so he was repackaged as an ambassador and sent off to the court of the Romanovs in Russia. We hope he liked vodka and caviar.

5. **Edwin Stanton served three presidents in their cabinets.** He was attorney general at the end of the Buchanan administration and served as secretary of war for both Lincoln and Johnson. He was loyal to Lincoln but played a double game in both the Buchanan and Johnson cabinets. His dismissal by Andrew Johnson led to Johnson's impeachment.

6. **Family friendships led to the appointment of James Speed.** Lincoln and James's brother, Joshua, were close friends dating back to Lincoln's early days in Springfield. James Speed was named attorney general in 1864. Lincoln also offered government posts to Joshua, but he declined them.

7. **The Maine man at treasury was William Pitt Fessenden.** Fessenden replaced Salmon Chase as secretary of the treasury but stayed less than a year before returning to the Senate.

8. **The most obscure award goes to Titian J. Coffey.** He was an obscure lawyer and assistant attorney general who stepped in when Bates left. Coffey served for only one week before giving way to James Speed.

9. **Montgomery Blair came from a politically powerful family.** He was the son of Francis Preston Blair, a longtime newspaper editor and political power, who was an informal adviser to Andrew Jackson and to many presidents who followed him, including Lincoln. The elder Blair was a Democrat who became a Republican but later returned to his Democratic roots.

10. **William Pitt Fessenden was the father of two generals.** The Maine senator turned treasury secretary had two sons who wore Union general's stars. Francis and James Deering Fessenden probably owed their promotions to their father's lofty status rather than to

their own military genius. Neither really distinguished himself, but Francis was wounded twice and lost a leg.

Matchup of Officers to States
1. **Edward Bates, (D) Missouri.** He was born in Virginia but was living in Missouri in 1860.
2. **Montgomery Blair, (C) Maryland.** He was Kentucky born but living in Maryland when the war began.
3. **Simon Cameron, (G) Pennsylvania.** He was one of the most powerful political leaders in the state.
4. **Salmon P. Chase, (F) Ohio.** He was probably the strongest abolitionist in the cabinet.
5. **William H. Seward, (E) New York.**
6. **Caleb Smith, (B) Indiana.** He was born in Boston.
7. **Gideon Welles, (A) Connecticut.**

8. Nomenclature

1. **Bohemian Brigade.** Northern newspaper writers applied this name to themselves. They saw themselves leading a footloose and happy but impoverished lifestyle.
2. **Arkansas toothpick.** A knife, usually a large one, like a Bowie knife. They were popular in frontier settings such as Louisiana, Texas, and Arkansas and were useful for a variety of tasks.
3. **Desecrated vegetables.** Dehydrated mixed vegetables were delivered in a dry brick and often used in stews. The official term is "desiccated vegetables," but the unofficial name was too good a joke for the soldiers to pass up.
4. **Housewife.** The sewing kit with needles, thread, buttons, and so on, that the soldier needed to repair his clothes. Many were made by loved ones at home, and some were highly elaborate in design.
5. **The Old Woman.** A soldier's tent mate, an obvious allusion to domestic life.

6. **Silent battle.** Also called acoustic shadow, it described the situation where people very near a battlefield could not hear it but those much farther away heard it clearly. Land contours and wind currents probably caused this phenomenon.

7. **Shinplasters.** Any paper money of questionable value but especially Confederate money. During the war, counterfeiting became rampant.

8. **Shoddy.** An inferior woolen yarn made from a combination of new and used wool and the fabric made from such yarn. Uniforms made from shoddy looked good new but quickly fell apart, especially when wet.

9. **Sherman's neckties.** Soldiers also used the term "Sherman's hairpins." When destroying railroads, soldiers would heat the rails on a fire until soft and bend them, usually around a tree. Later in the war, soldiers also found a way to twist them so they could not be straightened.

10. **Salt horse.** The name given to salted or pickled beef referred to the processes that preserved the meat. The process worked fairly well, but the meat could taste quite bad and was not ideal fare from a nutritional standpoint.

11. **Contraband of war.** Maj. Gen. Ben Butler used this term to describe escaped slaves who sought refuge with Union forces. His legal basis for not returning escaped slaves to their masters was that the Confederates would use them to help them wage war. The policy and the term stuck, with both the army and the slaves themselves referring to the escaped slaves as "contrabands."

12. **Havelock.** A white cap cover with a flap in the back to protect the neck from the sun. It was a British Army item that the Union forces tried early in the war but quickly discarded.

13. **Graybacks.** Union soldiers used this term to describe Confederate soldiers, body lice, and sometimes Confederate money.

14. **Gabions.** Baskets filled with dirt or rocks that were used in building fortifications.

15. **Zouaves.** Units that adopted the colorful uniforms, drill, and fighting methods of the French/Algerian soldiers. Both the North and South had such units.

16. **Dog robbers.** Northern term for cooks. The implication is that they were serving the men food meant for dogs.

17. **Cracker line.** A supply route, usually associated with the effort to supply Union troops in Chattanooga after the battle of Chickamauga.

18. **Infernal machines.** Any hidden explosive device, either in water or on land. The armies usually placed them around fortifications, but later in the war the Confederates used them in roads. Union soldiers considered that practice inhumane.

19. **Spooning.** Soldiers sleeping together, back to breast, to keep warm. When two or more soldiers did so, the others had to be notified when one man decided it was time to roll over.

20. **Quaker guns.** Dummy guns that resembled actual cannon and were so called to reflect the pacifist aims of the Quakers. From a distance the guns often fooled even veteran scouts.

9. Language of War

1. An **abatis** is a network of felled trees in front of an entrenched position with the sharpened branches interlaced and facing the enemy. It is placed there to form an obstacle to attacking troops. It filled the purpose of barbed wire in later wars.

2. **Angle and return** refers to a turn made in a fortified line so that troops at one point in the line can fire on troops storming another section.

3. The **Napoleon** was the most common field artillery gun, a 12-pounder with a range of sixteen hundred yards. The **Parrott** was a rifled gun, usually a 10- or 20-pounder, and with a range of thirty-five hundred yards. The Napoleon had a smoothbore barrel, while the spiral grooves of the Parrott's barrel made the projectiles spin as they exited the gun, thereby improving accuracy.

4. A **demonstration** is a show of force where no attack is made. It is usually done to draw attention away from the real attack.

5. **Echelon** is an attack formation where the units are placed in line side by side and one unit moves out before the next goes into action. This arrangement produces a formation in a sort of stepped pattern that hits the enemy line while delivering a series of individual blows.

6. To **enfilade** is to attack the flank of the enemy position and fire into the side of the unit. It was good for the attacking unit because if the soldiers missed their targets, their bullets still might strike another man farther down the line. It was difficult for the unit being attacked to respond.

7. To **envelop** is to attack both flanks of the enemy simultaneously in an attempt to reach his rear and encircle him.

8. A **lunette** is a fortification consisting of a salient angle with the two flanks open to the rear like a crescent moon. In colonial times, they were called demi-lunes.

9. A **redan** is an earthwork thrown up around an individual field gun to protect it and its crew. It was usually built in a V shape with the point in the direction of the enemy.

10. To **refuse** a line is to turn the end backward to give protection in case of a flank attack. The term is also applied to lines anchored on a natural obstacle such as a body of water.

11. In a **retrograde** movement, troops are moving away from the enemy or from their previous position. It's a polite word for "retreat."

12. A **return** is the portion of the line that comes from a salient, or projection, to the main line.

13. A **salient** is a bulge in a line of entrenchments. The best-known salient in this war was the Mule Shoe at Spotsylvania.

14. A **screen** is an attempt by the cavalry to keep the enemy from getting close enough to see what the rest of the army is doing. An army usually used the tactic when on the move.

15. A **stand of arms** was a weapon (usually a rifled musket) plus the bayonet, cartridge belt, and cap box needed for its use.

16. **Unlimbering** was the act of detaching the field piece from the limber, which was the two-wheeled cart pulled by six horses or mules. The gun traveled hitched to the limber, and when it reached the battlefield, it was pulled into position, "unlimbered," and made ready for action.

17. The **van** is the advanced guard of a moving army. It was considered an honor to be placed in the van. It was a more dangerous position, but it also minimized the amount of dust the soldiers inhaled.

18. A **works** is a defensive military fortification and can be anything from a simple line of trenches to a full-scale fort.

10. Toehold at Port Royal

1. **Federal planners also considered Bulls Bay, South Carolina.** It's very large—six miles long and a mile and a half wide—and offered access to Charleston and the Santee River through interior shallow water routes. Port Royal was large enough, however, to accommodate the entire Union Navy, offered a range of inland waterways for operations against both Charleston and Savannah, and was a good jumping-off place for operations against all ports in South Carolina, Georgia, and North Florida.

2. **Brig. Gen. Tom Sherman commanded the army troops.** A longtime army veteran and a major of artillery when the war began, the native Rhode Islander seemed a good choice to lead the operation, but he fell into the interservice rivalry trap. The lack of cooperation between the army and navy prevented greater gains than he might otherwise have made. A spiderweb of rivers offered backdoor attack routes to both Charleston and Savannah, but they were never fully exploited.

3. **Samuel Francis Du Pont commanded the naval forces.** The nephew of the founder of the huge Delaware chemical company, Du Pont had a long and successful prewar naval career. His Port

Royal victory on November 7, 1861, at Port Royal Sound made him a national hero, but even with this valuable base, his ships could not stop the blockade-runners. The army was hard to work with, and Assistant Secretary of the Navy Gustavus Fox wanted to exclude the army from any operations so the navy would get all the credit. Lincoln pressed Du Pont for more victories. When ordered to attack Charleston without a corresponding army campaign, he dragged his feet but finally did. The attack failed, and it cost Du Pont his career.

4. **Brig. Gen. Thomas Drayton commanded Fort Walker.** He was a West Pointer who left the army and was engaged in planting and politics in South Carolina. At the time of the attack he commanded all the Port Royal defenses. One of the Union gunships attacking him was the USS *Pocahontas* commanded by his brother Cdr. Percival Drayton, who would later command Rear Adm. David Glasgow Farragut's flagship, USS *Hartford*, at Mobile Bay, Alabama. Thomas Drayton put up a good defense but was forced to spike his guns and retreat. Later, Robert E. Lee found him wanting as a brigadier general, so Lee broke up his brigade and relegated him to desk duty.

5. **The army landing was delayed because it lacked shallow-draft steamers and supplies.** The expedition hit a major storm on the way south that scattered the fleet. Some of the small steamers had to turn tail and head back to Fort Monroe, Virginia, so they were not available to land the army troops. In addition, the men had loaded the ships incorrectly, piling long-term baggage on top of the ammunition and other items that were needed first. Thus the attack became purely a navy show. General Sherman and his soldiers would be spectators.

6. **The fort on the north side of the bay was Fort Beauregard.** It was on Phillip's Island and the weaker of the two forts; therefore, it received less attention early in the battle. By the time Fort Walker fell and the fleet turned its attention to Beauregard, however, twelve of the fort's nineteen guns had been knocked out of action. Col.

Richard Dunovant ordered his 619 men to retreat. They needed no
encouragement and left without their camp equipment and without
destroying their military property. The battle of Port Royal Sound
was over and Du Pont had his base on Hilton Head Island. He
would expand and develop it as a coaling station and ship supply
and repair facility. Incidentally, Perry's Island, near Phillip's Island,
is now the site of the famed Marine Corps' boot camp Parris Island.
Marines from Du Pont's force made landings there too.

7. **Robert E. Lee made the decision to move defenses inland.** Port
    Royal seemed to demonstrate the danger of holding fortifications
    that could be reached by large shipboard guns. The Confederacy
    had lost a great deal of valuable ordnance at Port Royal, so pulling
    back farther inland to positions the larger ships could not reach
    seemed wise. The decision was not popular, especially with the
    bellicose South Carolinians. Lee was coming off his unsuccessful
    West Virginia service, where he was ridiculed as "Granny Lee" and
    the "King of Spades" for his caution and use of entrenchments.

8. **The first Georgia port targeted was Savannah.** Fort Pulaski was a
    masonry fort at the mouth of the Savannah River on tiny Cockspur
    Island. Union troops seized Tybee Island, which gave them a position
    to place heavy guns and reduce Pulaski. That action would pretty well
    halt blockade-running in the Savannah River; however, it would not
    shut down the port of Savannah, which had several other ways to
    enter it, including Wassaw Sound and Ossabaw Sound. Combined
    army and navy operations also captured Brunswick, Georgia.

9. **The first Florida port attacked was Fernandina.** It was a good
    blockading port because it was the terminus of the Florida Railroad
    and only lightly defended as the Confederacy chose to invest its
    limited resources to more important ports, such as Charleston,
    Wilmington, Mobile, and New Orleans. Later, Union forces
    captured and occupied St. Augustine and went up the St. John's
    River to capture Jacksonville. Despite its status as a railhead, the
    Union Army chose not to continuously occupy Jacksonville, but the
    navy periodically patrolled the river.

10. **Lincoln personally revoked David Hunter's Emancipation Proclamation.** Hunter was a strong abolitionist who had gained Lincoln's ear. He was recovering from a serious wound at First Bull Run when the army had lost patience with Tom Sherman's slow pace in reducing Fort Pulaski and sent Hunter to replace him. Initially, Hunter charmed his navy associates, but he quickly became controversial. On April 11, the day after Fort Pulaski fell, he proclaimed the slaves who were in his control free. Later, he expanded it to all slaves in his department. This declaration far exceeded his authority, and Lincoln, ever sensitive to holding the border states, annulled the order. Hunter was replaced by Maj. Gen. Ormsby MacKnight Mitchel, who promptly died of yellow fever, and Hunter returned to the command.

11. Double Vision

1. **George Washington established an intelligence system.** During the Revolution, Washington put in place and made very good use of spies and scouts. However, after the war his network was allowed to dissolve. Americans had a deep distrust of a standing army and feared that spies might be used inappropriately. At the outbreak of the Civil War, the army had no formal intelligence-gathering and analysis operations.

2. **As commander of Washington's defenses, Joseph King Fenno Mansfield was initially handed the intelligence job.** The nation's capital was surrounded by slave territory and was a Southern city in virtually every way. Many of its citizens identified with the Southern cause and were willing to take action to help the South. Mansfield put Connecticut-born lawyer William C. Parsons in charge of intelligence. Parsons did not have to worry about finding Confederate forces. They were right on the other side of Chain Bridge and in sight in the city of Alexandria. He spent most of his energy chasing down spies and finding hidden caches of arms.

3. **George McClellan brought in Allan Pinkerton to handle intelligence.** He brought in experienced detectives and dedicated most of his energy to counterintelligence operations. Eventually, he would dedicate resources to learning the size and disposition of Confederate forces and their affairs in Richmond; however, he was never really effective at scouting enemy forces to discover their size and plans. He seems to have had an agreement with McClellan to keep all troop strength estimates on the high side and assumed, for example, that all enemy regiments had seven hundred men, a number they knew to be unrealistically high. After identifying all regiments that opposed them, they then assumed that they must have missed a large number and factored them in too. Estimates were commonly two or three times the real number.

4. **Winfield Scott's cloak and dagger man was Lafayette Curry Baker.** History has pronounced him a thoroughly unsavory character. When Winfield Scott made him a special agent, Baker used his connections with Stanton and Seward to gain a post in the provost marshal's office to root out corruption in the war effort. He held the rank of colonel for most of the war and was promoted to brigadier general after playing a role in running down the Lincoln assassination conspirators. He also collected a share of the reward money. Later, he authored the book *A History of the Secret Service* that is totally unreliable except as a window to Baker's dark soul.

5. **Maj. Gen. John Adams Dix was handed the job of evaluating those held.** A veteran of the War of 1812, he was successful in politics, the law, and railroading before returning to the army for the Civil War. He was commanding in Maryland when he received the assignment of working with Judge Edwards Pierrepont to evaluate the many prisoners being held. The most famous one was Rose O'Neal Greenhow, who was judged more of a nuisance than a threat and sent off to Richmond.

6. **Timothy Webster was the most daring Pinkerton man.** He was an English-born mechanic from New Jersey who joined the Pinkertons

and made several trips to Manassas and Richmond. He played the double agent game, acting as a courier between a Richmond newspaper and informants in Baltimore. He was allowed to come and go, though he obviously drew the attention of Richmond detectives. He obtained passes from Confederate secretary of war Judah Benjamin and boasted of dining with Jefferson Davis. Closely watched, he fell ill in Richmond. Two Pinkerton operatives sent to find him were arrested and gave him up to save their own lives. Webster was tried and found guilty of espionage and sentenced to hang. He asked for a firing squad, but his request was denied. The hanging was botched when the rope broke. He was hauled back up on the scaffold, and the second try proved fatal.

7. **The intelligence interpretation job fell to Robert and Louis-Philippe d'Orléans, two French noblemen, who were volunteer aides to McClellan.** Louis-Philippe, Count of Paris, was a claimant to the French throne. Robert was the duke of Chartres. Pinkerton was passing along a flood of information to McClellan but was not analyzing it. McClellan handed that job to the two French noblemen, who did a good job with the assignment. However, they were called back to Europe in July 1862.

8. **Army maps were unreliable as to the Warwick River.** Federal maps showed it running parallel to their line of march. In fact, it ran across the peninsula from near Yorktown to the James River and created a natural defensive line. The Confederates had created a series of dams that flooded large areas, making the crossing more difficult yet. Lacking reliable maps proved a constant problem for Union armies. Especially early in the war, the Union forces had failed to make an effort to correct the few sketchy maps in their possession.

9. **Former Chicago architect John C. Babcock was the army's best mapmaker.** He was a twenty-five-year-old private when Pinkerton plucked him from the ranks because he could draw accurate sketches of fortifications. McClellan took him from Pinkerton to map the peninsula. Babcock did a superb job, scouting ahead on his warhorse, Gimlet. It was dangerous but productive work.

McClellan praised his maps as did Lincoln. After McClellan was sacked, and Pinkerton after him, Col. George Sharpe took over the intelligence service with Babcock as his deputy.

10. **The lack of enough good cavalry hindered Union intelligence efforts.** Believing it would be a short war and cavalry was expensive to create, the Union had few units while the South had James E. B. "Jeb" Stuart and plenty of eager horsemen. Stuart easily penetrated Union lines and learned the size and location of Union troops. At the same time, he screened the Southern infantry so that Union generals often did not know their numbers, where they were, or where they were headed. This Union shortcoming lasted until mid-1963 when Joseph "Fighting Joe" Hooker reorganized the cavalry and it began to produce results.

11. **Hot air balloons were used to get a better look at enemy lines.** Both sides tried them, but they were cumbersome to move around and highly vulnerable in the air. Perhaps the most imaginative use of a hot air balloon occurred when Confederate Edward Porter Alexander loaded one on a barge on the James River during the Seven Days Campaign, thereby inventing the aircraft carrier.

12. **John Pope's campaign came to grief when his intelligence sources dried up.** Contrary to his image as a fumbler and bumbler, Pope had done a good job early in his tenure as commander of the three-corps army trying to cover Washington, Northern Virginia, and the Shenandoah Valley. With the help of good cavalry and intelligence work, he located Maj. Gen. Thomas J. "Stonewall" Jackson's attacking force and held it in place. However, when his cavalry burned out and intelligence sources dried up, he failed to recognize the arrival of Maj. Gen. James Longstreet's corps. Pope was trying to buy time while McClellan's army returned from the peninsula. As McClellan took his time, Pope's army, with minimal help from a small part of McClellan's force, suffered a costly defeat at Second Bull Run.

SECTION III

NO EASY PATH TO VICTORY

The short war theory died at First Bull Run. The South would not be a pushover. The North would not quit. Lincoln's seventy-five thousand men for three months would not even begin to do the job. Many dark and trying days lay ahead. Both sides began to gear up for a long and bloody struggle. In the east, Maj. Gen. George Brinton McClellan built a powerful army but it could not get the better of the

In the summer of 1862, Maj. Gen. George McClellan took his magnificent army to Fort Monroe and up the peninsula to the gates of Richmond. Victory was tantalizingly close, but Robert E. Lee put the Confederates on the offensive and pushed McClellan back to the James River. The final action of the Seven Days Campaign was fought here at Malvern Hill, where McClellan's superior artillery inflicted a costly loss on the Southern army. Almost three years would pass before Union soldiers would finally march into the Confederate capital. *Photo by the author*

smaller force under Robert E. Lee. West of the mountains, the Confederacy stumbled as Union armies drove their Confederate rivals deep into Tennessee and Mississippi.

QUIZ 1
Island Number 10

Early in 1862, Union forces in Missouri went after a Confederate stronghold in the southeast corner of the state. The almost bloodless victory catapulted the Union field commander to center stage and pushed the rebel front line all the way south to Memphis. Let's test your knowledge of the campaign.

1. Name the Union commander who won fame at Island Number 10 only to have his reputation destroyed while leading an army in the East.
2. What nearby Missouri city was a part of the Confederate defense system?
3. What aspect of river geography made the island strategically important?
4. Name the third-rate Confederate leader who built the first defenses there.
5. Name the Union department commander who pumped more troops into the action while ordering his field commander to break off and join Brig. Gen. Ulysses Grant (who was promoted to major general during that campaign).
6. Island Number 10 got its name by being the tenth island from what place?
7. Name the fretful Confederate commander who grossly overestimated the size of the Union force descending on him.
8. Name the Connecticut Yankee saltwater sailor who reluctantly furnished the gunboats to support the Union's field force.
9. What engineering feat did the Yankees pull off that totally changed the strategic situation?
10. One of the Union division commanders was the great-grandson of one of George Washington's generals. Name him.

11. Two Union gunboats ran past the Island Number 10 batteries and to the south of the island, effectively sealing its fate. Name the gunboats.

12. What prevented the final Yankee assault on the island?

Quiz 2
Stones River

Fought in two different years over a three-day period, the Battle of Stones River (which the Confederates called Murfreesboro) stands as a narrow but important Union victory. Coming as it did less than a month after the Union debacle at Fredericksburg, the victory was politically important. Let's see what you know about this Tennessee action.

1. An Ohio-born West Pointer commanded the Union troops. Who was he?

2. The Confederate army was commanded by a West Pointer from North Carolina. Name him.

3. The Confederate commander used his cavalry to good advantage in the early stages of the battle. Who commanded the cavalry?

4. How did the Union's battle plan differ from the Confederate plan?

5. Who led the initial Confederate assault?

6. What up-and-coming young brigadier commanded the division that absorbed this first assault and bought time for the Union to patch together a second line?

7. What natural obstacle proved a major stumbling block for the Confederate attackers?

8. What Union position in the center of the line stopped the Confederates cold?

9. Who was the brigade commander who held that hot spot?

10. When action resumed, who was the Confederate general who led the assault?
11. Name the Union colonel who served as chief of staff and who was killed in the battle.
12. The Union had a numerical superiority. Which number best describes the difference? (A) 6,700 men. (B) 9,200 men. (C) 12,500 men.
13. Which side experienced the most casualties?
14. Which side had the highest casualty rate?

Quiz 3
Field Artillery

Napoleon said that the best generals were those with artillery experience. Civil War leaders quickly realized that a well-placed and well-supported battery could stop an infantry charge in its tracks. Let's see what you know about this important arm of Civil War armies.

1. How many men constituted a Civil War field artillery gun crew?
2. How many guns were in a battery?
3. What was the proper rank of a battery commander?
4. What was the difference between a shot and a bolt?
5. Which crew member aimed the gun?
6. What was the number of the crew member who actually fired the gun?
7. What were the fuses made of?
8. How many horses did each battery have?
9. What was a brass Napoleon made of?
10. In case or shrapnel shot, what was packed inside the shell along with the balls?
11. What was a handspike used for?
12. How many shots per minute could be fired?

13. What was a sabot and how was it used? _
14. What was a thumbstall and how was it used?

Quiz 4
To Horse

It can be argued that the North began to win the Civil War when it achieved equality with the South in cavalry. The South entered the war with an important advantage in the mounted arm. The Union needed almost two years to catch up, but by the end of the war, the Union was dominant. Let's look at the early days of Union horsemen.

1. At the outbreak of the Civil War, the U.S. Army had three different types of mounted units. Name them.
2. How many mounted regiments did the army have when Lincoln was inaugurated?
3. Initially, Gen. Winfield Scott and Secretary Simon Cameron refused to accept mounted volunteer units. Why?
4. How many companies were in a cavalry regiment?
5. What weapon was called the wrist breaker?
6. The Sixth Pennsylvania Cavalry had the most unusual weapon. What was it?
7. When a cavalry unit came in from the field, what was the first duty of each trooper?
8. According to the 1860 Census, how many horses were in the United States?
9. What was considered the ideal age for a cavalry horse?
10. What clearly outmoded cavalry tactic was idealized in theory but dumped in practice?

QUIZ 5
Rail Junction

After bloody Shiloh, the Union's western army caught its breath and then began a slow advance toward Corinth, Mississippi. At stake was a strategically vital railroad junction. The South could ill afford to lose it and the Union wanted it. Let's see what you know of this campaign.

1. Name the two Confederate railroad lines that crossed in Corinth.
2. The Union Army had a new field commander. He was?
3. What was General Grant's new assignment?
4. Name the Confederate general defending Corinth.
5. What additional army joined the Confederates?
6. What additional army joined the Union forces?
7. What was the Union's strategy?
8. What was the Confederate strategy?
9. What young Union cavalry officer, a major star by war's end, took part in a successful raid on the railroad south and east of the city?
10. What was the determining factor in forcing the Confederates to evacuate Corinth?
11. As a result of that evacuation, what other key points were abandoned or fell?
12. After the withdrawal, what happened to the Confederate commander?
13. What was the Union commander's next assignment?
14. What did Grant select for his next objective?

Quiz 6
Capital Conquests

One by one, the capitals of the Confederate states fell to Union armies, usually as a stubborn rear guard exited one end of town while a long column in blue marched into the other. When the war ended, only two remained unoccupied. Let's see if you can match up the capital cities with the circumstances and dates of their fall.

1. The first rebel capital to fall had become untenable when a major Confederate fort upriver from it surrendered unconditionally. What was the city?

2. The governor gave a spirited call to defense but led the rush out of town. Union forces held a mock session of the legislature and voted it back into the Union before continuing their grand march. Name the town.

3. It might well be called the capital that would not stay captured. It fell in May 1863 and was abandoned, only to be recaptured in July. It was?

4. Union artillery across the Congaree River shelled and poked some holes in the new state capitol building. Large stars mark those holes today. Name it.

5. To this day, city residents boast it was never captured; however, their ancestors did abandon it when another city to its south fell. It was?

6. This capital was occupied without a fight, but the Rebels came back in August 1862 and made a determined but unsuccessful attempt to retake it. Name it.

7. Two days after the surrender at Appomattox, this Southern capital was occupied. It was the last to fall. It was?

8. Located farthest from the center of the war, this Confederate capital never fell but was covered by the final surrender of Confederate forces. Name it.

9. The day Lee surrendered at Appomattox, cavalry under Brig. Gen. James Harrison Wilson occupied this Deep South capital unopposed. It was?

10. A force under Union Gen. John Newton was turned back at a place called Natural Bridge on March 6, 1865, and this Southern capital remained in Confederate hands until May 10, 1865. Name it.

11. On September 10, 1863, a Union corps under Gen. Frederick "Fred" Steele restored this state capital to the Union. It was?

12. If the seat of government rests with the head of state, where was the rebel capital on May 10, 1865, when a troop of Union cavalry captured Jefferson Davis?

Quiz 7
Shenandoah Lightning

Many students of the Civil War believe that General Jackson's 1862 Shenandoah Valley Campaign was the most brilliant of all. From late March to early June, he confused and defeated several Union armies and kept Washington in a state of agitation. Let's test your knowledge of the great Stonewall in action.

1. Before he could begin, Jackson needed reliable maps. Who did he turn to for them?

2. Who commanded Jackson's cavalry during the campaign?

3. Remarkably, this brilliant campaign started with a tactical defeat. Where did that battle take place?

4. Name the Union commander who defeated Jackson.

5. Next, Jackson headed south and west to head off a Union force. Where did the next battle take place?
6. Name the two generals who commanded the Union forces in the second battle?
7. In the third major action of the campaign, Jackson captured a Union garrison. Name the place.
8. A famous female spy provided the Confederates with important information that led to the victory. Name her.
9. Jackson followed up that victory with an attack on a federal army led by Gen. Nathaniel Prentiss Banks. Name the place.
10. Union forces tried to trap Jackson between three converging armies, but he slipped away. Where was that trap to be sprung?
11. In Jackson's final and perhaps most impressive action, he defeated two Union forces in two days. Name the two actions.
12. Name the two Confederate generals who were Jackson's principal subordinates.

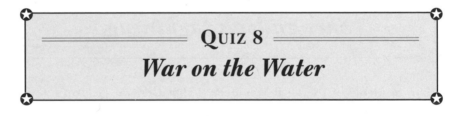

Quiz 8
War on the Water

Most Civil War readers focus on the army and the land battles. However, the Union's domination of the rivers and its blockade of Southern ports were also vital elements of the North's victory. This quiz looks at the salt and freshwater side of the Civil War.

1. When it came to capturing major cities by ship, Rear Adm. David Farragut wins the prize, capturing Mobile and New Orleans. In both cases, he had to force his way past two forts to do it. Name the forts and the cities they guarded.
2. This old salt commanded the gunboats on the Tennessee and Cumberland Rivers that backed up Grant's important victories at

Forts Henry and Donelson. He suffered a wound at Fort Donelson that forced him into a less active role, and he died in 1863. Name him.

3. The U.S. secretary of the navy was Connecticut Yankee Gideon Welles. His Confederate counterpart was born in Trinidad and grew up in Florida. He was?

4. Blockade-running was profitable. Confederate cotton sold for three cents a pound and could be sold in London for forty cents to a dollar a pound. A thousand bales on a fast steamer could turn a $250,000 profit in two weeks. But what was the chance of getting caught? (A) One in two. (B) One in six. (C) One in twelve. (D) One in twenty.

5. Two of the great ship duels of the war were the CSS *Alabama* against the USS *Kearsarge*, and the USS *Monitor* against the CSS *Virginia*, formerly the *Merrimack*. Name the officers who commanded the ships.

6. In a time of innovation these four men made names for themselves through invention or development. Name what the following men were famous for: John A. B. Dahlgren, John Ericsson, Horace L. Hunley, and Charles Ellet Jr.

7. The *Trent* Affair in November 1861 found the North in hot water after a U.S. warship stopped the British mail ship *Trent* and captured Confederate diplomats James Murray Mason and John Slidell. Eventually, Lincoln had to back off and release the captives. Name the ship and its captain.

8. Robert E. Lee had a brother in the Confederate navy. Name him.

9. David Dixon Porter was a sailor with family connections. What were they?

10. Yankee gunboats often used their firepower to rescue the army from harm at such battles as Malvern Hill and Shiloh. But one soldier, Ohio-born Joseph Bailey, saved a Union fleet. Where and how did he do it?

Quiz 9
The Union Navy

The considerable contribution of the Union Navy is often overlooked, lost in the tales of great land battles and huge armies. Most Civil War readers can identify Gideon Welles, David Dixon Porter, and David Farragut, but how about some of the others who contributed to victory on both salt and fresh water? See if you can identify the contributors to the Union's naval successes.

1. He was an adviser to Gideon Welles and led the expedition that captured Hatteras Inlet and Fort Clark, but he was considered too old for active duty at sea and retired.

2. This great-grandson of Benjamin Franklin ran a coast survey project before the war, and the data he developed was of great value to the Union in initiating the blockade.

3. This South Carolinian remained loyal to the Union despite his brother's being a Confederate general. He commanded Farragut's flagship, USS *Hartford*, at the Battle of Mobile Bay.

4. He commanded the naval forces during Burnside's 1862 North Carolina Campaign and later captured Norfolk, Virginia.

5. The commander of the Washington Navy Yard and a favorite of Abraham Lincoln's, he was primarily known as an inventor and engineer.

6. Although he commanded the upper Mississippi squadron and won victories at Fort Pillow and Memphis, he was not considered up to the job and was replaced by David Dixon Porter.

7. He served in both the army and navy of his native land but never in the United States. His design of an odd little ironclad, however, may have saved the day versus CSS *Virginia*.

8. A boyhood acquaintance of Navy Secretary Gideon Welles, he helped win important victories at Fort Henry, Fort Donelson, and Island Number 10.

Quiz 10
How Big Was an Army?

Prior to the Civil War, no American general had ever commanded an army of more than twenty thousand men, but this war would be different. The scale and organization of both the Union and Confederate armies broke new ground for America. Let's see how much you know about the armies and their organization.

1. What was the basic unit of organization for Civil War infantry?
2. How many men were in an infantry company?
3. What was the standard rank of a regimental commander?
4. How were officers selected?
5. What unit did a one-star general command?
6. How many of those units were in a division?
7. How many divisions were in a corps?
8. How did army units replace losses?
9. Cavalry regiments differed from infantry in size. How?
10. Field artillery batteries or companies were a part of a larger organization. What was it?
11. How many companies were in a heavy artillery unit?
12. Most Union armies were named for a certain geographic feature. It was?

QUIZ 11
The Social Scene

When we think of Civil War Washington, we think of a grim military camp, but even in the throes of war, the nation's capital was the scene of an active, if not totally gay, social life. Let's see if you can match some of the high-profile players to the roles they played.

The Roles

1. Prior to the war, a New York congressman shot and killed his wife's lover in Lafayette Park across from the White House and beat the rap. Who was the victim?

2. James Buchanan was a bachelor during his presidency, so who served as the White House hostess?

3. She was the beautiful daughter of a powerful cabinet member who married a wealthy former governor and senator, but after a series of unfortunate events, she died in poverty. Who was she?

4. She was one of the belles of prewar society, but when she elected to remain in Washington to spy for the South, she ended up in Old Capitol Prison.

5. Lincoln's private secretaries called their employer the Tycoon and referred to Mrs. Lincoln as the Hellcat. Name the two secretaries.

6. Mrs. Lincoln's mulatto dressmaker became her closest friend and confidante. Who was she?

7. The White House went into mourning four times during the war. Name the four persons for whom the Lincolns mourned.

8. What was the name of the New England senator's daughter, though plain and plump, who was said to be engaged to actor John Wilkes Booth?

9. When the Grants begged off an invitation to Ford's Theatre with the Lincolns, a senator's daughter and her fiancée were drafted. They were?

10. At the other end of the social ladder, this young woman was the subject of a sensational trial for running a bawdy house one block from the White House.

The Players

A. Col. Edward D. Baker
B. Col. Elmer Ellsworth
C. Rose O'Neal Greenhow
D. Lucy "Bessie" Hale
E. Clara Harris
F. John Hay
G. Gen. Ben Hardin Helm
H. Elizabeth Keckley
I. Philip Barton Key II
J. Harriet Lane
K. Willie Lincoln
L. John Nicolay
M. Maj. Henry Rathbone
N. Maude Roberts
O. Kate Chase Sprague

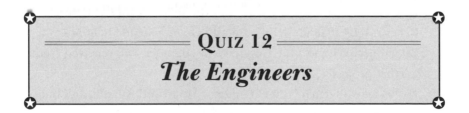

QUIZ 12
The Engineers

The logistics of war can be as important to victory as the fighting units themselves. The infantry, artillery, and cavalry received the glory, but the engineers built the bridges, kept the railroads open, repaired the roads, made the maps, built the fortifications, and scouted the battlefields. Let's see what you know about them.

1. With forty thousand men starving in Chattanooga, this engineer designed the famous "cracker line" that would save the day. Name him.

2. This Connecticut-born engineer commanded the U.S. Army Corps of Engineers throughout most of the Civil War. He was?

3. This engineering officer earned a statue, field glasses in hand, on the famous hill he helped to save. Name him.

4. A West Pointer who left the army soon after graduation, he returned to the army to keep the trains running. He was?

5. This New York–born West Pointer was considered the leading expert on pontoon bridges. He spent most of the war on Gen. Henry Halleck's staff. Name him.

6. Although the war was half over before he graduated from West Point, he made a name for himself on the Dutch Gap Canal and bridging the James River for Grant's army. He was?

7. The greatest engineering failure of the war may have been the delay of pontoon bridges in reaching Fredericksburg, Virginia. What engineering officer was relieved from duty for it?

8. Engineers spanned some wide rivers during the war, but the longest pontoon bridge was built across the Ohio River in 1861. What Kentucky town did it serve?

9. One of the great success stories was the spanning of the James River in 1864 that allowed Grant and George Meade to attack Petersburg. Who was the Connecticut engineer who received credit for that project?

10. He became Sherman's chief engineer, destroyed Atlanta, and built the roads and bridges for the March to the Sea and into the Carolinas. Name him.

ANSWERS

1. Island Number 10

1. **The general who captured Island Number 10 was John Pope.**
    After a great start in Missouri, he came east and made something
    of a fool of himself with lofty speeches and dispatches. Then
    General Lee and Maj. Gen. Stonewall Jackson soundly beat him at
    Second Bull Run. He spent the rest of the war chasing Indians.

2. **New Madrid was part of the Confederate defensive system.** The
    Confederates had built two forts, Thompson and Bankhead, and
    considered the city a strong position. Pope resisted the temptation
    to attack and simply bypassed it.

3. **The island was important because the river makes a large S curve
    there.** The forts at New Madrid and on the island effectively
    stopped shipping in the Mississippi. Large curves give land-based
    guns more time to fire on their targets.

4. **Initial defenses were built by Gideon Pillow.** He was President
    Polk's law partner and a volunteer general in the Mexican War, but
    his Civil War career ended when he handed the command of Fort
    Donelson over to Brig. Gen. Simon Buckner to surrender.

5. **Gen. Henry Wagner Halleck pumped in reinforcements.** "Old
    Brains" was his usual vacillating self, veering wildly from hot to cold
    on the project. Fortunately, Pope ignored Halleck's order to
    withdraw and won.

6. **The island was the tenth from Cairo, Illinois.** The mile-long island
    was 450 feet wide and vulnerable to high water because it sat barely
    10 feet above low water. Cairo (pronounced Ka-row) is an
    important point on the Mississippi because it is located where the
    Ohio River enters.

7. **Brig. Gen. John McCown was the island's defender.** Maj. Gen.
    Leonidas Polk picked him and he was a poor choice. He was an old-
    line regular with little ability, and the assignment seemed to terrify

him. He continually demanded more troops from General Beauregard, who finally told him to make do with what he had.

8. **Cdre. Andrew Foote reluctantly supported Pope.** His fleet had taken a pounding at Fort Donelson, where he was wounded. He vowed to his wife that he would never again sail that close to land fortifications, but under pressure from Assistant Secretary of War Thomas Scott, he finally went to Pope's assistance. It was obvious that on the major rivers, a combined land-naval operation was necessary.

9. **To bypass the island's guns, the Yankees built a canal.** It bypassed the island and allowed the Union Army to move transports into position without running past the fortifications first. They used huge swing saws to cut underwater obstructions. Grant would try the same strategy at Vicksburg but without success.

10. **The great-grandson of one of Washington's generals was Brig. Gen. Schuyler Hamilton.** He was Alexander Hamilton's grandson and great grandson of Gen. Philip Schuyler. He was a West Pointer with a fine record in the Mexican War but malaria forced him from active duty in late 1862.

11. **USS *Carondelet* and USS *Pittsburgh* ran by the island.** The *Carondelet* under Cdr. Henry Walke went first. Two nights later the *Pittsburgh* followed. Neither was seriously damaged, and Island Number 10 was made virtually untenable with their presence below it.

12. **The Confederates surrendered before a final assault could be launched.** Gen. William W. Mackall realized the Confederates' situation was hopeless and saved his men. The Confederates lost about forty-five hundred men killed, wounded, and missing (mostly captured) in the campaign. The Union lost thirty-two men.

2. Stones River

1. **The Union commander at Stone's River was William Starke Rosecrans.** He was highly regarded early in the war. He won the

Thanks of Congress for his performance at Stones River, but he was slow to move after the battle and ran into disaster at Chickamauga.

2. **Rosecrans's Confederate opponent was Braxton Bragg.** His skills as a military commander were often overshadowed by his tendency to battle with his subordinates. Bragg came close to winning a major victory at Stones River, but when he retreated he gave the Union the chance to claim victory.

3. **Joseph "Fighting Joe" Wheeler commanded the Confederate Cavalry.** As usual, he served well at Stones River and throughout the war. After the war, he practiced law and was Alabama's representative in Congress. He again led troops in Puerto Rico and the Philippines during the Spanish-American War. He is one of the few Confederates buried in Arlington National Cemetery.

4. **There was no difference; both battle plans were the same.** Both generals planned to strike the right flank of the other army on the morning of the thirty-first. Bragg simply moved his troops earlier and almost won the day. Had Bragg been successful, he would have cut Rosecrans off from his lines of supply, communication, and retreat back to Nashville.

5. **William Joseph Hardee commanded the Southern attack.** "Old Reliable" was an excellent division and corps commander. Prior to the war he was one of the most highly regarded officers in the army. However, he served throughout the war in subservient positions and never had a chance to lead a large army of his own.

6. **The attack struck troops commanded by Philip "Little Phil" Sheridan.** The stubby West Pointer commanded Maj. Gen. Alexander McCook's Third Division. He lost all three of his brigade commanders but probably saved the day for the Union. After the war, virtually every one of his commanders claimed credit for "discovering" him and advancing his career.

7. **The attack was impeded by cedar forests.** Bragg's tactics would have worked fine on an open field, but dense patches of woods slowed the Confederates' advance and prevented them from

moving up their artillery. Meanwhile, the Union forces created a line of artillery that stopped the Confederates before they could reach the Nashville Pike.

8. **The most solid Union position was called the Round Forest.** This forested rise of ground was the only Union position to hold for the entire first day of battle. The first attack came at 10 a.m. and was smashed with heavy losses. The second came within 150 yards but met with equally heavy losses.

9. **The commander in the Round Forest was Col. William Babcock Hazen.** This Vermont-born West Pointer was an excellent officer who rose to corps command. The monument to his brigade in the Round Forest, erected in 1863, is said to be the nation's oldest Civil War battlefield memorial.

10. **John C. Breckenridge led the Confederate attack.** The attack was launched on January 2 after a day off between battles. Breckenridge hit the Union left flank from east of Stones River, chasing off a small Union guard but sustaining 1,800 hundred casualties in the process. Again, well-placed Union artillery was too much for the attacking Confederates.

11. **Rosecrans's chief of staff Lt. Col. Julius Garesché was killed.** He was riding beside General Rosecrans near the Round Forest when a cannonball decapitated him.

12. **The Union outnumbered the Confederates by (A) 6,700 men.** The two forces were fairly close in size by Civil War standards. According to Thomas Leonard Livermore, the Federals had 41,400 men to 34,739 for the Confederates. Military tradition says that the attacking force should significantly outnumber the defenders, but while the Confederates rarely did, they still launched many attacks, some of which were remarkably successful.

13. **The Union suffered greater casualties.** They lost 12,906 compared to 11,739 for the Confederates. Most of the Union's losses probably came early in the fight when the Confederate attacks caught many units unready.

14. **The Confederates lost a higher percentage of their men.** They lost 33.8 percent of their force compared to 31 percent Union losses. The South had trouble making up for those losses. Bragg might have been wiser to retreat before the battle. This pattern would often repeat itself. By the final year of the war, the South had lost far too many good men and all hope of winning.

3. Field Artillery

1. **Eight men in a gun crew.** The gunner, usually a corporal, called the commands, and seven privates, each with a number that denoted his duties, carried out those commands. All the men knew each other's jobs, and should a man become a casualty, the men knew who they would have to replace.

2. **There were usually four guns in a battery, but sometimes it had five or six.** A four-gun battery was divided into two sections of two guns each. A lieutenant commanded each section. Occasionally, the two sections were separated on the battlefield, but they usually fought as a unit.

3. **The battery commander was a captain.** Occasionally a first lieutenant would be in command, but the job called for a captain. An infantry company, which was about the same size, also had a captain in command. The battery commander, however, had a much greater impact and often communicated directly with generals

4. **Shot was round while bolts were elongated.** Smoothbore guns usually fired round shot. Bolts, which were fired by rifled guns, would spin in flight. That created a more predictable path and therefore greater accuracy.

5. **The gunner usually aimed the piece.** He sighted the tube, set the elevating screw, and called for the correct type of ammunition, powder charge, and fuse setting. His job was ensuring accuracy.

6. **Actual firing was done by number 4.** Crew member number 4 grasped the lanyard and, on the command "fire," pulled it to cause an immediate discharge.

7. **Fuses were made of either wood or paper.** Early in the war wooden fuses were used, but later both sides switched to paper. The fuse was round and tapered to a point. Men filled it with gunpowder soaked in alcohol or whiskey. They cut it to the proper length so it would explode as it reached the target.

8. **Batteries had forty to sixty horses for a four-gun battery.** A four-horse team pulled a caisson with the field gun attached. The battery needed other horses for the officers, for pulling limbers and other supply wagons, and for providing the men's transportation. Everybody rode, either on the wagons or on horseback. As soon as the guns went into battery, some of the spare men took the horses to a point close by but out of danger. Horses suffered high mortality rates. An estimated million horses were killed in the war.

9. **Brass Napoleons were made of bronze.** They were commonly called brass but actually were actually bronze. Brass, an alloy of bronze, is too soft for cannon. After the war, many Confederate bronze guns were melted down and used to make lapel buttons for members of the Union's powerful veterans association, the Grand Army of the Republic.

10. **Case or shrapnel shot contained sulfur or coal tar.** The secondary explosion of this material spread out the shot and created more casualties. Forces used this anti-infantry ammunition from medium distances against massed troops. When they grew closer, the batteries switched to canister, which had balls packed in sawdust. With fuses cut short, it was like running into a giant shotgun. Incidentally, Shrapnel was the name of the British artillery officer who invented the murderous stuff.

11. **A handspike was used to move the tail of the gun.** It was a stout wooden bar that the men inserted into the tail of the gun to make it easier to move when the gun was in battery, that is, when it was in a firing position. The gun rolled backward as each shot was fired and had to be repositioned afterward every time.

12. **A trained crew could fire two to three shots per minute.** That rate is about the same as for an infantryman firing a muzzle-loaded

rifle, but the artillery gun's effect was potentially far more devastating. In a close fight, crews sometimes exceeded this rate by not swabbing out the gun between rounds. These crews were taking a long chance, however: sometimes sparks were left inside the tube, and ramming a fresh charge of powder on top of sparks was tempting fate.

13. **A sabot was a round piece of wood joining the projectile and the charge.** The round piece of wood usually had a hole in the middle with round shot resting in the hole. The charge was beneath the sabot and the combination strapped together. The sabot helped give the projectile its spin when fired from a rifled gun. *Sabot* is a French word meaning "wooden shoe." The word "sabotage"—to damage something by hammering it with your wooden shoe—also comes from it.

14. **A thumbstall is a leather sleeve worn on the thumb to block the vent.** Crewman number 3 kept the vent blocked during swabbing and loading to prevent accidental premature firing. The vent was hot so he wore the leather thumb cover.

4. To Horse

1. **The three types of mounted units were Cavalry, the Mounted Rifles, and Dragoons.** The Dragoons were the oldest service, established in 1832, and trained to fight either mounted or dismounted. The mounted rifles fought dismounted, and the cavalry was trained to fight from horseback. The cavalry uniforms had yellow piping, the Mounted Rifles green, and the Dragoons orange.

2. **The regular army had five mounted units: two of Dragoons, one of mounted infantry, and two of cavalry.** Soon after the war began, a third cavalry regiment was authorized. All mounted regiments were then redesignated as cavalry. The First and Second Dragoons became the First and Second Cavalry, and the Mounted Rifles became the Third Cavalry. The First Cavalry became the Fourth,

the Second as the Fifth, and the new regiment as the Sixth. This change caused trouble in the First and Second Cavalry, whose men took pride in their old designations and resented losing them.

3. **Army leadership was reluctant to accept volunteer cavalry units because of time and money.** Expecting a short war, they decided it would take too much time and cost too much money to turn raw recruits into cavalry. They only accepted one unit—a company from the District of Columbia—and only because its captain bankrolled it. They soon found that the war would not be over shortly and that they desperately needed more cavalry.

4. **By the book there were twelve companies in cavalry regiments, but in practice, they usually featured ten.** Set in 1861 the standard for regulars was twelve, which provided 174 extra troopers. The law called for twelve companies, or three battalions of four companies each. Each battalion consisted of two squadrons of two companies each. Five field officers—a colonel commanding, a lieutenant colonel, and three majors for the battalions—led the regiment. However, many volunteer units were accepted with only ten companies each. They were later expanded to twelve.

5. **The Model 1850 Straight-Blade Saber was called the wrist breaker**. It was heavy and required a great deal of arm strength to wield it. Officers spent many hours drilling their men in its use. By 1863 the army was phasing it out in favor of a lighter, curved model that is closer in design to a sword. Many men preferred using the pistol but found it almost impossible to reload while they were riding in the saddle. Confederates disliked the sabers and often called on Union cavalry to put their sabers away and fight like men.

6. **The Sixth Pennsylvania Cavalry used lances.** Known as Rush's Lancers, two companies of the regiment were armed with 8.5-foot lances made of Norwegian fir. They had an 11.5-inch blade and were decorated with a scarlet pennant. The brainchild of General McClellan, they were totally impractical on the American battlefield. Even Chief of the Cavalry George Stoneman Jr. called them "those damned poles." Eventually, the army replaced them with carbines.

7. **A cavalryman's first duty was to care for his horse**. The trooper had to brush and comb his horse, check its hooves, and feed and water it. The process took about an hour. Only after the horse was cared for could the trooper see to his own needs. Cavalry horses had to carry about fifty pounds of equipment on their backs in addition to the trooper's weight. Often the horses were saddled fifteen hours a day, and sore backs were an epidemic. Hard service took a frightful toll on the horses.

8. **The United States had 4.5 million horses (actual count: 4,504,854) according to the 1860 census.** The United States had more horses than any other country in the world. The majority of the horses were in states that did not secede; however, not all of them were suitable for cavalry use. In the first two years of the war, the government provided 284,000 horses for 60,000 cavalrymen. Of course, the army needed thousands more for the field artillery and the miles of wagon trains.

9. **The ideal age for a cavalry horse was six years old.** Specifications called for a horse fifteen hands high at the shoulder and a minimum of 950 pounds. The cavalry wanted a horse that was mature but not too old. The average cavalryman was no taller than five feet seven, was in his late teens or early twenties, and unmarried. The combination of horses that had never been ridden and men who had never been on a horse's back before was sometime lethal. Horses threw, kicked, and bit the men. Horses even would rub up against trees to try to rid themselves of their riders and saddles. Before the war between men could be fought, first they had to win the struggle with the horse.

10. **The saber charge was clearly outmoded.** The Mexican War produced a couple of successful charges and they seemed exciting and heroic, but modern weapons had made them as impractical as the lance was. The cavalry attempted a few saber charges, but they almost always were a disaster. No doubt, the glory of the charge attracted some young men into the cavalry, but others joined for more practical reasons—less walking and no trench duty. That

attraction is summed up in the language of a recruiting poster of the era: Less Fatigue! Less Mortality!

5. Rail Junction

1. **The railroads crossing in Corinth were the Memphis & Charleston and the Mobile & Ohio.** The former connected the East Coast to the Mississippi River. The latter connected the Gulf with the Mississippi and Ohio Rivers at Columbus, Kentucky. The Corinth crossroad was a strategically vital point for both armies.

2. **The new field commander was Henry Halleck.** "Old Brains" was the commander of all Union forces in the West. Shocked by the thirteen thousand casualties in Grant's near disaster at Shiloh, Halleck took field leadership of the Union armies under Grant and Maj. Gen. Don Carlos Buell.

3. **Grant was named second in command to Halleck.** In other words, Grant was on the shelf with nothing much to do unless Halleck left or was incapacitated. It almost drove him crazy, and he considered resigning.

4. **Confederate forces were commanded by P. G. T. Beauregard.** He took command when Gen. Albert Sidney Johnston was killed at Shiloh.

5. **Brig. Gen. Earl Van Dorn's Confederate Army of the West joined Beauregard's army.** It marched in from western Arkansas. Johnston had hoped to use these troops at Shiloh, but they were too late in arriving.

6. **Halleck was reinforced by John Pope's Army of the Mississippi.** Coming from a victory at Island Number 10, these fresh troops brought Halleck's army to about 120,000 men, or double the number Beauregard commanded.

7. **Halleck's strategy was to move slowly and entrench at each stop.** After Shiloh, Halleck was being super careful so that the Confederates would not have a chance to catch his army in the open. As a result, the army moved at a snail's pace.

8. **Beauregard hoped to catch a part of Halleck's army isolated from the rest and destroy it.** Halleck's strategy, while painfully slow, prevented this.

9. **Col. Phil Sheridan struck the railroad south and east of the junction.** He commanded the Second Michigan Cavalry. Along with the Second Iowa and under the command of Col. Washington Elliott, the raid tore up a lot of railroad and telegraph equipment and destroyed important Confederate supplies.

10. **The Confederates abandoned the town because it lacked good water.** The shortage of good drinking water and the disease that spread among the men when they drank the bad water forced Beauregard to give up Corinth.

11. **The loss of Corinth led to the loss of Fort Pillow and Memphis, Tennessee.** The loss of Corinth flanked Fort Pillow, which had to be evacuated. With Fort Pillow no longer guarding the river, Memphis fell soon afterward.

12. **Beauregard went on sick leave without permission and was sacked.** Davis disliked Beauregard. When he left the army without Davis's permission, Davis relieved him and selected a worse general, Braxton Bragg, to replace him.

13. **Halleck was called to Washington to become general in chief.** He replaced George McClellan, who was bogged down on the Virginia peninsula. Ironically, when the administration replaced Halleck, it chose Grant, his former subordinate.

14. **Grant decided to take Vicksburg.** With the railroads in hand, Grant began his long campaign to capture the city and control the Mississippi River.

6. Capital Conquests

1. **First Confederate state capital to fall was Nashville, Tennessee.** When Fort Henry on the Tennessee River and Fort Donelson on the Cumberland River fell, Nashville could no longer be defended. Buell's troops marched in February 24, 1862, driving out the

cavalry under Col. Nathan Bedford Forrest. The loss was shocking to the Confederacy.

2. **Sherman's army had fun when they captured Milledgeville, Georgia.** Governor Joe Brown, despite earlier fiery rhetoric, led the dash to Macon as Sherman's army marched into the Georgia capital on November 22, 1864. Union soldiers took over the legislature, opened the session with bourbon, followed it up with mock speeches and brandy, and concluded by voting Georgia back into the Union.

3. **Jackson, Mississippi, would not stay captured.** Grant captured it from Joe Johnston in May and turned to capture Vicksburg. After Vicksburg fell in July, Grant sent Sherman east to capture Jackson again. He did after a weeklong siege; however, given that the city had little strategic value, the Union made no attempt to occupy it continuously.

4. **Sherman's artillery poked holes in the capitol building at Columbia, South Carolina.** If Sherman and his "bummers"—or foragers—made Georgia howl, they made South Carolina pay. As they saw that state as the center of the secession trouble, many Union soldiers showed no mercy. The Rebels complained that Sherman issued two matches for every bullet. On the night of February 17, 1865, a huge section of the city burned while Union soldiers ran wild. Sherman denied any intent, but the result was disaster for Columbia.

5. **The people of Richmond, Virginia, boast that their city never surrendered.** When the Union Army broke through at Petersburg, Richmond had to be evacuated. Ironically, the first Union troops to march in were black soldiers, most of them former slaves. Their first job on arrival was to fight fires that the Confederate Army had set to destroy the city's cotton and military stores. The death throes of the Confederacy had begun.

6. **Baton Rouge, Louisiana, was taken without a fight.** After the fall of New Orleans, Union forces seized the capital city May 12, 1862. Earl Van Dorn's attempt to retake it in August initially met with

success but came to grief when the Confederate flagship CSS *Arkansas* developed engine trouble and ran hard aground. While the Confederates were driven back, the Union commander, Brig. Gen. Tom Williams, was killed. The city remained in Union hands.

7. **Raleigh, North Carolina, was occupied two days after Appomattox.** Gov. Zebulon Vance opened negotiations to try to spare the capital. Joe Johnston was under orders to head south to carry on the war, but he knew the end was near. Sherman got into trouble by drifting into political issues, and Grant had to go to his rescue. But when the surrender was signed at Durham Station on April 26, 1865, the war was over.

8. **Austin, Texas, never fell but was included in the final surrender.** After Vicksburg fell, the Trans-Mississippi theater was cut off from the rest of the Confederacy and was almost irrelevant to the Union. Austin, the last capital to capitulate, was covered by the surrender that Gen. Edmund Kirby Smith and Maj. Gen. John Bankhead Magruder signed on June 2, 1865, aboard the steamer USS *Fort Jackson* in Galveston Bay.

9. **Union cavalry captured Montgomery, Alabama, the day Lee surrendered.** After the battle of Nashville, Maj. Gen. George Thomas sent Wilson raiding in the South. After capturing Selma, he moved on to Montgomery and eventually to Columbus, Georgia.

10. **A campaign to take Tallahassee, Florida, failed.** By the end of the war, large areas of Florida were in Union hands and the state had become a haven for deserters and draft evaders. The situation was made more chaotic when Gov. John Milton committed suicide. The Confederates defeated Newton's force of largely black soldiers at Natural Bridge, and the capital remained in the rebel hands until Maj. Gen. Edward McCook occupied the city in May.

11. **On September 10, 1863, Gen. Fred Steele captured Little Rock, Arkansas.** The Confederate government viewed the Trans-Mississippi area as secondary and sent many troops from Missouri, Arkansas, Louisiana, and Texas east of the river. Missouri was in

Union hands early in the war, and Union forces quickly pressed south into Arkansas. The South could only respond with secondary troops led by generals of questionable skills.

12. **On May 10, 1865, the Confederate government was near Irwinville, Georgia.** The president and his aides were only twenty miles from the Florida state line when a Union cavalry patrol swooped down on them. President Davis ran for a horse with a shawl over his shoulders. That shawl led to stories that Davis was disguised as a woman when captured.

7. Shenandoah Lightning

1. **Stonewall Jackson's mapmaker was Capt. Jedediah "Jed" Hotchkiss.** A New Yorker who ran an academy for boys in western Virginia and did mapmaking on the side, Hotchkiss received a request from General Jackson: make a map of the Shenandoah Valley from Harpers Ferry to Lexington, showing all of the points of offense and defense. Hotchkiss became the foremost mapmaker of the war. More of his maps appear in the official records than those of any other topographical engineer.

2. **Jackson's cavalry was commanded by Gen. Turner Ashby.** He was a successful planter, grain dealer, and politician in the area and rose quickly to command the Seventh Virginia Cavalry and then Jackson's cavalry brigade. He was killed in a skirmish at Harrisonburg as Jackson started to leave the valley to join Lee.

3. **Jackson's campaign started with a defeat at Kernstown.** Jackson's assignment was to keep the various Union armies from joining McClellan on the peninsula. When he learned that troops north of his position at Mount Jackson were leaving, he marched north and attacked the Union forces at Kernstown just south of Winchester. Jackson thought he was up against a rear guard, but the Federals had him outnumbered about two to one. He was forced to retreat but, while defeated, still achieved his objective. Plans to reinforce McClellan were dropped.

4. **The man who defeated Jackson was Brig. Gen. James Shields.**
   This Irish-born politician once challenged Abe Lincoln to a duel.
   He fought in the Black Hawk War, was a volunteer brigadier
   general in the Mexican War, and carried that rank into the Civil
   War. His later actions in the Shenandoah Valley showed his
   limitations, and after a year of "awaiting orders" he resigned. In his
   different terms in the Senate, Shields represented three states:
   Illinois (1849–1855), Minnesota (1858–1859), and Missouri (1879).

5. **The next battle took place at McDowell.** Learning that two
   brigades of John Frémont's force were moving into the
   Shenandoah from West Virginia, Jackson moved to McDowell to
   block them. The Union forces attacked his position on Sitlington's
   Hill. After four hours of hard fighting, the Union forces were
   forced to withdraw to Franklin, West Virginia.

6. **Maj. Gen. Robert Milroy and Brig. Gen. Robert Schenck led
   Union forces at McDowell.** They were typical of the decidedly
   third-rate team operating against Jackson. But the greatest
   shortcoming was in the Lincoln administration's failure to provide
   a unified command. This situation allowed Jackson to defeat them
   individually.

7. **Jackson captured the garrison at Front Royal.** Another Stonewall
   surprise! He started north toward Winchester but passed over the
   Massanutten at New Market Gap and up the Luray (Page) Valley,
   surprising and capturing most of the Union garrison there.

8. **At Front Royal, Jackson received valuable aid from Isabelle
   "Belle" Boyd.** Her father ran a hotel in Front Royal, and as the
   Confederates approached, she rode out to meet them and
   delivered detailed information on the Union forces' strength and
   positions. This intelligence allowed Jackson an easy and thorough
   victory. Belle Boyd was a character right out of fiction and central
   casting, but she was a really big help to Stonewall, who made her a
   captain and honorary aide-de-camp.

9. **Jackson next attacked General Banks at Winchester.** It was the
   first of three major battles that would be fought there. The town

changed hands seventy-two times during the war. When Banks learned of the strike at Front Royal, he was told that it was a raid, but he wisely ignored the faulty information and pulled back. Jackson caught him in Winchester and inflicted heavy losses on the outnumbered Union army. However, the Confederates lost the opportunity to destroy Banks's army.

10. **Union forces tried to trap Jackson at Strasburg.** One of the keys to Jackson's success was his excellent intelligence. Operating on home ground, every civilian was a spy for him. And because his cavalry was superior to the Union cavalry, he could screen his own actions and keep his adversaries in the dark. Jackson was also frustratingly secretive, even with his own top subordinates.

11. **The Union suffered consecutive defeats at Cross Keys and Port Republic.** With Union forces in hot pursuit, Jackson retreated with forced marches up the valley. Frémont's troops pushed him while Shields followed down the Luray Valley to the east. On June 8, a portion of Jackson's army stopped Frémont at Cross Keys directly south of Harrisonburg. The following day, Jackson turned east to the river town of Port Republic and attacked Shields. By driving him back, Jackson prevented the Union forces from combining the two armies, a combination that might have spelled his doom.

12. **Jackson's primary subordinates were Maj. Gen. Richard Stoddert Ewell and Brig. Gen. Dick Taylor.** Ewell, a West Pointer and veteran dragoon, led the Confederate victory at Cross Keys. Later he would succeed Jackson as corps commander but would fail at that job. Taylor, son of Zachary Taylor, studied at Harvard and Yale and was a planter and politician before the war. After his brilliant service under Jackson, he went to Louisiana, where he defeated General Banks in the Red River Campaign.

8. War on the Water

1. **Forts St. Philip and Jackson flanked the Mississippi River below New Orleans. Forts Morgan and Gaines flanked the opening of**

Mobile Bay. In April 1862, Farragut first tried to reduce the Mississippi River forts, but despite a long pounding they held out. Farragut then ran his fleet past them, succeeding in moving thirteen gunboats upriver. The largest city in the South was forced to surrender. Two years later, at Mobile Bay, Farragut ran his fleet past Fort Morgan on the east side of the bay entrance and "damned" the torpedoes. Torpedoes then were really floating mines. One monitor ironclad ship did strike one and sank, but the others entered the bay, where they chased off or sank smaller ships before defeating and capturing the huge ironclad CSS *Tennessee*. The city did not fall immediately, but Mobile was out of business as a port for blockade-runners.

2. **The Yankee sailor who backed Grant was Andrew Hull Foote.** He was born in New Haven, the son of a prominent state and national politician, and became a midshipman in 1822. He fought pirates in the West Indies and suppressed the slave trade off Africa before heading to China for more adventure right before the Civil War. Foote assembled the naval force to back Grant's victories at Fort Henry and at Fort Donelson, where he was wounded in the foot. Those river victories allowed the Union Army to drive south all the way to southern Tennessee and Mississippi.

3. **Stephen Mallory was Confederate secretary of the navy.** He was a lawyer and a judge and fought in the Second Seminole War. He was a senator when the war broke out and proved a good choice as Confederate secretary of the navy. He had been a member of the Senate Committee on Naval Affairs and chaired the committee for much of that time. Jeff Davis knew little of naval matters and left much of them up to Mallory but did not always give him the support he needed. Mallory's decisions on the use of steam and ironclads helped keep kept the South in the war for four years.

4. **(B) For the war, the chance of a blockade-runner being caught was just one in six.** Only one in ten of blockade-runners were caught in 1861 and one in eight in 1862, but by 1863 the Union fleet was catching one in four. By the end of the war, it was

catching half of them, probably because fewer ports were open to the runners. This vital supply line to Europe via Bermuda, the Bahamas, and Cuba provided vital supplies to the Confederate war effort.

5. **Commanders in the great sea battles: The *Monitor* was commanded by Lt. John Lorimer Worden** with a crew of 58. The huge but slow-moving ***Virginia* (*Merrimack*) was commanded by Capt. Franklin Buchanan** with a crew of 250. More closely matched in size, the ***Alabama* was commanded by Maryland native Raphael Semmes** and the ***Kearsarge* by Capt. John A. Winslow**. The *Monitor-Virginia* battle was technically a draw but actually resulted in a Union victory because it allowed the North to maintain the blockade. Eventually, the Confederates themselves destroyed the *Virginia* because they could not move it upriver. The *Kearsarge* victory over the *Alabama* off the French coast was a huge lift for the North, but it made little difference in the war's progress.

6. **The inventors: Dahlgren, rifled guns; Ericsson, the monitor; Hunley, a submarine; and Ellet, steam rams.** John Dahlgren was the Philadelphia-born son of the Swedish consul and became a career naval officer who invented a rifled naval gun and boat howitzers on iron carriages. Lincoln relied heavily on his judgment on technical armament issues. Swedish-born engineer John Ericsson invented the screw propeller and the ironclad monitor. Horace Hunley was the force behind the Confederate submarine that both bore his name and sunk the sloop USS *Housatonic*, which was blockading Charleston Harbor. Charles Ellet, a Pennsylvania-born engineer, designed and built a fleet of high-speed naval rams that were highly successful against the Confederates. Ellet was the only casualty on the ram fleet at the Battle of Memphis. His brother, Alfred, succeed him in command of the unit.

7. **The *Trent* was stopped by Capt. Charles Wilkes commanding USS *San Jacinto*.** Wilkes was a hero briefly, but he nearly brought the nation to war with Great Britain. After the fracas subsided, Wilkes was shipped off to command the West Indies squadron. There he

repeated his mistake and seized another British vessel, the *Peterhoff*, bound for Mexico with cargo that Wilkes claimed was bound for the Confederacy. The courts ruled against him, and he was retired in 1864. Prior to the war he was a well-known explorer of the Arctic and the Pacific.

8. **Gen. Robert E. Lee's naval officer brother was Capt. Sidney Smith Lee.** Smith Lee was a U.S. Navy captain who joined the Confederacy when the war began. Civil War diarist Mary Boykin Chesnut declared him more handsome and better company than his brother Robert. Smith Lee was the father of Confederate Gen. Fitzhugh Lee.

9. **David Dixon Porter was the son of Cdre. David Porter, brother of Cdre. William "Dirty Bill" Porter, foster brother to David Farragut, and cousin of Gen. Fitz John Porter.** The talented but sometimes difficult David Dixon Porter started his career at age eleven, sailing with his father against West Indian pirates, and was a midshipman in the Mexican Navy (which his father commanded) before moving to the U.S. Navy at age sixteen. Ambitious to a fault, he frequently clashed with army officers; however, he got along well with both Grant and Sherman. They worked together to capture Vicksburg.

10. **Army engineer Joseph Bailey saved a Union fleet by damming the Red River to allow Union ships to cross the Alexandria rapids.** Colonel Bailey, an Ohio engineer, devised a method of partially damming the Red River at Alexandria, Louisiana, and floating the fleet to safety when rapidly falling water had threatened to leave it high and dry in Banks's ill-fated 1864 campaign. The feat made him one of only fifteen army officers to win the Thanks of Congress.

9. The Union Navy

1. **Silas Horton Stringham captured Hatteras Inlet but was too old for shipboard duty.** Already a veteran of the War of 1812, the Algerian War, and the Mexican War, he provided valuable advice to

Gideon Welles in the first days of the war. Initially, he commanded the blockade squadron and led the attacks on Hatteras Inlet and Fort Clark, North Carolina, one of the Union's earliest victories. However, he was too old for sea duty and, ashore, ran afoul of Gustavus Fox and retired.

2. **The man with great knowledge of the coast was Alexander Dallas Bache.** This great-grandson of Benjamin Franklin was a West Pointer who graduated first in the class of 1825 without receiving a demerit. After a career as a military engineer, he entered the academic life. In 1843 he became superintendent of the U.S. Coast Survey, and the data he developed about the southern coast was of great value to Union naval operations.

3. **Farragut's flagship commander was South Carolinian Percival Drayton.** Captain Drayton took part in the Battle of Port Royal Sound and later commanded a monitor. Among his many duties, he was transferred to the West Blockading Squadron. His brother Confederate Brig. Gen. Thomas Drayton graduated from West Point with Jefferson Davis.

4. **The Navy commander for Burnside's North Carolina campaign was Louis M. Goldsborough.** This veteran naval officer commanded the blockade of Virginia and North Carolina and personally led the naval support of Burnside's successful Carolina Campaign of 1862. Goldsborough also captured Norfolk, although his performance there was unspectacular. General McClellan also criticized him for his lack of support in the Peninsula Campaign. When he failed to force his way past Drewry's Bluff for an attack on Richmond, he was relieved from active duty and served the rest of the war on desk duty.

5. **Lincoln's favorite naval officer was John A. Dahlgren.** As noted previously, this Pennsylvania ordnance expert invented the eleven-inch Dahlgren gun. Following his duty running the Washington Navy Yard, he took command of the South Atlantic Blockading Squadron. His son Col. Ulric Dahlgren was killed in a raid on Richmond in 1864.

6. **Charles Henry Davis held important commands but was pushed aside.** He had a long career, was promoted to rear admiral, and took part in many actions including victories on the Mississippi. However, after the Vicksburg campaign, he was sent off to a desk job as head of the Bureau of Navigation. He later headed the Naval Observatory and was a founder of the National Academy of Sciences.

7. **John Ericsson invented the monitor.** After service in the Swedish military, he went to England to try to sell his inventions. When the effort failed, he landed in debtor's prison. He had better luck in the United States, where he was allowed to develop the navy's first steam-powered vessel, the *Princeton*. However, in 1844, when a gun exploded on its deck, killing the secretaries of state and the navy and almost killing President John Tyler, Ericsson was unfairly blamed. Gustavus Fox turned to Ericsson when he was looking for an ironclad design in 1861, and Ericsson showed him a mock-up for the monitor. It was built in less than four months and arrived at Hampton Roads in time to drive off CSS *Virginia* (resurrected *Merrimack*) and preserve the blockade.

8. **Andrew Hull Foote was a boyhood friend of Gideon Welles.** This veteran Connecticut-born salt spent forty years in the navy. His cooperation with Grant early in the war helped produce victories at Fort Henry and Fort Donelson, where he was wounded, and at Island Number 10. The wound forced him ashore. He died in June 1863 while on his way to take command of the South Atlantic Blockading Squadron.

10. How Big Was an Army?

1. **The regiment was the basic unit of organization.** At full strength, a regiment consisted of about a thousand men. They were designated by number and state, for example: the Eighth Connecticut, Twelfth Missouri, Eighteenth Virginia. The initial

Union regiments were enlisted for only three months' service, but most of the later ones were enlisted for three years.

2. **An infantry company at full size was about a hundred men.** Regulations called for a captain, a first lieutenant, a second lieutenant, a first sergeant, four sergeants, eight corporals, two musicians, a wagoner, and sixty-four to eighty-two privates. Each company then had 83 to 101 men total. Ten companies were in a volunteer infantry regiment.

3. **A regimental commander was usually a colonel.** Regimental officers included a colonel, a lieutenant colonel, a major, an adjutant (a lieutenant), a surgeon, two assistant surgeons, a chaplain, a sergeant major, a quartermaster sergeant, a commissary sergeant, and a hospital steward. Therefore, a regiment could be, at full strength, anywhere from 842 to 1,022 men. On active duty, these numbers dropped quickly as disease, battle, and desertion took their toll.

4. **Initially, officers were elected.** At least that's the way the arrangement started; however, as the war progressed and this method was found unsatisfactory, superior officers took over the process of awarding promotions. Initially, the governor designated a prominent local citizen or experienced soldier to raise a regiment. He, in turn, authorized others to go out and recruit companies. The understanding was that the man raising the regiment would be the colonel and those raising the companies would be captains. Much of the time it worked out that way, but sometimes politics and popularity upset this process.

5. **A brigadier general commanded a brigade.** At least in theory he did, but there were many exceptions. A brigade comprised four regiments and sometimes more as regiments shrunk later in the war. In the event of the general's promotion or incapacitation, the senior colonel led the brigade. Very late in the war, even lieutenant colonels led some.

6. **A division consisted of three brigades.** At full strength, it would have 12,000 men, but in practice the total more likely came to 7,500

to 10,000 men. While three brigades were typical, some divisions had two and a few had four. Major generals commanded some divisions with others being commanded by brigadiers.

7. **There were two or more divisions in a corps.** The legislation that created them did not specify and left it up to the War Department. General McClellan wanted to wait until he saw his division commanders in action, but the Lincoln government pressed him. When he failed to make the appointments, Lincoln named the new corps commanders himself: veteran officers Edwin Vose Sumner, Samuel Heintzelman, Erasmus Keyes, William Franklin, and Irvin McDowell. Sumner served well for two years but died in 1863. The others were all dropped and did not hold major commands at the end of the war. The Confederates, meanwhile, had larger corps. General Lee initially had only two corps commanders—James Longstreet and Stonewall Jackson, until Jackson's death.

8. **Union units tried to refill their ranks by sending men home to recruit.** Remarkably, the government went on accepting new regiments but had no system in place to fill the depleted ranks of the older regiments. Men were sent home to find recruits, but that effort did not produce anywhere near the number needed. The draft, started in 1863, produced a few but not in the quality or quantity needed. Regiments that had marched away a thousand strong were almost all down to five hundred or fewer men and regiments of fewer than three hundred men were not unusual.

9. **Cavalry regiments consisted of twelve companies rather than ten.** Cavalry companies were also called troops. Early in the war, Union cavalry was vastly inferior to that of the Confederates and was parceled out to divisions and even to brigades to work with them. For the most part, they were wasted in such small numbers. When Joe Hooker took over the army in early 1863, he put the cavalry on a proper footing, and when Phil Sheridan assumed command in 1864 he made use of it as a powerful force.

10. **Field artillery batteries were part of artillery regiments.** A regiment consisted of twelve batteries. Batteries typically had two two- or three-gun sections. Regiments were assigned to divisions or corps, and some of the batteries were assigned to work with divisions or brigades. The remainder was held in a reserve, to be sent into action as needed.

11. **Heavy artillery regiments consisted of twelve companies.** These units were assigned to man the heavy guns in the Washington defenses or in harbor fortifications. It was safe duty until the spring of 1964 when Grant, in need of additional troops, converted several of these large regiments into infantry. They were three or four times the size of the average regiment by then, and they paid a terrible price as casualties mounted during Grant's Overland Campaign.

12. **Union armies were usually named for rivers.** Their names included the Army of the Potomac, the Cumberland, the Tennessee, the James, the Ohio, and the Mississippi. The Confederates' two main armies were the Army of Northern Virginia and the Army of the Tennessee.

11. The Social Scene

1. **The unfortunate lover was (I) Philip Barton Key II.** Called the handsomest man in Washington society, he was shot by the cuckolded Congressman Daniel Sickles, who later became a Civil War general. He assembled a crack legal defense team, much as O. J. Simpson did in modern times, and was found not guilty by reason of temporary insanity. The jury recognized Sickles's right to defend his marriage to the beautiful young Teresa.

2. **The White House hostess was (J) Harriet Lane.** She was Buchanan's orphaned niece, and he raised her and several other nieces and nephews. A Civil War gunboat was named in her honor.

3. **The beautiful daughter of a cabinet officer was (O) Katherine "Kate" Chase Sprague.** She was hostess for her widower father, the

treasury secretary, and her brains and beauty made her a star of Washington society. She was young, slender, and beautiful, so, of course, Mary Lincoln hated her. Her marriage to Senator William Sprague IV of Rhode Island seemed made in heaven, but when Sprague turned to drink and lost his fortune, they divorced. Later, poor Kate died broke on a small farm.

4. **The society belle who spied for the Confederates was (C) Rose O'Neal Greenhow.** Some credit her spying with the victory at First Bull Run, but it landed her in jail. She would come to a sad end when the British blockade-runner she was aboard ran aground off Wilmington, North Carolina, and when she attempted to get to shore she was thrown into the water. The weight of the gold she had sewn into her clothing pulled her to her death.

5. **Lincoln's two young secretaries were (F) John Hay and (L) John Nicolay.** History owes them a debt of gratitude for leaving us a realistic look at the Lincoln family, the Lincoln presidency, and Washington in wartime. Both wrote extensively afterward.

6. **Mary Lincoln's mulatto dressmaker, friend, and confidante was (H) Elizabeth Keckley.** The former slave held an almost magical spell over Mary Todd Lincoln and was one of the few people who could handle her during her emotional outbursts.

7. **The White House mourned (B) Col. Elmer Ellsworth, (G) Gen. Benjamin Hardin Helm, (A) Col. Edward Baker, and (K) Willie Lincoln.** Colonel Ellsworth was a personal friend of the Lincolns and one of the first conspicuous casualties of the war. Confederate general Helm was the husband of Mrs. Lincoln's youngest half-sister, Emilie Todd. Colonel Baker was a close friend of the Lincolns dating back to Springfield, Illinois, and the only sitting senator to be killed in the war. Their son Edward (Eddie) was named for him. Saddest of all was the loss of their son Willie to typhoid fever in 1862. Of any of the boys he was probably the most like his father.

8. **The senator's daughter was (D) Lucy "Bessie" Hale.** Booth led his family to believe that he was engaged to Bessie, and he carried her

picture. That relationship, however, did not keep him away from his mistress or, for that matter, many other women. Bessie was the daughter of Senator John P. Hale of New Hampshire, a Free Soil Democrat. It seems an unlikely union.

9. **Drafted to join the Lincolns were (E) Clara Harris and (M) Maj. Henry Rathbone.** Clara was the daughter of Senator Ira Harris of New York. Booth stabbed and seriously injured Major Rathbone during the attack. The couple married and moved to Germany, where Rathbone went mad and murdered Clara years later.

10. **The madam of the neighboring brothel was (N) Maude Roberts.** The trial caused quite a sensation, in part because Maude was a pretty young woman and in part because her partner in the commercial venture was a former army officer who attended the trial in uniform. One wonders about their list of clients.

12. The Engineers

1. **The designer of the cracker line was William Farrar "Baldy" Smith.** With Rosecrans's army trapped inside Chattanooga and starving, Smith designed a plan to open a supply line to Bridgeport, Alabama, on the Tennessee River. When Grant came with reinforcements, Smith's plan was used and worked perfectly. Later, Grant gave Smith the chance to command a corps, but his performance was lackluster. By the way, Baldy Smith was not bald. As a West Point cadet, his classmates noted his light blond hair and felt it made him look bald, hence the nickname.

2. **Joseph Totten commanded the engineers through most of the Civil War.** Born in New Haven, Connecticut, he was only a year younger than the Constitution, had fought in the War of 1812, and was Winfield Scott's chief engineer in Mexico. He served as a colonel until 1863 when the Topographical Engineers were integrated into the Engineer Corps and Totten received his star as a brigadier. He died of pneumonia in 1864 after almost sixty years in the army.

3. **Carved in bronze is Gouverneur K. Warren.** His bronze likeness stands atop Little Round Top at Gettysburg, watching the approach of Longstreet's men. The true story is a tad less heroic. Meade sent him down to Little Round Top to check things out. Before he arrived there, Warren stopped to chat with someone and sent an assistant, Washington Augustus Roebling, to the top of the hill. Roebling actually saw and reported the danger, but Warren sprang into action, commandeered the brigade of Col. Strong Vincent to hold the hill, and the rest, as they say, is history. Warren later was given a corps to command, but Sheridan dumped him during the drive to Five Forks. After the war, Washington Roebling, who was not memorialized with a statue, built the Brooklyn Bridge.

4. **Herman Haupt kept the trains running.** One of the great unsung heroes of the war, he grew up in Philadelphia and graduated from West Point in 1835, but he quickly resigned his commission to become a civilian engineer. He was one of America's best railroad builders when, at the start of the Civil War, he was lured back to the army to build and repair railroads for the Union. Interestingly, he initially demanded that he be allowed to serve without wearing a uniform, but he relented when he was reminded that the uniform would establish his authority. After the war, he returned to railroading, extended the Baltimore & Ohio Railroad, through the mountains to Pittsburgh, and worked on the famous Hoosac Tunnel in the Massachusetts Berkshires.

5. **George W. Cullum was the expert on pontoon bridges.** A West Point graduate in 1833, he was a veteran engineer and became a brigadier general early in the war. He served on Halleck's staff in Missouri, where he developed pontoon trains and did work developing the India rubber pontoons. He remained on Halleck's staff when Halleck became general in chief, but when Grant replaced Halleck, Cullum became superintendent of the Military Academy. Very much an admirer of Halleck, he married his widow. Cullum is best known for publishing a biographical register of West Point graduates.

6. **The young engineer with a big reputation was Peter Smith Michie.** Born in Scotland and raised in Cincinnati, Michie graduated second in the West Point class of 1863 and was quickly in the thick of things, rapidly rising from lieutenant to colonel. He stayed in the army, taught physics at West Point, and wrote extensively about the war. His son Lt. Dennis Mahan Michie fielded the first football team at the academy but was killed at San Juan Hill in Cuba. Michie Stadium at West Point is named for the son. The family name is pronounced Mike-E.

7. **Daniel Woodbury paid a heavy price for poor communications.** One of the prominent New Hampshire Woodburys, he was placed in charge of the pontoon train that was to meet Burnside in Falmouth and bridge the Rappahannock River. Unfortunately, no one notified him of the urgency, and when he arrived there six days late, Lee was already in place, fortifying the heights above the town. Burnside completed the tragedy by crossing and attacking those strong positions. It was more Halleck's fault than anyone else's, but General Woodbury was relieved and assigned to Fort Jefferson in the Dry Tortugas, a sort of hot-weather Siberia. He contracted yellow fever and died there in 1864, the final casualty of the ill-fated Battle of Fredericksburg.

8. **The longest pontoon bridge was build at Paducah, Kentucky.** When Leonidas Polk broke Kentucky's neutrality by occupying Columbus on the Mississippi River, Grant countered by occupying Paducah on the Ohio River. Engineers assembled river barges into a pontoon bridge there that was at least three-quarters of a mile long. Some estimates placed it closer to a mile long, but it was probably about 4,200 feet. The record stood for the entire war.

9. **Henry Benham built the James River bridge that allowed Grant's army to reach Petersburg.** He is living proof that good engineers do not necessarily make good field commanders. Early in the war he had a line command but fell into disfavor with Rosecrans and was sent south. After success at Fort Pulaski, he led a movement against Secessionville near Charleston that turned into a disaster. It

not only cost him his general's star but he also was sent back to engineering duty in Massachusetts. In 1863, Lincoln reinstated his volunteer rank, and he was assigned as chief engineer of the Army of the Potomac, where he performed very well.

10. **Sherman's chief engineer was Orlando Poe.** A West Pointer, class of 1856, he served on McClellan's staff before getting a promotion to brigadier general. He led troops at Second Bull Run and Fredericksburg, but when his temporary appointment ran out, he returned to engineering duty as a captain. He caught Sherman's eye for his work at the siege of Knoxville and served Sherman for the remainder of the war. After the war he built lighthouses and locks on the Great Lakes. The Poe Lock at Sault St. Marie is named in his honor.

SECTION IV

YEARS OF HARD WAR

They would fight on with great battles at Manassas, Sharpsburg, Fredericksburg, Chancellorsville, and Gettysburg, but the situation in the East changed but little. In the West, under the emerging leadership of Ulysses S. Grant, Southern armies were driven south into Mississippi and Georgia. When the North was victorious at

Heading the list of Confederate casualties was Gen. Thomas J. "Stonewall" Jackson of Virginia, who was accidentally wounded by his own men. He lost his left arm but seemed on the road to recovery when pneumonia set in that would cost him his life. His loss was devastating. Lee never won another major battle after Jackson died. He was laid to rest in the Old Presbyterian Cemetery in Lexington. Today, it is the Stonewall Jackson Memorial Cemetery. The memorial statue is by Edward V. Valentine. Visitors often leave lemons on Jackson's grave at the base of the statue. Legend has it that Jackson favored the fruit to battle his chronic dyspepsia. *Photo by the author*

Gettysburg and Vicksburg on July 3 and 4, 1863, prospects seemed to be brightening for the Union. However, the war was far from over, and even greater loss and devastation lay ahead.

This ordinary building, the office of Fairfield Plantation at Guinea Station, Virginia, would become hallowed ground to the South. It was here Stonewall Jackson would be taken to recover from his wounds, and it was here he would die. A shudder went through the people of the Confederacy. Their greatest hero was gone. The war would last almost two years longer, but Jackson's death can be said to mark the beginning of the end for the Confederacy. *Photo by the author*

QUIZ 1
1863

The year started with the issuance of the Emancipation Proclamation, which changed the nature of the war. Stonewall Jackson was killed in May. In July, the fortunes of war tilted sharply toward the North. Lee's invasion of Pennsylvania was a costly failure. The following day, Vicksburg surrendered. The South would win its greatest western victory at Chickamauga in September, but Grant would quickly reverse it. These incidents were some of the big events of 1863, but how about some of the smaller ones?

1. On the second day of the year, a former vice president led an unsuccessful attack that ended a major battle. Name him.
2. A new state joined the Union in a manner never used before or since. The state was?
3. Congress created two new territories. Name them.
4. In New York City, a protest of the new draft law resulted in a riot, putting the police commissioner, who was also acting superintendent, on the spot. Name him.
5. At what age could you no longer be drafted?
6. The fall of Vicksburg did not quite open the Mississippi River. The fall of another fortification several days later did. It was?
7. In June, Ambrose Burnside shut down a major newspaper that was violently against the Lincoln administration. Lincoln reversed the order three days later. The paper was?
8. Armies under Robert E. Lee and George Meade engaged in extensive maneuvering, ending in a standoff by a Virginia stream. Name it.
9. A distinguished orator gave a two-hour-long speech in Pennsylvania that was widely heralded. History remembers a shorter one that day. Where was it given?
10. Abraham Lincoln created a new holiday. It is?

QUIZ 2
War in Far Distant Places

Most of the Civil War took place in Virginia, Tennessee, Georgia, Mississippi, and South Carolina, but some events happened far away from the main theaters of the war. Let's see what you know about these more remote actions.

1. Which one of these battles was *not* fought in West Virginia? (A) Rich Mountain. (B) Carnifex Ferry. (C) Kings Mountain. (D) Philippi.
2. Only one real battle took place in Florida. Name it.
3. The land battle of Honey Springs was unusual in that it did not take place in either a state or an organized territory. Where did it happen?
4. When students of the war mention the western theater, they're usually talking about Tennessee or Mississippi, but the westernmost battles of the war took place far west of the Mississippi River. Name the two battles that took place in New Mexico.
5. Gettysburg is generally considered the northernmost point of the war, but Confederates struck a Northern town far north of Pennsylvania. Name the town and state.
6. On the far side of the Atlantic Ocean, USS *Kearsarge* sank the Confederate raider CSS *Alabama*. Out of what port did the *Alabama* sail to her doom?
7. Most battles took place in rolling countryside, but one was fought in a place so high and steep it was known as the Battle above the Clouds. Name it.
8. What foreign power launched a Mexican adventure during the Civil War?
9. Two points on the Texas coast were the site of military and naval actions. Name them.

10. We think of the Civil War as ending at Appomattox Court House in Virginia, but the final "surrender" took place many miles west of that location. Where was it and who surrendered?

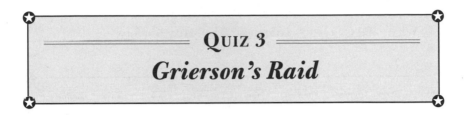

QUIZ 3
Grierson's Raid

In the spring of 1863, General Grant needed someone to lead a cavalry raid into central Mississippi as a diversion from his own planned campaign against Jackson and Vicksburg. He picked Benjamin Grierson, who performed brilliantly. Let's see what you know about that bold venture.

1. An incident in Grierson's youth made him seem an unlikely candidate for cavalry leadership. What was it?
2. In his early years, he followed a career that called on his artistic rather than his military talents. What path did he pursue?
3. Grierson became a friend and supporter of an up-and-coming politician from his home state. Name him.
4. Grierson almost missed his date with destiny. Why?
5. From what Tennessee town did the raid begin?
6. How big was the raiding party? (A) 600 men. (B) 1,100 men. (C) 1,700 men. (D) 2,500 men.
7. What was the mission of the Quinine Brigade?
8. Which regiment had the job of decoying the rebel pursuers and cutting the Mobile & Ohio Railroad?
9. What did Grierson's gray-clad scouts call themselves?
10. Grant launched another cavalry raid at the same time as Grierson's. Who led it and where did it go?
11. What was Grierson's primary objective and what did he plan to do when he got there?

12. As the main column was about to cross the Strong River, a dramatic event took place. What was it?
13. Who was the Confederate commander who tried to coordinate the effort to trap Grierson?
14. Where did Grierson plan to reach the safety of Union lines?
15. Where did Grierson's command finally reach safety?

QUIZ 4
KIA/CSA

The Civil War was hard on generals, especially on the side of the Confederate States Army (CSA). Of its 425 generals, 77—a staggering 18 percent—were killed in action (KIA) or mortally wounded. Among them were such important leaders as Stonewall Jackson, Albert Sidney Johnston, Leonidas Polk, and Jeb Stuart. Let's see if you can match these slain Confederate generals with the battlefields on which they fell.

Confederate Generals
1. Bernard Bee Jr.
2. Lawrence O'Bryan Branch
3. Archibald Gracie Jr.
4. States Rights Gist
5. Maxcy Gregg
6. Ben Harden Helm
7. Ambrose Powell (A. P.) Hill
8. Ben McCulloch
9. William Dorsey Pender
10. Lloyd Tilghman
11. William Henry Talbot (W. H. T.) Walker
12. Felix Kirk Zollicoffer

Battlefields
A. Sharpsburg/Antietam
B. Atlanta
C. Champion's Hill
D. Chickamauga
E. First Manassas/First Bull Run
F. Franklin, Tennessee
G. Fredericksburg
H. Gettysburg
I. Logan's Cross Roads/Mill Springs, Kentucky
J. Elkhorn Tavern/Pea Ridge, Arkansas
K. Petersburg breakthrough
L. Petersburg trenches

QUIZ 5
KIA/USA

The Civil War was hard on generals in the Union Army too. Of the 583 who served, 47, or 8 percent, were killed in action or mortally wounded. Let's see if you can match the slain Union generals with the battlefields on which they fell.

Union Generals	*Battlefields*
1. Philip Kearny	A. Antietam
2. Nathaniel Lyon	B. Atlanta
3. William Haines Lytle	C. Chantilly
4. Joseph King Fenno Mansfield	D. Chickamauga
5. Daniel McCook Jr.	E. Gettysburg
6. James Birdseye McPherson	F. Kennesaw Mountain
7. Jesse L. Reno	G. Shiloh
8. John Fulton Reynolds	H. South Mountain
9. John Sedgwick	I. Spotsylvania
10. Joshua Woodrow Sill	J. Stones River
11. James Samuel Wadsworth	K. Wilderness
12. William Harvey Lamb	L. Wilson's Creek
"Will"(W. H. L.) Wallace	

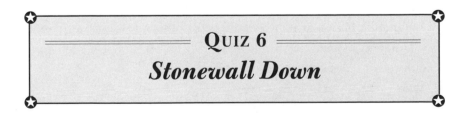

QUIZ 6
Stonewall Down

Perhaps no event in the Civil War harmed the South as much as the accidental wounding of General Jackson. He fell at the apex of his greatest triumph, brought down, ironically, by a volley fired by his own men. Jackson would lose his left arm, but Lee had, in his own words, lost his right arm. Let's test your knowledge of this cataclysmic event.

1. How many times was Jackson hit?
2. Was he struck by the first shots fired?
3. Who commanded the brigade that fired the shots?
4. What horse was Jackson riding?
5. What order did Jackson issue before leaving the field?
6. Jackson received yet another injury before he reached safety. How did it happen?
7. Jackson's personal physician arrived with an ambulance. Name him.
8. What general took over Jackson's corps after he was wounded?
9. Why did he not remain in command?
10. Who was the next man to command the corps?
11. Who finished the battle in command?
12. To what location was Jackson evacuated?

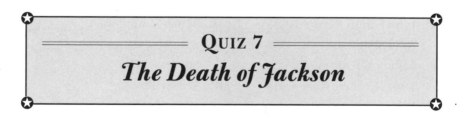

Quiz 7
The Death of Jackson

The wounds General Jackson received on May 2, 1863, at the Battle of Chancellorsville did not initially seem to be mortal. Despite the necessity of amputating his left arm, he seemed well on his way to recovery when new problems loomed that would eventually take his life. Let's test your knowledge of this catastrophic loss to the Southern cause.

1. Who amputated Jackson's arm?
2. What was Jackson's first concern after surgery?
3. An hour and a half after surgery, Jackson received a caller. Who was it and what was his mission?

4. To what house in Guinea Station was Jackson taken?
5. What additional malady struck Jackson on the fifth day after the amputation?
6. Who arrived at his bedside on May 7, five days after his wounding?
7. Who informed Jackson that he was dying?
8. In his final delirium, to what subordinate commander did Jackson issue orders?
9. What were his final words?
10. Where is Jackson's first "grave"?
11. Where was Jackson buried?
12. What item dear to Jackson do visitors leave on his grave?

QUIZ 8
Father of Waters

A major part of the Civil War in the West was played out on the mighty Mississippi and its various tributaries. Let's see if you can identify the people, places, and events that made news on these waterways.

1. Initially, Kentucky declared itself neutral, but the South lost the state when a Confederate general lost patience and seized the Mississippi River stronghold at Columbus, Kentucky. Who was he?
2. This fledgling Union commander came downriver to Belmont, Missouri, opposite Columbus and was lucky to get his troops back onto the transports before they were cut off by aggressive Confederates. Name the Union general.
3. This Tennessee River fort was so badly designed it flooded periodically. The capture of the fort and its small garrison was child's play for the Union, but the victory lifted spirits in the North.
4. A bigger chore was the capture of Fort Donelson on the Cumberland. Who was the Confederate general in command when

the Union attacked and who eventually had to surrender to Grant "unconditionally"?

5. The Union used an exciting new weapon in the capture of Memphis, Tennessee. A fleet of rams virtually destroyed the enemy fleet and captured the city. Provide the name and rank of the commander of the ram fleet.

6. The navy under David Farragut and David Dixon Porter did the heavy work in capturing New Orleans as they forced their way past the Confederate forts. However, a brash army general sailed up to the city and claimed victory. Who was he, and who was the Confederate general defending the city?

7. On the Mississippi River north of Memphis, Fort Pillow fell to Confederate forces in April 1864. Who commanded the Southern troops who probably killed many black Union soldiers when they were trying to surrender?

8. In early 1862, the Union Army in Missouri captured the strategic Mississippi River town of New Madrid and opened the river all the way to Fort Pillow. Who was the Yankee general propelled to promotion and short-term fame by this action?

9. During the Union campaign to capture Vicksburg, Mississippi, a Union Army and Navy expedition was stopped at the hastily built Fort Pemberton. Name the stream the men were ascending.

10. Adm. David Dixon Porter tried another river to enter Vicksburg, was stopped at a place called Rolling Fork, and was almost bottled up there. Sherman's troops came to his aid in a night march in which the men illuminated their way with candles stuck in their rifle barrels. Name the river.

Quiz 9
Salisbury Prison

Everybody knows about the hell of Andersonville and the misery of Libby Prison. But many other places, both North and South, kept men heaped inhumanely with their fellow men. Let's look at the history of another such place, the Salisbury Prison in North Carolina.

1. The Salisbury compound included one large building. What had it been before the war?
2. Early in its existence, Salisbury Prison was remembered for two excellent features that made life there comfortable. What were they?
3. A well-known painting shows Salisbury prisoners engaged in a popular activity of the day. Name it.
4. What event in August 1864 suddenly swelled the prison population at Salisbury?
5. Salisbury was the fourth-largest town in North Carolina. What was its approximate population?
6. The prison was designed for 2,500 prisoners. At what number did the prison population peak?
7. Salisbury had ten commandants, but the best-known one was brought to trial for war crimes. He was?
8. An ill-fated escape attempt was thwarted when a Confederate unit rushed back and fired into the compound. Name it.
9. Two Union civilians imprisoned there escaped and returned north to tell the story of suffering at Salisbury. Who were they?
10. In February 1865, prisoners who could walk were marched out. Where did they go?
11. The sicker men were sent by rail. Where were they sent?
12. Three days after Lee's surrender, Union cavalry arrived at Salisbury. Name the commander.

All the ingredients were there for a tragic event: a remote outpost held by inexperienced troops under an inexperienced leader; a tough, aggressive attacker with a chip on his shoulder; a badly designed fortification; and a controversy about the treatment of prisoners. But was it really a massacre? Let's look at this controversial 1864 battle and its aftermath.

1. Perched on a bluff overlooking the Mississippi River north of Memphis, the works were named for a prominent Tennessean. He was?

2. Just prior to attacking Fort Pillow, Nathan Bedford Forrest's command had been repulsed elsewhere. Where had his earlier unsuccessful attack taken place?

3. Name the officer who commanded Fort Pillow at the time of the attack.

4. Which of Forrest's generals commanded the troops that first entered the fort?

5. Southern troops hated black Union soldiers, but they hated another group inside Fort Pillow as much. That group was?

6. When Forrest demanded surrender in twenty minutes or else, what flag did the Union garrison say he was hoisting?

7. The Union garrison was incensed when Forrest moved troops for they felt he had no right to do so. Why?

8. What was the South's explanation for that move?

9. What was the approximate ratio of Union casualties to Confederate losses?

10. Who did the Union government send to investigate the affair?

Quiz 11
War Rides the Rails

The American Civil War was the first conflict in which railroads played a major part. Both sides made innovative use of the relatively new technology. Railroads dictated lines of attack and where many major battles would be fought. Let's look at how this technology impacted the war.

1. The technology was new. In what year were the first railroad lines in the United States started?

2. Between 1850 and 1860 railroad building boomed. By what percent did trackage expand? (A) 72 percent. (B) 147 percent. (C) 181 percent. (D) 334 percent.

3. Why was it impossible to travel long distances without changing trains?

4. When Confederate Gen. Joe Johnston started sending his troops to Bull Run, from what location did they depart?

5. What future Confederate general put the Baltimore & Ohio Railroad out of business for a year and a half at the start of the war?

6. What made Corinth, Mississippi, an important strategic place?

7. Who commanded the U.S. Military Railroad Command?

8. What general commanded the largest railroad troop movement of the war?

9. What major battle did the Confederates win because they shipped reinforcements from Lee's army by rail?

10. What was the longest railroad supply line of the war?

11. At Petersburg, Lee was forced to evacuate the city when a railroad line was cut. Name it.

12. The war ended when Grant's army kept Lee from reaching this Virginia railroad depot. It was?

ANSWERS

1. 1863

1. **The former vice president leading the attack was John Cabell Breckinridge.** The Battle of Stones River or Murfreesboro started on the final day of 1862. The first day of the new year saw action primarily limited to cavalry attacks on the Union's communications. Late afternoon on January 2, Breckinridge attacked Union troops occupying high ground. He succeeded in driving them off, but when his troops pursued, they encountered fifty-eight massed cannon. The Confederates lost 1,700 men and were pushed back to their starting point. Stones River might have been remembered as a drawn battle had not Braxton Bragg retreated the following day. It would be six months before William Rosecrans would go on the offensive again.

2. **The new state was West Virginia.** The twenty-five mountainous counties in western Virginia remained loyal to the Union and created a revolution within a revolution when they seceded from Virginia. The Constitution forbids the creation of a new state from the territory of another without the approval of the legislature of the former. However, citing wartime powers, Congress admitted West Virginia to the Union on June 20, 1863. Many still believe the process was unconstitutional.

3. **The two new territories were Arizona and Idaho.** Arizona was the western portion of the New Mexico Territory. Idaho borrowed territory from Washington, Utah, Dakota, and Nebraska. Despite the distraction of the war, Manifest Destiny continued to march westward.

4. **The New York City police commissioner dealing with the draft riot was Thomas Acton.** He was a self-made man and prominent in business and civil affairs in New York. In fact, he is credited as the father of the city's first professional fire department. His obituary in the *New York Times* gives him credit for quelling the New York

draft riot, but in fact it did not fully end until troops from the Army of the Potomac arrived. Riots also occurred in Indiana, Wisconsin, and Boston.

5. **Men aged forty-six or older could not be drafted.** The law required all white males, including aliens who declared intention to become citizens, ages twenty to forty-five to register. The fact that the rich could buy themselves out of it or find a replacement did not sit well with most people. A state applied the draft when it could not meet its assigned quota of new recruits through voluntary enlistment. Most states resorted to cash bounties to try to avoid using the draft.

6. **The last Confederate position to fall on the Mississippi River was Port Hudson, Louisiana.** Gen. Nathaniel Prentiss Banks had been besieging the stronghold on the east bank of the Mississippi, twenty-five miles north of Baton Rouge. Five days after Vicksburg fell, Gen. Franklin Gardner surrendered the city and his 5,500 men. Banks took the bows for it, but with Vicksburg gone, Port Hudson was no longer defensible. The twin victories placed the Mississippi's entire eastern bank in Union hands.

7. **Gen. Burnside shut down the *Chicago Times*.** The paper was started in 1854 in support of Stephen Douglas. During the war, the editor was Wilbur Storey, an outspoken Copperhead, who castigated the Lincoln government and all its works. Ambrose Burnside, then military department head, was offended and closed the paper down. Lincoln wisely reversed his decision.

8. **Meade and Lee maneuvered to a standoff at Mine Run in Virginia.** Lee pulled his army into a strong defensive position behind Mine Run near the village of Orange Court House. Lee was minus two divisions, which were with James Longstreet in Tennessee, but Meade decided that Lee's position was too strong so he withdrew into winter quarters. Lee remained in the area for the winter, bracing for the hard campaigning he knew would come in 1864.

9. **The long and short speeches were delivered at Gettysburg, Pennsylvania, at the cemetery dedication.** Edward Everett was one

of the great orators of his day, having served as a Unitarian minister; the president of Harvard; congressman, senator, and governor of Massachusetts; the minister to Great Britain; and the secretary of state. He was also the vice-presidential candidate in 1860 on John Bell's Constitutional Union Party ticket. His impressive two-hour talk is all but forgotten while Lincoln's five-minute address, which followed Everett's and was considered a failure then, even by Lincoln, is now immortal. Everett was getting on in years and had prostate problems. He requested a tent for his personal use near the stage; however, he had a great deal of trouble achieving his purpose because so many wanted to come in and shake his hand.

10. **Lincoln made official the first Thanksgiving.** At the urging of Mrs. Sarah Josepha Hale, the president declared a national day of Thanksgiving for the last Thursday in November. Of course, Lincoln was not the first, or the last, to advocate such a celebration. It is equally true that he probably did not envision a day to feast or watch football, but rather a day to praise the Almighty for Union victories. Incidentally, Mrs. Hale also wrote the nursery rhyme "Mary Had a Little Lamb."

2. War in Far Distant Places

1.   **(C) Kings Mountain was not a West Virginia Civil War battle.** It was a Revolutionary War battle that took place in South Carolina. The rest were Union victories in 1861 in western Virginia, later West Virginia. Philippi was known as the Philippi Races because the heavily outnumbered Confederates lost little time getting out of town. It is considered the first organized land battle of the war. A month later, George McClellan and William Rosecrans defeated those Confederates dug in on Rich Mountain. McClellan received most of the credit for the victory while Rosecrans did most of the fighting. Two months later, Rosecrans defeated a Confederate force at Carnifex Ferry on the Gauley River. West Virginia remained largely in Union hands for the balance of the war.

2. **The Battle of Olustee or Ocean Pond was Florida's only real
   battle.** It was fought on February 20, 1864. Troops under Brig.
   Gen. Truman Seymour were marching from Jacksonville toward
   western Florida when they met Confederates under Brig. Gen.
   Joseph Finegan. Union objectives included cutting off a supply of
   beef cattle to the Confederates and freeing more slaves for military
   service. Although the sides were about even—with 5,500 troops
   each—it was clearly a Southern victory, with the North taking the
   greater number of casualties and retreating.

3. **Honey Springs was fought in Indian Territory, present-day
   Oklahoma.** It was a Union victory. Initially, the tribes in Indian
   Territory sided with the Confederates, but when a Union column
   under Brig. Gen. James Blunt arrived from Kansas, some switched
   sides. Confederate troops under Brig. Gen. Douglas Cooper were
   hampered by wet gunpowder and suffered a stinging reverse. White
   troops were the minority in this battle. A large portion of the
   Confederate force comprised Indian units. Union troops included
   both Indian guard units and the First Kansas Colored Infantry.

4. **The New Mexico battles were Valverde and Johnson's
   Ranch/Glorietta Pass.** Both battles—Valverde on February 21,
   1862, and Johnson's Ranch/Glorietta Pass on March 26–28, 1862—
   were small affairs. The westernmost action, though, was fought at
   Picacho Peak in Arizona on April 15. It was really only a tiny
   skirmish fought between ten Confederates out of Tucson against
   thirteen California Column cavalrymen headed east from Yuma.
   After having three of their number killed and three more
   wounded, the Union patrol headed home, taking three prisoners.
   Two other Confederates were wounded. The Confederacy had its
   eye on southern California as a Confederate base on the Pacific.

5. **The northernmost land action was at St. Albans, Vermont.**
   Confederate agents and escaped rebel soldiers crossed the Canadian
   border and raided St. Albans on October 18, 1864. Under Lt. Bennett
   Young, who was one of John Hunt Morgan's officers, the raiders'
   primary target seems to have been the local banks. They robbed three

banks and planned to use the money for further Confederate operations. They escaped back into Canada. The U.S. government protested, but Canada took no action other than to return $88,000 taken from the raiders when they returned to Canada.

6. **The sea battle took place off Cherbourg, France, on June 19, 1864.** Locals gathered on shore and in boats to watch the action. When the *Alabama* sank, its captain, Raphael Semmes, was saved from capture when a private English yacht rescued him and spirited him away to England. In its brief career, the *Alabama* took sixty-five Northern merchant ships and two thousand prisoners.

7. **The Battle of Lookout Mountain, Tennessee, was fought above the clouds.** On November 24, 1863, troops under Joe Hooker scaled the steep mountain, which rose more than eleven hundred feet above the river, and drove off the Confederate defenders. The battle was an important part of a complex series of moves that lifted the siege of Chattanooga and drove the Confederates out of southern Tennessee and into Georgia.

8. **France sent troops to Mexico.** When President Benito Júarez suspended interest payments on the national debt, France, Britain, and Spain launched an expeditionary force to Mexico. When Spain and Britain discovered French emperor Napoleon III intended to invade, stay, and occupy the territory, they withdrew. France initially lost the Battle of Puebla on May 5, 1862, the victory Mexico celebrates as Cinco de Mayo. Eventually the French army won, and Napoleon brought in Austrian prince Maximilian Ferdinand and his wife, Belgian princess Charlotte (Carlota), to be king and queen. The invasion alarmed the Lincoln government, which feared an alliance between the Confederates and the French. However, as Union victory came to appear more certain, Napoleon lost interest and withdrew his troops. Maximilian ended the adventure in front of a Mexican firing squad as Phil Sheridan camped on the Mexican border with fifty thousand men.

9. **The Texas coastal battles were Sabine Pass and Galveston.** In September 1862 Union forces seized Sabine Pass at the mouth of the

Sabine River, which forms the boundary between Texas and Louisiana, as a part of the blockading effort. A year later Texas forces occupied the area. Deadly accurate fire from the Confederate fort turned back an effort by the Union Navy and General Banks. Meanwhile, the Union had captured Galveston Island in October 1862, but the Confederates under John Magruder recaptured it in January 1863. Banks's Red River Campaign was also aimed at Texas.

10. **Brig. Gen. Stand Watie surrendered at Fort Towson in Indian Territory.** It was not until June 23, 1865, more than two months after Appomattox, that Confederate general Watie commanding the First Indian Brigade, Trans-Mississippi Department, ended the Civil War by signing a cease-fire. He was born in Georgia and was a Cherokee tribal leader who favored relocation to Indian Territory, or modern-day Oklahoma. When the Civil War began he sided with the Confederates and led Indian cavalry in many battles, distinguishing himself at Pea Ridge, Arkansas. He was one of two Native Americans to hold the rank of brigadier general. The other was Ely Parker, a Seneca, who was on General Grant's staff. Parker's rank was by brevet.

3. Grierson's Raid

1. **As a boy, he was kicked by a horse.** At age eight he was seriously injured when a horse kicked him in the cheek and forehead, leaving him permanently disfigured. Understandably, after that experience, he did not like horses.

2. **By occupation, Grierson was a music man.** He taught music and organized bands and entertainments. Not exactly your typical training for cavalry leadership!

3. **Grierson was a supporter of Abraham Lincoln.** Grierson wrote several songs for Lincoln's 1858 Senate campaign, and Lincoln stayed at Grierson's home on one occasion during that campaign. The friendship may have played a role in Grierson's rapid rise in the military, but he proved himself an excellent cavalry leader.

4. **He almost missed the raid because he was home on leave.** When he learned of his assignment in the Vicksburg Campaign, he took a boat to Memphis and a late train to his base, arriving with only a few hours to spare. Had he arrived too late, instead of Grierson's Raid, we would know the event as Hatch's Raid.

5. **The raid started from La Grange, Tennessee.** It is located between Corinth and Memphis on the Memphis & Charleston Railroad.

6. **Grierson led (C) 1,700 men.** The party included the Sixth and Seventh Illinois Cavalry and the Second Iowa Cavalry plus six small guns of Battery B, First Illinois Artillery.

7. **The Quinine Brigade's job was deception.** Grierson weeded out about 175 men who were unable to continue due to illness, exhaustion, or broken-down horses. Riding in columns of four and pulling one gun, the Quinine Brigade was to ride out the same route the raiders had used coming in and obliterate their tracks, making the Confederates think the raiders had departed.

8. **The job of cutting the railroad went to the Second Iowa Cavalry under Col. Edward Hatch.** His regiment was to swing back north, strike the Mobile & Ohio Railroad at West Point, destroy a key bridge, and then head home. Hatch was successful in drawing off Col. Clark Barteau's Tennessee Cavalry but a sharp skirmish at Palo Alto, Mississippi, kept him from doing serious damage to the Mobile & Ohio Railroad.

9. **Grierson's gray-uniformed scouts called themselves the Butternut Guerrillas.** Led by Richard Surby of the Seventh Illinois and dressed and armed like local militiamen, they rode ahead to scout and keep the main column out of traps.

10. **Grant's other raid was led by Col. Abel Streight in middle Tennessee and Alabama.** Streight was unfortunate in being up against Bedford Forrest, who captured him and most of his command. Streight ended up in Libby Prison and was a part of the great escape from it.

11. **The primary objective was Newton Station, where they planned to wreck the Vicksburg Railroad.** The line from Meridian through

Jackson to Vicksburg was the main supply route for the embattled Confederate strongpoint. Grierson's men destroyed two trainloads of ammunition, a nearby Confederate military facility, plus the depot, tracks, bridges, culverts, and telegraph.

12. **Company B of the Seventh Illinois caught up to the main column at the Strong River.** Capt. Henry Forbes and his three dozen men had been sent off on a feint against the Mobile & Ohio Railroad at Macon days earlier. Grierson was about to burn the bridge when they arrived, so their last-minute appearance probably saved them from capture.

13. **Lt. Gen. John C. Pemberton was trying to trap Grierson's men.** The Pennsylvanian rebel received so many reports of Yankees in so many places that he became confused. Grierson's ruses worked. Pemberton also had to watch Streight's raid and another force under Brig. Gen. William Sooy Smith, who was marching south from Memphis.

14. **Grierson was headed for Grand Gulf, Mississippi.** He hoped to come up behind the Confederate army as Grant's army crossed the Mississippi River in the Grand Gulf–Bruinsburg area, but a skirmish at Union Church forced him back eastward.

15. **Grierson's raiders reached Union lines at Baton Rouge, Louisiana.** Exhausted after traveling six hundred miles, Grierson's cavalry quickly became the toast of Baton Rouge and New Orleans. The raid was a huge success.

4. KIA/CSA

1. **Bernard Bee at (E) First Manassas/First Bull Run.** A South Carolinian and West Pointer, class of 1845, he didn't make much of a mark during the war because he was mortally wounded in its first major battle. But during the battle, Bee gave fellow Brig. Gen. Thomas J. Jackson his colorful nickname when he told his troops, "There stands Jackson like a stone wall."

2. **Lawrence O'Bryan Branch at (A) Sharpsburg/Antietam.** This pampered and talented son of North Carolina was raised by his

uncle, governor of the state, and tutored by Salmon P. Chase. After attending the University of North Carolina and graduating from Princeton, he became a lawyer and newspaper editor. He fought in the Seminole War and led troops at New Bern, on the peninsula, and at Second Bull Run before being killed at Antietam.

3. **Archibald Gracie Jr. at (L) Petersburg trenches.** A West Point graduate, class of 1854, he served in eastern Tennessee and fought at Chickamauga. Then he headed east to lead troops from the Wilderness to the Petersburg trenches, where he was killed. He had New York roots, and his family once owned Gracie Mansion, now the official home to the mayor of New York.

4. **States Rights Gist at (F) Franklin, Tennessee.** The man with the ultimate Confederate name was educated at South Carolina College (now the University of South Carolina) and Harvard. He was leading a brigade at Franklin when his horse was killed. Proceeding on foot, he was killed, one of five Confederate generals to die there.

5. **Maxcy Gregg at (G) Fredericksburg.** He was a South Carolina lawyer and leader of the secession faction who had fought in the Mexican War. As a Confederate brigadier, he fought from the peninsula onward, only to be mortally wounded at Fredericksburg, a battle in which the South suffered relatively few casualties.

6. **Ben Hardin Helm at (D) Chickamauga.** He was a Kentuckian and a West Pointer, class of 1851. He left the army to become a lawyer and legislator. He led the First Kentucky Brigade, or the "Orphan Brigade," in the West before being mortally wounded at Chickamauga. His death put the Lincoln White House into mourning because he was married to Mrs. Lincoln's younger half sister.

7. **Ambrose Powell (A. P.) Hill at (K) Petersburg breakthrough.** A Virginian, Hill was a West Point graduate, class of 1847. When he discovered that Union infantry had broken through at Petersburg, he rode out to rally his troops only to ride into Union troops from the 138th Pennsylvania and be shot dead. Interestingly, in delirium

on their deathbeds, both Stonewall Jackson and Robert E. Lee called for Hill.

8. **Ben McCulloch at (J) Elkhorn Tavern/Pea Ridge, Arkansas.** He was a colorful character: a buddy of Davy Crocket's, a hero of San Jacinto, and a Texas Ranger. He fought in the Mexican War, went to California for the gold rush, and became a peace commissioner to the Mormons in Illinois. He commanded the Confederate army at Wilson's Creek, but a sharpshooter's bullet killed him at Elkhorn Tavern.

9. **William Dorsey Pender at (H) Gettysburg.** He was a North Carolinian and West Pointer, class of 1854, with a distinguished record. He became a major general at age twenty-nine and was wounded at Malvern Hill, Fredericksburg, and Chancellorsville. On the second day at Gettysburg he was severely wounded and evacuated to Staunton, Virginia, where he died after an amputation.

10. **Lloyd Tilghman at (C) Champion's Hill.** He was a West Pointer, class of 1836, from Maryland who sided with the South. He was captured at Fort Henry and, after a prisoner exchange, served under Maj. Gen. William Wing Loring at Vicksburg. Tilghman was killed at the battle of Champion's Hill as Pemberton came out of his entrenchments to meet Grant.

11. **William Henry Talbot Walker at (B) Atlanta.** He was a West Pointer, class of 1837, who served in the Seminole War and was so severely wounded in Mexico that he was not expected to live. Despite continuing health problems, he stayed in the U.S. Army until 1860 when he resigned to serve his home state. He was part of the anti–Jeff Davis faction, won praise from Joe Johnston, and served ably at Chickamauga and in Mississippi before being killed in the Battle of Atlanta. In January 1864, he and Maj. Gen. Patrick Cleburne proposed arming the slaves to fight for the South. While the leadership sternly dismissed the plan, it was finally put into action late in the war but too late to help the South.

12. **Felix Kirk Zollicoffer at (I) Logan's Cross Roads/Mill Springs, Kentucky.** He was a printer, a lieutenant in the Seminole War, and

later a newspaper editor who was a powerful Whig in Tennessee. As a brigadier general in the Civil War, he commanded a brigade, first in Tennessee and then in Kentucky. His weak eyes proved his undoing at Mill Springs, Kentucky—also known as Logan's Cross Roads—where he rode up to some troops to tell them they were firing into their own men. They proved to be Union men from the Fourth Kentucky, and their colonel, Speed S. Fry, shot Zollicoffer dead.

5. KIA/USA

1. **Philip Kearny at (C) Chantilly.** He entered the army after graduating from Columbia College and studying law, but he proved himself a great warrior. Kearny won distinction in the Mexican War, where he lost his left arm. He fought with the French army in Italy and won the Legion of Honor for his service in the Battle of Solferino. At Chantilly in 1862 he accidentally rode into enemy lines and tried to fight his way out but was killed. Kearney, New Jersey, is named for him.

2. **Nathaniel Lyon at (L) Wilson's Creek.** The little redheaded captain from Connecticut, West Point class of 1841, helped Congressman Frank Blair keep Missouri in the Union. His reward was a general's star. He later drove Confederate forces from the state but died while attacking a larger force at Wilson's Creek, Missouri.

3. **William Haines Lytle at (D) Chickamauga.** The Ohioan wanted to go to West Point but bowed to family pressure and became a lawyer. He set aside his law practice to fight in the Mexican War and in the Civil War and could always be found where the action was hottest. He was killed leading a charge on the second day at Chickamauga. He was also a well-known poet, who was best remembered for his piece "Anthony and Cleopatra."

4. **Joseph King Fenno Mansfield at (A) Antietam.** He was one of the Union's oldest field commanders at fifty-nine years old. He graduated from West Point, class of 1822; won three brevets in

Mexico; and was army inspector general with the rank of colonel when the war began. Mansfield commanded the XII Corps for only two days before he received a mortal wound while leading it into the fight at Sharpsburg, Maryland.

5. **Daniel McCook Jr. at (F) Kennesaw Mountain.** One of the numerous Fighting McCooks of Ohio, he was a prewar law partner of Thomas Ewing Jr., William Sherman, and Hugh Boyle Ewing. All four would become Union generals. Sherman selected McCook's brigade to lead the assault at Kennesaw Mountain. McCook must have seen the hopelessness of the task because he addressed his troops using a stanza from Thomas Macaulay's "Horatius," which begins, "And how can man better die than facing fearful odds?" He was killed on the enemy's works.

6. **James Birdseye McPherson at (B) Atlanta.** First in his West Point class of 1853, he rose rapidly under Grant and Sherman, leading the Army of the Tennessee at age thirty-five. He tried to cut across what he thought was open ground during the battle of Atlanta and rode into Confederate troops. He was shot trying to escape.

7. **Jesse L. Reno at (H) South Mountain.** Here's another good veteran officer with a city named in his honor—Reno, Nevada. The family name was Renault when they came from France, but they simplified it. He was born in Virginia but raised in Pennsylvania. His high standing in the West Point class of 1842 won him an assignment to ordnance, and he commanded a field artillery battery in Mexico. The IX Corps he commanded was the remains of Burnside's North Carolina expedition. He was killed leading the IX Corps as it tried to force the pass at Fox's gap at South Mountain in 1862 on its way to Antietam.

8. **John Fulton Reynolds at (E) Gettysburg.** A highly regarded soldier, he was a West Point graduate, class of 1841; taught there; and became superintendent of cadets. He won two brevet promotions in the Mexican War. In the Seven Days' battles in 1862 he made a fine defense at Beaver Dam Creek but was captured at Gaines's Mills. He led the I Corps onto the field on the first day at

Gettysburg and was killed within minutes. Ironically, he had been offered command of the army but countered with conditions that the Lincoln government would not accept. The job went to fellow Pennsylvanian George Meade.

9. **John Sedgwick at (I) Spotsylvania.** The beloved leader of the VI Corps was the victim of a sharpshooter, ironically while assuring his men that the Confederates could not "hit an elephant from this distance." They may not have been his exact words, but "Uncle John," as the men called him, was trying to calm them. He was a West Pointer, class of 1837, and had a long and distinguished career before the Civil War.

10. **Joshua Woodrow Sill at (J) Stones River.** This West Pointer, class of 1853, from Ohio served in West Virginia, Kentucky, and Tennessee. He was leading a brigade at Stone's River when he was killed. Fort Sill in Oklahoma is named for him. The James Andrews's Raiders who stole the locomotive The General from the Western & Atlantic Railroad and touched off the great locomotive chase were from his command.

11. **James Samuel Wadsworth at (K) the Wilderness.** He was a graduate of both Harvard and Yale and read law under Daniel Webster. One of the richest men in the country, Wadsworth left the army briefly to run for governor of New York. Defeated, he returned to the army. In 1864 he was mortally wounded and captured in the confused fighting in the dense Virginia undergrowth as General Grant began his campaign to capture Richmond.

12. **William Harvey Lamb "Will" (W. H. L.) Wallace at (G) Shiloh.** Will Wallace was an Illinois lawyer who had served in the Mexican War. He fought well at Fort Donelson and replaced Charles Ferguson Smith in command of a division when Smith was injured. At Shiloh, Wallace played a major role in defending the "Hornet's Nest," buying six important hours for Grant to piece together a new defensive line. Wallace was wounded while retreating and left for dead on the battlefield, but the next day his men found him still breathing. For the next three days, he was

nursed by his wife, who had arrived in the rear during the battle, but he died. He was promoted to brigadier general while on his death bed.

6. Stonewall Down

1. **Jackson was hit three times.** One bullet hit the palm of his right hand. A second went into his left wrist and out his left hand. The third struck his upper left arm between the elbow and the shoulder. The large bone was splintered to the elbow, and the wound bled dangerously.

2. **The first shots missed, but the second volley hit him.** Startled by the sound of horses in their front and fearing a night attack, the Eighteenth North Carolina, serving as the Confederate picket line in that sector, fired an initial volley. Jackson was unhurt, and someone in his party shouted an order not to fire. Suspecting a Yankee trick, someone on the Confederate line ordered another volley, this one wounding Jackson.

3. **The men firing were commanded by Brig. Gen. James Lane.** Once a student and later a colleague of Jackson's at Virginia Military Institute (VMI), the general had a distinguished combat record from Big Bethel to Pickett's Charge to Appomattox, but he never received another promotion after his troops mortally wounded Jackson. A small but passionate man, after the war while he was teaching at what would become Virginia Polytechnic Institute and State University (Virginia Tech), his difference with the college president over policy resulted in a fistfight.

4. **Jackson was riding Little Sorrel.** The horse bolted toward Union lines, but Jackson somehow got him turned. Staff officers rode to his aid and stopped the runaway horse. Though Jackson is gone, Little Sorrel lives on, sort of. A taxidermist stuffed his hide, which is now on display at VMI.

5. **Before he left the field, Jackson ordered Dorsey Pender to hold his line.** Jackson was helped into Pender's line and the general told

Jackson that he might have to fall back. Jackson issued his final order: Pender must hold his present position.

6. **The men dropped his stretcher.** One of the men carrying him was hit by enemy fire, and Jackson was thrown to the ground, causing him great pain.

7. **Dr. Hunter McGuire treated Jackson.** Dr. McGuire stopped the bleeding using finger pressure until he could adjust the tourniquet.

8. **Ambrose Powell Hill replaced Jackson.** Civil War command followed a strict rank and seniority system that was seldom circumvented. Hill was the senior division commander and probably the best man in the corps to replace Jackson.

9. **Hill too was wounded.** Soon after taking command, Hill received a painful leg wound and could not continue fighting. The command fell to the next senior division commander.

10. **Corps command moved to Brig. Gen. Robert Rodes.** If Hill had been a logical choice, Rodes was less certain. He quickly assessed the situation and decided that a night attack was out of the question owing to the fatigue and disorganization of his troops. He planned to move again in the morning.

11. **Jeb Stuart finished the battle.** This move was highly irregular and apparently engineered by officers from the staffs of Hill and Jackson. They called in Stuart. Rodes stepped aside because Stuart outranked him. After the fact, General Lee was notified and expressed his approval. Most observers think that Stuart did an excellent job, but he returned to the cavalry when the battle ended.

12. **Jackson was evacuated to Guinea Station.** Lee was concerned that the Federals might recross at Ely's Ford, and he wanted Jackson moved to safety as soon as his condition would allow it.

7. The Death of Jackson

1. **Dr. Hunter McGuire performed the amputation.** He first removed the bullet from Jackson's right hand. Then he removed the left arm two inches below the shoulder. Dr. Coleman administered the

chloroform and Dr. Walls tied the arteries. Dr. Black monitored Jackson's heart during the operation. The operation was performed in a heated tent and the arm was carefully preserved. Generals received first-class treatment in those days too.

2. **Jackson feared that he might have said something inappropriate.** Assured that he had not, he said he felt it wrong to administer chloroform to anyone near death but admitted it was one of the most delightful physical sensations he had ever experienced. He spoke of hearing wonderful music but said he would not want to enter eternity in such a condition.

3. **An hour and a half after surgery Maj. Alexander "Sandy" Pendleton called on Jackson.** Jeb Stuart sent Jackson's assistant adjutant general to Jackson to ask for direction. Dr. McGuire initially denied him entrance but relented when Pendleton said the fate of the army might hang on the conversation. However, Jackson simply told Pendleton that Stuart would have to do what he thought best.

4. **Jackson was removed to the Chandler house at Guinea Station.** It was being used as a hospital. Jackson was put into a separate office building because an officer in the main house had erysipelas.

5. **Five days after the amputation, Jackson contracted pneumonia.** His progress was excellent for four days before a major change took place. Jackson experienced nausea and pain. Wet towels were applied but did no good. An examination revealed pleuropneumonia on the right side. He was treated with mercury, antimony, and opium.

6. **Five days after Jackson was wounded, his wife and youngest child arrived.** Mary Anna Jackson and five-month-old baby Julia were delayed getting there by George Stoneman's raid. She was assured that the general was doing "pretty well," but she could see for herself that his condition was less promising.

7. **His wife told him he was dying.** One of the doctors at his bedside was Dr. S. B. Morrison, Mrs. Jackson's brother. On Sunday, May 10, he told her that the end was near. Mrs. Jackson told her husband

that he would soon be with God. The general, a deeply religious man, seemed almost to welcome the news.

8. **In his final delirium, he was issuing orders to A. P. Hill.** In his delirium, Jackson ordered Hill to prepare for action and pass the infantry to the front rapidly. Then he mentioned Major Hawks but stopped talking.

9. **His final words were, "Let us cross over the river and rest under the shade of the trees."** He smiled as he said it, and death came quickly. The old soldier had found peace.

10. **His "first grave" is at Ellwood, the Lacy home near Wilderness Tavern.** Beverly Lacy was the chaplain for the corps. Jackson's arm was amputated in a field hospital near Wilderness Tavern. The following day, his arm was buried about a half mile away in the Lacy family's plot, where it rests to this day.

11. **Jackson was buried in Presbyterian Cemetery in Lexington, Virginia.** It is now known as Stonewall Jackson Memorial Cemetery. Initially, Jackson was buried in the family plot, but he was later moved to a more central location. He currently rests under an impressive standing statue of himself that Edward V. Valentine sculpted. His original headstone remains in the family plot, hence Jackson has three graves.

12. **Some visitors leave lemons at the grave.** Jackson suffered from dyspepsia and believed that sucking on lemons gave him relief. He did that frequently. He also had some strange ideas about blood circulation and rode with one arm raised in the air. It must have been a strange sight.

8. Father of Waters

1. **Leonidas K. Polk ended Kentucky's neutrality.** He was a West Pointer but with little actual military experience. For many years he had been an Episcopal bishop. He convinced his commanding officer, Albert Sidney Johnston, to let him seize Columbus, Kentucky, gaining the strategic Mississippi position but losing the

even more strategic state. Ulysses Grant moved quickly to seize Paducah, Kentucky, and announced that he had come to protect the state from invaders. His new base at Paducah effectively flanked Polk's position at Columbus, and Polk would eventually have to give it up. Kentucky stayed divided, but it also remained in the Union.

2. **Ulysses Grant was lucky to get his troops out of Belmont.** His move on Belmont, Missouri, was ill conceived and unwise. He would gain little by capturing the position across the river from heavily fortified Columbus, Kentucky. It also put his command at considerable risk. Polk sent reinforcements across the river and turned the action into a minor defeat for Grant, who managed to get most of his command back on the ships and headed back up river. The last man to board the transports was Grant himself.

3. **Fort Henry was badly sited.** It fell to the navy before the first army troops under Gen. Charles Smith could even get there. Confederate Gen. Lloyd Tilghman made a stand with about a hundred men but wisely sent most of the garrison off to Fort Donelson. The fort was situated on swampy ground and was so badly flooded during the action that the men could fire only a few of the fort's guns. Naval personnel coming in to take the surrender came right into the fort by boat.

4. **John Buchanan Floyd commanded at Fort Donelson, but Simon Bolivar Buckner had to surrender it.** Floyd commanded the fort but escaped before the surrender, supposedly because he feared legal action against him from his days as secretary of war under President Buchanan. His second in command, Gideon Pillow, also escaped and left Buckner to surrender to his old friend Grant. The victory opened the Cumberland River all the way to Nashville, which became the first Confederate state capital to fall.

5. **Col. Charles Ellet Jr. was father of the ram fleet.** An experienced engineer, Ellet convinced Secretary of War Stanton to let him build a fleet of rams for the army. Ellet was commissioned an army colonel and led his fleet to spectacular success at Memphis. The

Union suffered but one casualty in the action: Colonel Ellet was mortally wounded.

6. **The glory hound was Benjamin Franklin Butler, and Mansfield Lovell defended the city.** Butler was the brash general who offended the navy by claiming victory and then became the most hated man in the South for his policies in governing New Orleans. Lovell was the city's defender and was blamed for the defeat, but his army had been stripped for the Shiloh Campaign. Lovell abandoned the city before Butler arrived, leaving the civilian authorities to surrender. He also removed supplies, creating hardships for the civilian population. Later, it was the much-hated Butler who fed the city's poor.

7. **Nathan Bedford Forrest commanded the Fort Pillow attack.** The major general usually is blamed for the Fort Pillow massacre, but the Confederate troops were under the direct orders of Brig. Gen. James R. Chalmers. Further, evidence suggests that Forrest and Chalmers actually tried to stop the slaughter once they arrived on the scene. The South held that the black soldiers were not soldiers at all but slaves taking part in a revolt against their legitimate masters.

8. **John Pope won that important river victory.** He did an able job at Island Number 10 in command of the Army of the Mississippi, and his reward was to be sent east to command the Army of Virginia, a defensive force left to guard Washington while McClellan tried to capture Richmond via the peninsula. After driving McClellan back to his ships, Robert E. Lee handed Pope a humiliating defeat at Second Bull Run. Pope had made enemies in both the North and the South with his vainglorious and boastful pronouncements. After his humiliating defeat, he was sent off to Minnesota to fight Indians.

9. **Fort Pemberton blocked the Tallahatchie River and the entrance to the Yazoo River.** The Union managed to get ships into the rivers via the Yazoo Pass. Confederates under Major General Loring hastily built Fort Pemberton on the Tallahatchie and blocked the

route, sinking a steamship in the channel to obstruct navigation. The fort was pretty minimal—cotton bales covered with earth—but the Tallahatchie was very narrow with overhanging trees and the ships had no room to maneuver. Accurate gunfire from the fort forced them to retire downriver.

10. **Admiral Porter almost got trapped in Steele's Bayou.** This expedition also was a spectacular failure. In an attempt to move beyond the Vicksburg flank defenses on the Yazoo River, Porter took his ships up Steele's Bayou and into Deer Creek. The creek proved too narrow for the flotilla, and Confederate forces under Col. Winfield S. Featherston felled trees both above and below the ships, trapping them in place. Porter sent for help, and troops under William T. Sherman made a forced march to his relief. It was yet another dead end in the efforts to find a way into Vicksburg.

9. Salisbury Prison

1. **The main building had been a cotton factory.** The state of North Carolina quickly saw the need for a military prison camp and purchased the sixteen-acre site complete with the twenty-year-old mill, which was three stories high plus an attic. Several other buildings were also on the grounds. A stockade fence was erected around most of the land.

2. **The prison was remembered for good water and shade.** Large oak trees provided the shade and several wells the good water. In addition, the first prisoners were allowed outside the compound on parole and locals even loaned them books. All in all, it was a pretty comfortable place.

3. **The picture shows prisoners playing baseball.** An artist named Otto Boetticher of the Sixty-Eighth New York, a prisoner at Salisbury, produced the popular painting that depicts an idyllic setting. Baseball profited from the war too. In the years following the war, baseball's popularity exploded and the first professional baseball team was formed in Cincinnati in 1869.

4. **The prison population boomed because of the end of prisoner exchanges.** Early in the war, prisoners were rarely held for more than a few months. When Grant came east in 1864, he decided to end large-scale exchanges but allowed some limited or informal exchanges. In August, that door slammed shut. Fearing Northern cavalry raids to free prisoners in the Richmond area, prisoners were sent south, and prison camps and supply systems were greatly strained.

5. **The population of Salisbury was two thousand.** As the prison population grew, the citizens of Salisbury grew alarmed. If the prisoners escaped or if a raid freed them, what would be the fate of the town and its people? It never happened, but the citizens of the "Old North State"—many of whom were lukewarm secessionists at best—feared the worst.

6. **The prison, designed for 2,500 prisoners, held 10,000.** Where once prisoners slept snugly in the mill or other buildings, now many were cast outside on their own in the cold and wet winter while all the buildings were converted to hospitals. Men slept under buildings, in crowded tents, or in "bear dens" dug into the ground. The death rate, once only 2 percent, skyrocketed to 28 percent. There was not enough food, clothing, shelter, or medicine.

7. **The best-known commandant was Maj. John Henry Gee of Florida.** Initial estimates claimed 11,700 prisoners died there. The modern accepted number is about 5,000, which is bad enough but not the disaster originally believed. Major Gee realized he could not properly care for the prisoners and wanted to resign but was not allowed to do so. After the war, he was brought to trial but found not guilty. The only other prison commandant brought to trial, Henry Wirz of Andersonville, was found guilty and hanged.

8. **The Sixty-Seventh North Carolina Junior Reserves rushed from their train to stop the break out.** The unit was made up of boys who were too young to serve in the army. Most of the prison guards were boys, "graybeards," and convalescents. The prisoners' attempt to rush the gate on November 25, 1864, was probably badly

planned and doomed to failure, but the men were growing desperate. One of the prisoners who was slightly wounded in the attempt was Frank Smith of the Fifth Maine, the grandfather of the author of this quiz.

9. **The civilians who broke out were Albert Richardson and Junius Browne of the *New York Tribune*.** Imprisoning newspaper reporters may seem strange, but the Confederates hated Horace Greeley and his abolitionist "rag" of a paper. The correspondents were captured near Vicksburg. They escaped into western North Carolina and over the mountains to Knoxville. On their return the stories they filed of the suffering in the prisons contributed to the reopening of prisoner exchanges and the release of the men at Salisbury.

10. **Men who could still march were sent to Wilmington.** Once they reached Greensboro, the 3,729 men were sent by train to Wilmington, where they were paroled at North Ferry on the Cape Fear River. For most of them, the war was over. Disease and lack of food and shelter had taken their toll, and few of the men were up to anything more taxing than light duty.

11. **The weaker men were sent to Richmond.** The 1,420 men who could not be marched were put on a train in Salisbury and sent to the Confederate capital. The prison camp was out of business, but 5,000 or more Yankee soldiers remained, lying shoulder to shoulder in eighteen trenches, each 240 feet long. They are there still.

12. **George Stoneman headed the Union troops who arrived at Salisbury.** He ordered the prison, now a supply depot, burned and had a fence erected around the cemetery. Salisbury was the only prison camp that the Union troops burned. Stoneman, himself a prisoner for a time after a failed attempt to free the Andersonville prisoners, had good reason to hate prisons; however, he was fully justified in burning the place because it was a supply depot. Stoneman received a brevet promotion to brigadier general in the regulars for his capture of Salisbury.

10. Fort Pillow

1. **The fort was named for Gen. Gideon Pillow.** He used his position as a law partner to James K. Polk to become a general in the Mexican War, but he did not perform well. He was second in command at Fort Donelson, but when he followed John B. Floyd in fleeing the fort and leaving the surrender to Buckner, Jefferson Davis relieved Pillow of field command. Later reinstated for the Battle of Stone's River, he failed again, hiding behind a tree when he should have been leading an attack. Pillow proved as unsuited to the job as was the fort named in his honor.

2. **Forrest had been repulsed at Paducah, Kentucky.** Only twenty days before the assault on Fort Pillow, Forrest went after the garrison at Paducah. Twice he attacked and twice he was repulsed with significant losses. He was forced to give up the attempt and depart. Black soldiers were part of that garrison. Forrest did not suffer many defeats, and when he did he tended to take them personally. He was probably still in a dark mood when he reached Fort Pillow.

3. **Maj. Lionel F. Booth commanded the fort.** Booth was from Philadelphia and had enlisted in the army in 1858 as a common soldier. As did many other experienced soldiers, he received his chance to be an officer by volunteering to serve in a colored regiment, which in his case was the Sixth U.S. Colored Heavy Artillery. He was killed early in the battle by a sharpshooter's bullet.

4. **James R. Chalmers commanded the attackers.** He was a Virginian, graduate of South Carolina College, and a lawyer in Mississippi. He entered the war as a captain and rose in rank through a solid combat record. After the war he served in Congress, where there were disputes over seating him.

5. **The much-hated loyal Tennesseans also defended the fort.** Southerners saw black soldiers as slaves in rebellion and regarded Southerners who remained loyal to the Union as traitors. They called them Tories and treated them as if they were criminals

rather than enemy soldiers. Further, they viewed white Northerners leading black troops—like Major Booth—as leading a slave rebellion.

6. **Forrest had, figuratively, hoisted the black flag, traditional sign of no quarter given.** He signaled that he would wage a battle to the death. Forrest was raiding into Union territory and could not engage in a prolonged battle. He counted on fear and terror to win quick, easy victories.

7. **Forrest moved his men during a flag of truce.** The Confederates had sent in a flag of truce to demand surrender, and as long as it was in existence neither side was supposed to take offensive action. Some of the Southern troops, however, moved to better positions during the truce.

8. **Forrest used the movements of a ship on the river as an excuse.** The Union gunboat USS *New Era* was offshore, and the Confederates said they feared it was about to land. Many students of the battle doubt this story and believe that the Confederates were cutting off escape routes. It also does not explain why the storming party on the land side of the fort simultaneously moved to better positions.

9. **The Union to Confederate casualty ratio was 5.5 to 1.** The discrepancy in killed was even greater, with 231 Union dead against only 14 Confederates. That difference is most unusual because an attacking force usually has greater casualties attacking across open ground. Clearly, most of the Union dead were killed after the Confederates were inside the fort.

10. **Ohio senator Benjamin Wade and Massachusetts representative Daniel Gooch went to investigate.** The men were members of the powerful Joint Committee on the Conduct and Expenditures of the War. They concluded that a massacre had taken place. They pointed to the fact that Forrest's men took 168 white prisoners but only 58 black ones as clear evidence. Modern studies by author Albert Castel and lawyer/author Richard Fuchs reached the same conclusion. Contemporary Southerners, meanwhile, maintain that

the Union soldiers had refused to throw down their arms and ran for the river to escape. General Forrest said he had proved that blacks could not stand up to Southerners.

11. War Rides the Rails

1. **The first American railroads were started 1830.** The first two railroads were the Baltimore & Ohio and the Charleston & Hamburg, both in slave states. The first steam engines ran on them in 1831. The engine on the Charleston & Hamburg was named the Best Friend of Charleston, but it blew up before the railroad was completed.

2. **(D) Remarkably, railroad growth was 334 percent.** In 1850 there were 9,000 miles of track in the United States. In 1860 that number had grown to 31,000 with 71 percent of it in free states. However, had the South been an independent nation, it would have stood fourth in the world with 9,000 miles. Railroads seemed tailor made for this big sprawling country.

3. **Railroad design and track size made long trips difficult.** Most railroads then did not go far and were not connected to other railroads. In addition, the railroads used a variety of gauges—the distance between the two rails—so it would not have been possible to connect many of them. The standard gauge did not become common until the transcontinental railroad was built. Lincoln approved that standard—4 feet, 8.5 inches—at the recommendation of engineer and general Grenville Dodge. Many cities preferred not to connect rail lines. They wanted to have travelers stay at local hotels and buy meals and other services. That model also kept local teamsters and porters fully employed.

4. **Johnston's army caught the trains at Piedmont, Virginia.** Union Maj. Gen. Robert Patterson was supposed to hold Johnston in place in the Shenandoah Valley and keep him from reinforcing General Beauregard at Manassas Junction, but Johnston marched his force to the Manassas Gap Railroad at Piedmont and put them on trains.

They reached Beauregard in time to turn the tide of the battle and give the South its first major victory of the war. It was a classic example of the use of "interior lines," and the less technologically advanced Confederates pulled it off smoothly.

5. **Col. Thomas J. Jackson, later the immortal "Stonewall," wrecked the Baltimore & Ohio Railroad.** In the opening months of the war, he commanded state troops at Harpers Ferry on the Baltimore & Ohio. He insisted that trains run through the area only at midday. As soon as he amassed a large number of them in a small area, he sprung his trap, capturing or destroying huge numbers of engines, cars, and tracks. He was not "Stonewall" yet, but he was obviously a formidable force.

6. **Corinth was an important place because two major rail lines crossed there.** The Memphis & Charleston Railroad, the South's most important east-west line, crossed the Mobile & Ohio Railroad in Corinth. Whoever controlled that crucial spot controlled transportation in the region. Otherwise regarded as an unhealthy and unimportant backwater, Corinth was twice the objective of major campaigns. The North won both times.

7. **Gen. Daniel McCallum ran the military railroads.** During Simon Cameron's brief stint as secretary of war he identified the need for the function and recruited McCallum, who formerly ran the Erie Railroad, to head it. With the help of Brig. Gen. Herman Haupt the U.S. Military Railroad Command recruited a professional workforce, took over and ran thirty-five railroads in the South, and controlled 2,100 miles of track, 419 engines, and 6,330 cars. They quickly repaired both damaged track and burned bridges, and they built new railroad lines where needed. The command is one of the greatest success stories of the war. McCallum designed prefabricated bridge trusses for quick replacement, causing the Rebels to comment that the Yankees traveled with two or three bridges in their pockets.

8. **Confederate Braxton Bragg made the war's largest move by rail.** In July 1862, Bragg's 30,000-man army was in northern Mississippi. He wanted to move to Chattanooga, but Grant and Don Carlos

Buell held the Memphis & Charleston Railroad, his most direct route. Instead, Bragg used ten railroads farther south to move his force 776 miles, some going as far south as Mobile, Alabama. From Chattanooga, he launched his fall invasion of Kentucky that climaxed at the Battle of Perryville.

9. **Reinforcements by rail helped win the Battle of Chickamauga.** After Gettysburg, the war in the east settled down with Meade unable or unwilling to attack Lee. Lee agreed to send James Longstreet with two of his three divisions to Bragg, whose forces Rosecrans had pushed back to Chattanooga. Longstreet's 12,000 men traveled eight hundred miles in twelve days and arrived in time to break Rosecrans's line and win a major victory. The reinforcements gave Bragg the rare luxury of outnumbering his Yankee opponents. However, the Union responded by sending Joe Hooker and two corps from the Army of the Potomac to reinforce Rosecrans. The 25,000-man force traveled a hundred miles a day for twelve days and helped to reverse the situation at Chattanooga.

10. **The Louisville–Atlanta supply line at 473 miles was the war's longest.** It had to supply 100,000 men and 35,000 animals, and that effort required five ten-car trains per day. Confederate cavalry commanders Nathan Bedford Forrest and Joe Wheeler did their best to disrupt it, but the Union kept the trains rolling and Atlanta fell. The length and vulnerability of the supply line, however, meant that Sherman could not remain there. He had to abandon the city and strike for the sea.

11. **Lee had to retreat when the South Side Railroad was cut.** Supplies coming into Wilmington, North Carolina, from blockade-runners and other items from the Carolinas came into Petersburg via the Weldon Railroad. When Union forces extended their lines to cut the Weldon, the Confederates rerouted supplies so they came in via the South Side line. Sheridan's victory west of Petersburg at Five Forks cut the South Side line and forced Lee to evacuate. It was the beginning of the end for the Confederacy.

12. **Lee was trying to reach supplies at Appomattox Station.** Union cavalry under George Armstrong Custer swooped in and captured two trains of supplies awaiting Lee's army. Meanwhile, both cavalry and infantry maneuvered in front of Lee's march at the nearby courthouse. Lee sent a message to Grant under a flag of truce. Lee was forced to do what he most dreaded. The war ended there.

⤖ SECTION V ⤖

WAR ON THE HOME FRONT

War is the work of the soldier, but in one way or another, wars touch every home and every citizen. Civil wars are even more dramatically touching, because the line between friend and foe is often blurred by family ties and longtime associations. No better example can be found than a death that sent the White House into

No civilian felt the war more painfully than Abraham Lincoln. Born in a slave state and married to a woman with brothers in the Confederate army, fate handed him the job of healing a union already broken. Somehow, he did. This statue of Abraham and son Tad is at the Richmond National Battlefield Park Headquarters at the Tredegar Iron Works on the James River. It is the work of David Frech and a gift from the U.S. Historical Society of Richmond. Its dedication in 2003 set off a firestorm of protests as well as praise. Old wounds heal slowly. *Photo by the author*

mourning in 1863 when Gen. Ben Harden Helm was killed in the Battle of Chickamauga. He was brother-in-law to the Lincolns, the husband of Mary Lincoln's younger half-sister, and a Kentuckian in Confederate gray who led that state's Orphan Brigade.

Quiz 1
Power Diplomacy

During the Civil War, American diplomats played a high-stakes game as the North tried to keep England and France neutral and the Confederacy tried to draw them into the struggle. Let's test your knowledge of some of the major players and the challenges they faced.

1. Lincoln tapped a congressman with a great family pedigree to be ambassador to Great Britain. He was?

2. Jeff Davis countered by sending a former senator from Virginia to represent the Confederacy. Name him.

3. The British government, clearly preferring a splintered America, leaned toward the South in the dispute. Who was the British prime minister?

4. The British foreign secretary was also seen as supporting the Confederates and took the blame when the *Alabama*, which he had been ordered to detain, escaped to sea to prey on Northern shipping.

5. What cabinet minister jumped into the fray and announced that Jeff Davis had created a nation and the time had come to recognize it?

6. Which charming and capable diplomat did the British government send to Washington as ambassador?

7. What European head of state continually pressed the British government to recognize the Confederacy and give approval to his other North American incursion?

8. A former vice-presidential candidate was Lincoln's choice as ambassador to France. He was?

9. Jeff Davis countered with a charming, French-speaking former senator from Louisiana. Name him.

10. The North's most loyal friend in Europe was Russia. Its first ambassador to Russia was an antislavery figure from Kentucky who would really rather have been a general. Who was he?

11. Jeff Davis countered with a fiery Mississippi congressman who was sidetracked in England and France and never went to Russia. He was?

12. When the first ambassador to Russia returned, Lincoln used the vacancy to rid himself of a problem in his cabinet. Who did he send next?

13. The most effective Confederate undercover agent in Britain was an official Confederate naval agent who played a key role in bolstering Southern sea power. He was?

14. The American ambassador to Britain was finally successful in keeping a pair of rams out of the Rebels' hands. What firm was building them?

15. What American event led to a British cabinet fight over recognition of the Confederacy?

16. Which British statesman was the greatest defender of the North in Parliament?

QUIZ 2
Old Thad

Lincoln lives in history as the Great Emancipator, but the Radicals of his party had been urging that momentous step on him for two years before he acted. Perhaps the most effective and the most dedicated of those radicals was Thaddeus Stevens. His impact on the Civil War cannot be overstated. Let's see what you know about him.

1. Stevens rose to prominence in Pennsylvania but it was not his native state. Where was he born?

2. What congenital deformity did he have?

3. His father was a business failure and a bankrupt drunkard who deserted the family twice, but his mother managed to find the money to send Thad to college. What college did he attend?

4. During his long political career, which of these charges was *not* leveled at him? (A) Having a black mistress. (B) Shamelessly currying favor with James Buchanan. (C) Murder. (D) Voting for programs that would line his own pockets.

5. When the Civil War broke out, what was his special wartime responsibility in the House of Representatives?

6. What Confederate military action was aimed personally at him?

7. Which of these men was *not* one of his fellow Radicals? (A) George Boutwell. (B) Zachariah Chandler. (C) Lyman Trumbull. (D) Salmon Chase. (E) Ben Wade.

8. Stevens used deadly riots in two Southern cities to convince moderate Republicans to vote with the Radicals during Reconstruction. Where were those riots?

9. Stevens is generally credited with being the father of two constitutional amendments. Which ones?

10. What landmark Supreme Court case threatened to undo all the gains made by the Radicals?

11. What was the first Confederate state to rejoin the Union?

12. In 1867, what Northern state with only a tiny black population voted against giving blacks the vote, thereby embarrassing the Radicals?

13. Why was Thaddeus Stevens called the Old Commoner?

14. What official party position did Stevens hold while battling for his radical agenda?

15. What official role did Stevens play in the impeachment of Andrew Johnson?

16. Why did Stevens elect to be buried in a remote cemetery in Lancaster, Pennsylvania?

QUIZ 3
Robert Todd Lincoln

Robert "Bob" Lincoln was the first son of Abraham and Mary and the only one who would live past adolescence. In many ways more of a Todd than a Lincoln, he had an uneasy relationship with his father and a bumpy one with his mother. Let's look at his long and successful life.

1. When Abraham came east in 1860 and gave his famous Cooper Union speech, he had another family chore to do. What was it?
2. Robert picked up a comic nickname that he detested. It was?
3. When Robert first visited Manchester, Vermont, where he eventually would build a home, where did he stay?
4. A small building on the grounds at Hildene attests to an unusual hobby that Robert Lincoln enjoyed. Name the hobby.
5. An unlikely stranger once saved Robert Lincoln's life. Name him.
6. Robert wished to leave Harvard Law and to enlist, but his father stopped him. Why?
7. Where was Robert when his father was assassinated?
8. Who was his politically well-connected bride?
9. Robert made a decision about his mother that caused a permanent estrangement. What action did he take?
10. Much of Robert Lincoln's wealth came from his long association with one of America's largest companies. Name it.
11. What cabinet post did he hold and to what nation was he ambassador?
12. In death, he is unlike any other family member. In what way?

QUIZ 4
Northern War Governors

The states played a major role in raising and equipping troops for the war, so the governors were important players. Many gave the Lincoln government outstanding cooperation, but a few opposed the administration and battled it. Let's look at these key political figures.

1. Openly an abolitionist, this governor may be best remembered today for raising a famous black regiment. He was?

2. This industrialist turned governor played an important role as a volunteer aide at First Bull Run and later married a famous Washington beauty. Name him.

3. This governor launched the career of a great general by putting him to work as a mustering officer for state troops. He was?

4. Lincoln backed his 1860 gubernatorial campaign by making six speeches in his state. He repaid Lincoln by being one of his most loyal supporters. Name him.

5. This governor backed the war effort but strongly opposed the Emancipation Proclamation and the enlistment of blacks as soldiers. He was?

6. This strong supporter of Lincoln is the only governor with a statue at Vicksburg. Name him.

7. He hosted the convention of the Loyal War Governors Conference in 1862 that backed emancipation. He was?

8. He was one of three famous brothers who gave strong support to the war. Name him.

9. One of Lincoln's most vocal critics later was a presidential candidate. He was?

10. This New York–born midwestern governor was not only against slavery but was a reformer who railed against capital punishment and for suffrage for blacks and women. Name him.

QUIZ 5
Southern War Governors

The South, ostensibly, fought for the rights of the states, but as the Davis government took control of the war, some of the governors found themselves as upset with Richmond as they had been with Washington. Let's look at some of the leaders of the Southern states.

1. After leaving the governor's office in the middle of the war he became an army officer and was captured with Jeff Davis. He was?
2. This Southern blue blood was a strong voice for secession and signed the first secession ordinance. Name him.
3. This governor was a Whig and then a Know-Nothing who led the Twenty-Sixth Regiment from his state early in the war. He was?
4. This Georgia-born governor believed death would be preferable to reunion. He practiced what he preached, blowing his brains out on April 1, 1865. Name him.
5. When this governor's term ended in 1862 he joined the state militia and served as a private for the rest of the war. He was?
6. He worked to avoid secession but supported it once his state seceded. In reprisal for his Confederate service, troops under David Hunter burned his home. Name him.
7. Though he favored secession, he was a powerful enemy of the Davis government, tried to keep his state's troops at home, and opposed the draft. When Union troops overran his state, he called for an end to the war. He was?
8. This Fire Eater was refused amnesty and was a fugitive until his death in 1867. His Confederate general brother had a famous bridge named for him. Name that governor.

9. He employed a soon-to-be-famous Union general right before the war. The general returned the favor by obtaining a pardon for him after the war. He was?

10. He was elected governor in 1858 and defied Lincoln when the president made his appeal for troops, but he died in office as the war was beginning. Name him.

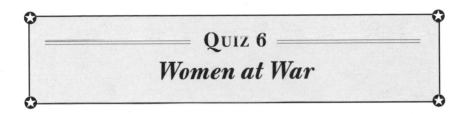

QUIZ 6
Women at War

Women did not take the military roles in the Civil War that modern women do in today's conflicts, but they were far from inactive. See if you can identify these women who made a real impact.

1. This Union hospital matron wielded so much power that Sherman said of her, "She outranks me. I can't do a thing." She was?

2. Disguised as a man this Canadian served in the roles of nurse and spy, terms she used in the title of her postwar book. She was?

3. This "Betsy Ross of the Confederacy" helped make the first three battle flags and later married a Confederate general. Name her.

4. This native of Oxford, Massachusetts, was a teacher, a nurse, and a humanitarian. She played a major role in identifying the Andersonville dead and went on to found the American Red Cross. She was?

5. President Lincoln credited her with being the "little lady who started the war." She was?

6. This controversial woman served the army as a surgeon and later became embroiled in controversy over her Medal of Honor. Name her.

7. She operated at the highest levels of Confederate society and wrote it all down with an acid-dipped pen. She was?

8. She was the only woman to be officially commissioned an officer in the Confederate Army. Name her.

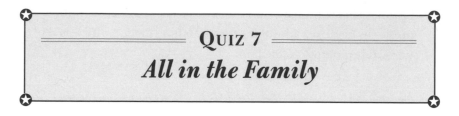

Quiz 7
All in the Family

The American Civil War was played out on a small stage. The nation had a population of only 31.5 million, most of them living east of the Mississippi. Many of the principal military leaders were bound together through their studies at West Point, their service in the army and the Mexican War, and their other close ties. This quiz concerns some of those close relationships.

1. Abraham Lincoln had a brother-in-law who was a general. Unfortunately for Lincoln, he wore gray. Name him.
2. Jefferson Davis also had a brother-in-law who was a general, but at least he was on Jeff's side. He was?
3. On several occasions, Confederate cavalry leader Jeb Stuart's men clashed with Union troopers under the leadership of Jeb's father-in-law. Who was he?
4. Confederate generals A. P. Hill and D. H. Hill each had a brother-in-law who was a prominent Confederate general. Who were they?
5. When General Grant was a young lieutenant stationed at Jefferson Barracks near St. Louis, a West Point classmate from that city used to take him to his family home. Grant eventually married that man's sister. The name of the classmate, please.
6. William Tecumseh Sherman was married to the sister of three Union generals. Who were Sherman's brothers-in-law?
7. General Sherman's brother John also played a major part in the war years but not as a soldier. In what role did he serve?
8. Politically powerful John Crittenden of Kentucky supported Lincoln and tried hard to head off the Civil War with his famous

Crittenden Compromise. His sons provide a classic footnote to the war. What was their distinction?

9. Brothers Daniel and John McCook of Ohio both served in the Union Army. How many Fighting McCooks served the Union cause? How many generals were in the lot?

10. When George Brinton McClellan was seeking the hand of Ellen Marcy, daughter of his colonel, he had competition from a fellow officer who went on to become a Confederate general. Who was he?

ANSWERS

1. Power Diplomacy

1. **The diplomat from the famous family was Charles Francis Adams of Massachusetts.** His grandfather John Adams and his father, John Quincy Adams—both of whom, of course, served as president—filled the position before him.

2. **Adams's Confederate counterpart was James Murray Mason.** With ten years' experience on the Senate Foreign Relations Committee, he seemed a good choice, but his crude style and reliance on the cotton famine did not play well in Britain.

3. **The British prime minister was Henry John Temple, Viscount Palmerston.** The Lincoln government thought of him as being strongly for the South, but he actually walked a cautious course of neutrality.

4. **Lord John Russell was British foreign secretary.** The North distrusted his motives, but he blamed the *Alabama* situation on his own gross negligence.

5. **The troublemaker was Chancellor William Ewart Gladstone.** Palmerston distanced the government from the position. Later in life, Gladstone admitted it was a mistake and denied any anti-Northern intention.

6. **Richard Bickerton Pemell, Lord Lyons, was British ambassador to the United States.** He was widely admired in the North for his honesty and reason and for keeping his government neutral.

7. **Napoleon III was strongly pro-Southern.** From the start, he pressed England to recognize the Confederacy and give legitimacy to the Maximilian government he had set up in Mexico. However, lacking British support, he would not go it alone.

8. **William Lewis Dayton was minister to France.** The New Jersey lawyer was John Frémont's running mate in 1856. Though he spoke no French and had no diplomatic experience, he was effective in dealing with the French government.

9. **John Slidell was the Confederacy's man in France.** The urbane Slidell should have been perfect for the job, but he made little headway. He played a key role in negotiating the disastrous Erlanger "cotton" loan in which the company marketed Confederate bonds backed by cotton. After the war, he moved to Europe. Like his counterpart, Dayton, he was born in the North.

10. **Cassius Marcellus Clay represented the United States in Russia.** He delayed his departure and organized a group of volunteers to protect the White House until federal troops arrived and the capital was safe. Itching for action, he returned from Russia to become a general but differed with the Lincoln government over the protection of slavery in the occupied South and refused the commission. Later, he returned to his Russian post.

11. **Lucius Quintus Cincinnatus Lamar was assigned to Russia by the Confederacy but never arrived there.** His official title was special commissioner to England, France, and Russia, but the Confederate Senate never confirmed him. He returned home to support Davis and served as a military judge. After the war he was a member of the U.S. Supreme Court.

12. **Lincoln solved a cabinet problem by sending Simon Cameron to the court of the czar.** Thaddeus Stevens joked about Cameron's alleged corrupt practices, saying that he would not steal a hot stove! He served in Russia for only a year but seems to have been effective.

13. **The Confederate naval agent was James Dunwoody Bulloch.** The former naval officer was a favorite uncle of young Theodore Roosevelt's. His successes are one of the great untold stories of the Confederacy.

14. **The rams were being built by William Laird & Son of Liverpool.** Ambassador Adams discovered the illegal contract and called it to the attention of the British government. It was too blatant to ignore, and the British government stopped it.

15. **Lee's 1862 invasion of Maryland sparked a debate on recognition.** Expecting news that Washington or Baltimore had fallen, the pro-Southern bloc in the English cabinet pushed for intervention.

However, when Lee's army was turned back, cooler heads prevailed. Many feel that Lincoln's release of the preliminary Emancipation Proclamation effectively ended future attempts to recognize the Confederacy.

16. **John Bright was the foremost defender of the North in Parliament.** The fearless leader of his majesty's loyal opposition was a bitter and effective force against slavery and privilege.

2. Old Thad

1. **He was born in Danville, Vermont.** Thaddeus Stevens was born April 4, 1792. His father, Joshua, was a shoemaker with an alcohol problem and left his wife to raise four boys on her own. Somehow she did it, but it must have been a life of grinding labor and poverty.

2. **He limped from a clubfoot.** Strangely enough, his older brother was born with both feet clubbed. In that time such deformities were viewed as the mark of the devil or punishment from God.

3. **Stevens was educated at Dartmouth College.** His mother sent him off first to the University of Vermont, but after three semesters, he transferred to Dartmouth where he graduated in 1814. Dartmouth started as a school for Indians.

4. **(B) He was never accused of shamelessly currying favor with James Buchanan.** Although both men lived in Lancaster, Pennsylvania, they detested each other. Regarding the other charges, on the one hand, Stevens did have a black woman living with him, he did support the building of a railroad that would have significantly aided his iron forge, and early in his career, while a young lawyer in Gettysburg, he was suspected by some to have murdered a young, pregnant black woman. On the other hand, the black woman in his home was officially a housekeeper, and there were whispers but no proof that Stevens had done anything improper with the pregnant black girl or had been involved in her death. As to the railroad, that sort of deal was hardly uncommon then or even now.

5. **Stevens was assigned to find a way to finance the war.** His efforts in the House of Representatives were outstanding. Stevens defended the government printing of "greenbacks," fiat paper money that was used to finance the war. The banking interests fought it because it had previously been their exclusive province and a source of revenue for them.

6. **The Confederates burned his ironworks.** On his way to Gettysburg, Jubal Early led a force to destroy Stevens's ironworks at Caledonia west of Gettysburg. Early expressed regret that the owner was not home. The Confederates justified the action because they said that Stevens defended Union armies in the South that were doing the same to Confederate property.

7. **(C) Lyman Trumbull was not a Radical.** Connecticut-born Lyman Trumbull was a senator from Illinois and considered a moderate. Stevens was one of the most radical of the Radical Republicans. Strangely, he had started as a Federalist, switched to the Anti-Masons, and then moved to the Whigs. However, his sympathy for the slaves and his egalitarian views not only sent him into the new Republican Party but also to the most extreme side of it.

8. **The riots were in Memphis and New Orleans.** In both cases, the police openly joined with Confederate veterans to beat and murder blacks. Stevens could see that, without interference by the North, the newly freed slaves would simply be pushed into a new form of slavery.

9. **Stevens is considered the father of the Thirteenth and Fourteenth Amendments.** The Thirteenth Amendment officially freed all slaves and the Fourteenth gave the freedmen the vote. Former Confederate states were forced to accept them as a condition of returning to full status. However, while the states might officially accept them, it did not mean they would honor them.

10. **The Supreme Court ruling in *ex parte Milligan* was trouble for the Radicals.** Despite the presence of five Lincoln appointees on the bench, the court ruled in 1866 that the government could only

resort to military courts where civilian courts were not in operation. This decision threw out the work of the Freedmen's Bureau courts and sent all issues to the state courts, which were reluctant to prosecute local whites in cases involving blacks.

11. **The first seceded state to rejoin the Union was Tennessee.** It was readmitted before the Radicals took over the Reconstruction process. Therefore, it escaped some of the conditions that the Radicals demanded of other states.

12. **Connecticut twice refused.** It rejected Negro suffrage in 1865 and 1867. Minnesota, Kansas, and Ohio also declined to give the Negro the vote. However, ratification of the Fourteenth Amendment made it the law of the land.

13. **He was called the Old Commoner because his service was entirely in the House of Representatives, and the voters directly elected him.** He was similar to William Pitt before him who was called the Old Commoner because he had spent his entire career in the House of Commons. Both men were champions of the common man and of the downtrodden. Neither was especially popular with the rich and powerful.

14. **Stevens served as majority whip.** His job was to line up votes for the Republicans on major pieces of legislation. He was ideal for the job because he knew how to wield power and could be very persuasive.

15. **In Johnson's impeachment trial he was a prosecution manager.** He was one of the seven managers from the House of Representatives who handled the prosecution. They function much as prosecuting attorneys in a criminal action do. Of course, an impeachment is a political trial and many rules differ.

16. **He wished to be buried in a cemetery that had no prohibition against blacks.** Thaddeus Stevens was more than an abolitionist. He was an egalitarian who believed that the black race was the equal of the white race. That position was very rare in America in his day.

3. Robert Todd Lincoln

1. **Lincoln planned to visit his son Robert in New Hampshire.** In 1859, Robert had attempted to enroll in Harvard College but flunked fifteen of sixteen subjects on the entrance exam. He was sent off to Phillips Exeter Academy in Exeter, New Hampshire, to prepare. Abraham considered Bob to be bright but probably questioned his work ethic. He was going to visit Bob and ensure he was ready to move to Harvard later in the year. The educational experience did the job. Bob was admitted to Harvard and graduated with the class of 1864.

2. **Robert hated the comic nickname the Prince of Rails.** It was a takeoff on the Prince of Wales and the Rail Splitter. Robert Lincoln was uncomfortable with his father's fame, but when he arrived at "largely Republican" Harvard as the son of the party's presidential nominee, his stock quickly rose. It went even higher when his father was elected.

3. **In his first visit to Manchester, Vermont, he stayed at the Equinox Hotel.** Mary Lincoln took sons Robert and Tad there in the summer of 1864. The rambling white buildings still exist as the Equinox Resort. Robert loved the area so much that he would eventually build his home, Hildene, down the road and overlooking the Battenkill River valley. Hildene, in Scottish, means "hill and valley."

4. **His hobby was astronomy.** He had an observatory built and installed an elaborate telescope for studying the heavens. That telescope is still in use today. Robert liked his gadgets. Hildene also features a large pipe organ that plays music from rolled punched sheets.

5. **Robert was saved by actor Edwin Booth, brother of his father's assassin.** On a trip to Washington from Harvard in 1864, Robert was on a railroad platform in Jersey City. The crowd jostled him, and he fell between the platform and the train as it started to move. Booth, standing nearby, grabbed young Lincoln's coat collar and

pulled him to safety. Lincoln recognized the popular actor and thanked him by name. Booth did not realize whom he had saved until a mutual friend told him some months later. Edwin was a loyal Union man and mortified by his younger brother's act. He took solace in the knowledge that he had saved the fallen president's son.

6. **Lincoln refused to let his son enlist because he feared that Mary could not bear the loss of another son.** Sons Eddie and Willie were already dead and Mary's emotional stability was fragile. Abraham knew he would take political heat for it, but he did not want to risk losing his son in combat. In early 1865, he relented to pressure from Robert and asked Grant to give him a staff position, which kept Captain Lincoln relatively safe. He was at Appomattox at the time of the surrender.

7. **Robert was at the White House.** Robert was invited to join his parents at the theater, but after a long trip from Appomattox, he begged off as too tired. Some accounts say he was asleep; others say that he was hanging out with Lincoln's secretary Johnny Hay. When the news came, he hurried to the Petersen house. He did his best to calm his mother and wept when his father died. Robert was close by during two other assassinations of American presidents— Garfield and McKinley. He warned later presidents not to stand too close to him for their own safety.

8. **He married Mary Eunice Harlan.** She was daughter of Senator James Harlan of Iowa, an ally of Lincoln's who favored freeing the slaves and enlisting them to fight for their own freedom. Later, Lincoln appointed him secretary of the interior, but Abraham was assassinated before Harlan moved into the post. Robert and Mary had three children, but the line died in 1985 with the death of Robert Todd Lincoln "Bud" Beckwith, Robert's grandson.

9. **Robert had his mother committed to a mental institution.** Alarmed by Mary's bizarre behavior, Robert brought her before a sanity hearing in 1875. She wallowed in grief, engaged in spiritualism, and alternately went on spending binges and then

cried poverty. When she was adjudged insane he had her committed to Bellevue Place in Batavia, Illinois. But Mary Lincoln was no pushover. She hired a lawyer, obtained her release, and was taken in by her sister Elizabeth Edwards in Springfield, Illinois, where she lived out her days. She never forgave her only living son.

10. **Robert was associated with the Pullman Palace Car Company.** It was the age of the railroad, and George Pullman's cars were helping to revolutionize travel in America. Initially, Robert was the company's general counsel, but he became president in 1897 when Pullman died. He held the post until 1911 when he became chairman of the board and served there until the end of his life in 1926.

11. **He held the posts of secretary of war and ambassador to Great Britain.** Rutherford B. Hayes offered him the post of assistant secretary of state, but he refused it. James Abram Garfield appointed him secretary of war, and Benjamin Harrison sent him to England. Between 1884 and 1912, he was prominently mentioned as a candidate for either president or vice president. Robert discouraged the talk saying, "What you really want is my father."

12. **He is not buried with the rest of the family.** Abraham, Mary, Eddie, Willie, and Tad lie in the family crypt in Springfield, Illinois. Robert, Mary, and son Jack were interred at Arlington National Cemetery. Ironically, his resting place is in proximity to yet another assassinated president. His grave is up the hill from that of John F. Kennedy.

4. Northern War Governors

1. **The strong abolitionist was John Albion Andrew of Massachusetts.** He was born in Maine and educated at Bowdoin College. Politically, he was a Whig, then a Free Soiler, and finally a Republican. He led an effort to obtain legal aid for John Brown and became governor of Massachusetts in 1861. He quickly prepared

the state militia for war and urged Maine and New Hampshire to do the same. He was an innovator who accepted men from other states to serve in Massachusetts regiments. He enlisted five hundred Californians into one of his regiments and sponsored the Fifty-Fourth Massachusetts, the famous black regiment depicted in the movie *Glory*.

2. **The industrialist turned governor was William Sprague IV of Rhode Island.** He came from a successful industrial family and became governor in 1860. He took a great interest in his Rhode Island Brigade and accompanied it to Bull Run as a volunteer aide to its commander, Ambrose Burnside. Sprague showed both bravery and skill in that action. He was an enthusiastic supporter of the war and married Kate Chase, daughter of the secretary of the treasury, considered the belle of Washington society. It was not a happy union. Sprague took to the bottle. Kate had an affair with Roscoe Conkling, divorced Sprague, and later died in poverty. Sprague remarried, but he, too, lost most of his fortune and died in France.

3. **Richard Yates of Illinois played a role in advancing the North's best general.** He was born in Kentucky and educated at Transylvania College in Lexington and at Illinois College. He served in Congress before the war. As a Republican governor, he gave strong support to Lincoln and gave Ulysses Grant his first war job as a mustering officer. After the war he was a senator. His son Richard was also an Illinois governor.

4. **William A. Buckingham of Connecticut received important support from Lincoln.** Born in Lebanon and educated at Bacon Academy in Colchester, he became a merchant and manufacturer in Norwich. After serving as Norwich mayor, he won the Connecticut governor's race in as a Republican 1860 by only 541 votes. When the war began, he was asked for ten companies, or one regiment. He raised fifty-four companies and $2 million to equip them. His support for the war was outstanding, and by 1865 his

electoral victory margin had risen to 11,000 votes. He later ran for the Senate.

5. **Initially supportive was David Tod of Ohio.** Tod supported the war, but many ensuing developments eroded that support. The Copperheads were strong in Ohio, and the state took five thousand casualties at Shiloh. Morgan's Raiders came into the state and draft riots occurred in Holmes County. A war Democrat, Tod opposed the Emancipation Proclamation and resisted enlisting blacks as soldiers. The bottom line was that Tod, as with many in his state, was lukewarm to the war.

6. **Oliver P. Morton of Indiana has a statue at Vicksburg.** Actually, his name was Oliver Hazard Perry Throck Morton. Initially a hatter, he took up the law and studied at Miami University in Ohio and Cincinnati College. Though a lifelong Democrat, he moved to the Republicans and gave strong backing to the war. He is considered one of the best wartime governors. His clout can be shown in that after appealing to him for help, a general from his home state, Brig. Gen. Jeff Columbus Davis, was never prosecuted for murdering Kentucky general William "Bull" Nelson.

7. **Andrew Curtin of Pennsylvania hosted the Loyal War Governors Conference.** He was educated at Dickinson College and its law school, and was a Whig turned Republican. He was governor from 1861 to 1867, and despite severe physical problems during his first two years in office, he gave the war his enthusiastic support. He organized the Pennsylvania reserves into fighting units and played a major role in repelling Lee's army during the Gettysburg Campaign. But his greatest contribution was organizing the 1862 Loyal War Governors Conference in Altoona in support of the Emancipation Proclamation.

8. **Israel Washburn Jr. was one of thee famous brothers from Maine.** Another Whig turned Republican, he was a lawyer and had sat in the House of Representatives with brothers Elihu (Washburne) of Illinois and Cadwallader (Washburn) of Wisconsin. While Israel was supporting the war as Maine's governor, Cadwallader became a

general and Elihu was busy in Congress promoting the career of General Grant.

9.   **Horatio Seymour of New York was no fan of Lincoln.** He gave tepid support to the war but continually attacked Lincoln for suppressing individual freedoms, centralizing power in Washington, and for proposing emancipation. He opposed the draft, and when draft rioting broke out in New York, he seemed to attempt to conciliate the rioters rather than put them down. Republicans called his efforts treasonous. His views played a role in his election loss in 1864. Four years later, he was the Democrats' candidate for president against Ulysses Grant.

10. **Austin Blair of Michigan was a real reformer.** Educated at Hamilton and Union Colleges, he studied law and moved to Michigan, where he entered politics as a Whig. He was instrumental in passing a law ending capital punishment and pushed for voting rights for women and blacks in the state. He became a Republican, and as governor, he gave strong backing to the war. Michigan, with a population of only 800,000, produced 90,000 soldiers for the Union. Blair served in Congress after the war, and his statue stands on the Michigan State Capitol grounds.

5. Southern War Governors

1.   **Francis Lubbock of Texas was a soldier after serving as governor.** A South Carolinian, he went to Texas in 1836 and became involved in politics. As a wartime governor he supported the draft and the controversial conscription of resident aliens. When his term ended he became a lieutenant colonel and served under Maj. Gen. John Magruder in Texas. He later served Jeff Davis as an aide, fled with him, and after being captured with him in Georgia, was imprisoned for eight months at Fort Delaware. Incidentally, the city and county of Lubbock, Texas, are named not for him but for his brother, Tom.

2. **Francis Pickens of South Carolina signed the first secession ordinance.** Grandson of a Revolutionary War general and son of a governor, he was also related to John Calhoun. He was educated at Franklin College, now part of the University of Georgia, and South Carolina College, now the University of South Carolina. He was a nullifier and an ardent secessionist and was at Charleston harbor as events led to war. His son-in-law was Confederate cavalry Brig. Gen. Matthew Butler.

3. **Zebulon Vance of North Carolina led a regiment before becoming governor.** He came from a slave-owning family and studied at Washington College in Tennessee. He attended the University of North Carolina Law School on a $300 loan from the college. He was a Whig in the state legislature and became a Know-Nothing while serving as the youngest congressman at the outbreak of the war. He led the Twenty-Sixth North Carolina at New Bern and was credited with a skillful withdrawal. The unlucky outfit was later decimated at Gettysburg, long after Vance left it to become governor in 1862. As governor, he clashed with Davis over the writ of habeas corpus, the rights to blockade goods, and conscription practices. After the war he defended Tom Dula in the murder trial that was made famous in the folk song "Tom Dooley." Vance served as an enlightened governor and as a U.S. senator.

4. **John Milton of Florida was true to his belief of "death before reunion."** Born in Georgia to a prominent family, he married twice and fathered fourteen children. In Florida, he became active in politics, served in the state legislature, and was an ardent secessionist. As governor, he moved the state toward secession and became an active supplier of food and salt to the Confederate army. His suicide at the end of the war certainly demonstrated his sincere support of the lost cause. One of his sons, Jeff Davis Milton, became famous for shooting bad guys. He was a Texas Ranger and a legendary lawman in Arizona.

5. **Henry Rector of Arkansas served out the rest of the war as a private soldier.** He was born in Kentucky and went to Arkansas as a

young man because he was related to many of the ruling families there. After failing in banking, he became a U.S. marshal and served in the state senate before becoming governor in 1860. Arkansas dragged its feet over secession but left the Union when Lincoln called for volunteers. After a turbulent two years, Rector was not eligible to run for reelection so he joined the state militia as a private soldier. By the end of the war he was ruined, and Yankee troops had burned his home near Little Rock.

6. **John Letcher of Virginia had his house burned by the Yankees.** A native of Lexington, Virginia, he attended Macon College and Washington Academy, now Washington and Lee. He was a newspaper editor and for eight years was a member of Congress, where he was known as Honest John for his opposition to government extravagance. When David Hunter launched his Shenandoah Valley Campaign in 1864, he burned the Virginia Military Institute and Governor Letcher's home.

7. **Joseph Brown of Georgia was a thorn in the side of Jeff Davis.** Determined to obtain an education, he drove a yoke of oxen 125 miles and exchanged them for a year of schooling in Anderson, South Carolina. He was a teacher and a lawyer before becoming a Georgia state senator. As governor, he used state railroad money for public education. Though he favored secession, he immediately clashed with Jeff Davis over state versus Confederate power. He was Davis's top foe on nearly every issue. After the war he was a Republican scalawag—a Southerner who supported Reconstruction— before returning to the Democrats and serving in the U.S. Senate.

8. **John Jones Pettus of Mississippi was a fugitive until his death.** He was the quintessential Rebel who said he would rather eat fire than sit down with the Yankees. On the lam after the war until his death, he is largely forgotten today. His brother, Edmund, a Confederate brigadier general, would be equally obscure but for the fact that a bridge was named in his honor. The Edmund Pettus Bridge in Selma, Alabama, was the scene of a violent attack by armed police officers against civil rights marchers in "Bloody Sunday" 1965.

9. **Thomas Moore of Louisiana was rescued by his former employee.** He was a successful planter and served in the state legislature before becoming governor in 1860. He was interested in education and helped select Yankee Capt. William T. Sherman to head the new Louisiana Seminary (now Louisiana State University). Of course, the Yankees took New Orleans early in the war, and the government retreated first to Opelousas, then to Shreveport. He left office in 1864, but he could not return to his plantation house, which had been burned. At war's end, he fled to Mexico and then to Cuba. General Sherman hand-carried Moore's application for a pardon directly to President Andrew Johnson, and through Sherman's intervention, Moore's land was restored to him.

10. **John Ellis of North Carolina died in office early in the war.** His correspondence shows a desire to take his state out of the union and his reply to Lincoln's appeal for troops is classic. He said, "I can be no party to this wicked violation of the laws of the country and to this war upon the liberties of a free people. You can get no troops from North Carolina." He died shortly afterward of natural causes at age forty. It turns out he was wrong about North Carolina troops being unavailable to the Union. More than five thousand white men from the Old North State, and countless former slaves, enlisted and helped to defeat the Confederacy.

6. Women at War

1. **Mary Ann Bickerdyke, called Mother Bickerdyke, was a widow who set up a hospital to care for the wounded at Fort Donelson.** She innovated by creating a hospital boat and became Grant's chief of nursing at Vicksburg. By the end of the war, she had established three hundred hospitals and was honored by riding at the head of the XV Corps in the Grand Review of the Armies in Washington.

2. **Sarah Emma Edmonds was a nurse and spy.** Born in Nova Scotia, she was living in Flint, Michigan, when she enlisted as Frank Thompson. She was one of about four hundred women who so

served. Serving as a male nurse for the Second Michigan, she
volunteered as a spy, making trips into enemy territory disguised
variously as a black man, a young Southerner, and an Irish peddler
woman. However, she contracted malaria and, fearful of being
discovered as a woman, deserted. After the war, she was the only
female member of the veterans' group, the Grand Army of the
Republic.

3. **Hetty Cary was a Confederate Betsy Ross.** She was a Baltimore
blue blood, related to the Jeffersons, the Randolphs, and
Pocahontas. Early in the war she and her sister, Jennie, recklessly
smuggled drugs and clothing into Virginia and were caught and
sent behind Confederate lines. In January 19, 1865, she married
Brig. Gen. John Pegram. He was killed eighteen days later at
Hatcher's Run. It was her sister Jennie who took James Randall's
popular poem "Maryland" and set it to music, resulting in
"Maryland, My Maryland." It was called the "Marseillaise" of the
South and is still the official state song.

4. **Clarissa "Clara" Barton helped identify the Andersonville dead.**
Her skills were organizational and managerial rather than medical.
Among her achievements was establishing a distribution system for
medical supplies, convincing the army to bring medical supplies
with them to the battles, and setting standards for hygiene and
cooking for the sick. Maj. Gen. Ben Butler named her as the "lady
in charge" and gave her great leeway. Later she became founder
and first president of the American Red Cross and campaigned for
black civil rights and women's rights. She went on to provide aid in
Armenia, Cuba, China, and finally Galveston, Texas, after the great
hurricane destroyed that city.

5. **Harriet Beecher Stowe was the little lady who started the war.**
Born into the powerful abolitionist Beecher clan of Litchfield,
Connecticut, she was educated by an older sister and married
abolitionist professor Calvin Stowe. The Stowes supported the
Underground Railroad, even hiding some escapees in their own
home. When the Fugitive Slave Law was passed in 1851, Harriet

wrote *Uncle Tom's Cabin* as a protest. It was immensely popular and helped sway public opinion in the United States and in England against Southern slavery. She went on to write more than twenty books and to champion other social causes, but the story of Uncle Tom and Little Eva was her masterpiece.

6. **Dr. Mary Edwards Walker was a Medal of Honor winner.** The graduate of Syracuse Medical College volunteered for military duty but initially was treated as a volunteer nurse. The army tried to keep her out of the field, but eventually she treated the wounded from Bull Run, Fredericksburg, and Chickamauga. She was captured and accused of being a spy, but then exchanged. General Sherman and Maj. Gen. George Thomas both recommended her for the Medal of Honor, which she received in 1866. Later the army revised the standards for the award and asked her to return it. She refused but was no longer listed as a winner. President Jimmy Carter officially restored the honor long after her death.

7. **Mary Boykin Chestnut penned a first-class diary.** Her diary is one of the great treasures of the war. The properly educated daughter of a South Carolina congressman and governor, she married James Chestnut Jr., who was a U.S. senator and became a wartime aide to Jefferson Davis. She was in Charleston to see Fort Sumter being attacked and on hand in Montgomery for Jeff Davis's inauguration. She was a buddy of President Davis's second wife, Varina, and faithfully recorded the Richmond social and political scene as Southern fortunes rose only to be smashed. Her writing style is still vibrant today.

8. **Sally Tompkins held a Confederate commission.** After First Bull Run, the Richmond government called on private citizens to set up hospitals for the wounded. Sally Tompkins set one up in the home of a friend, Judge John Robertson. She quickly distinguished the Robertson Hospital with her superior care. When the government issued a rule that hospitals could only be run by Confederate officers, Jefferson Davis issued Sally a commission as a captain in the cavalry. Captain Sally operated the hospital throughout the

war, tending to 1,333 wounded soldiers with only 73 deaths. When she passed away many years later, she was buried with full military honors.

7. All in the Family

1. **Kentuckian Ben Hardin Helm was Lincoln's brother-in-law.** He was a West Pointer, class of '51, who practiced law and married Mary Todd Lincoln's youngest half-sister, Emilie. Lincoln tried to persuade him to stay with the Union, offering him a regular army commission as a paymaster, but he joined the Confederate army and led the Kentucky Orphan Brigade, so called because they could not go home. When he was mortally wounded at Chickamauga, the White House went into mourning.

2. **Gen. Richard "Dick" Taylor was Davis's brother-in-law.** In 1835, Jeff Davis left the army to marry Sarah Knox Davis, daughter of his colonel, Zachary Taylor, and sister of future Confederate general Dick Taylor. Dick was a Yale graduate and a planter when the war started. He proved a very capable military leader, first under Stonewall Jackson in the Shenandoah and later in his native Louisiana, where he won a brilliant victory on the Red River.

3. **Philip St. George Cooke was Jeb Stuart's father-in-law.** The Virginia-born West Pointer stayed with the Union, but his son-in-law, Jeb Stuart; his son, John Rogers Cooke; and his nephew, author John Esten Cooke all joined the Confederacy. During the 1862 Peninsula Campaign, Jeb Stuart rode with his cavalry command and encircled the Union Army. Cooke gave chase but could not catch him. Thereafter, Cooke was placed on court-martial duty and given administrative and recruiting posts. He retired from the army in 1873.

4. **A. P. Hill was brother-in-law to John Hunt Morgan and D. H. Hill was brother-in-law to Thomas J. Jackson.** Ambrose Powell Hill married John Hunt Morgan's sister, while Daniel Harvey Hill's wife was the sister of Stonewall Jackson's second wife. Before the Civil

War, Harvey Hill taught at Washington College and married Isabella Morrison, daughter of a prominent clergyman. Later, Professor Thomas J. Jackson of VMI married Isabella's younger sister, Mary Anna. Powell Hill was once engaged to Ellen Marcy, who later married George McClellan. Hill later married Kitty Morgan McClung, which made him the brother-in-law of two future Confederate generals—John Hunt Morgan and Basil Duke.

5. **Ulysses married the sister of classmate Frederick Tracy Dent.** He spent the first half of the war in California before coming east and getting into the action. He became a brigadier general of volunteers in April 1865. He served on his brother-in-law's staff, and after Grant became president, Dent served as his military secretary.

6. **William T. Sherman was brother-in-law to Thomas, Charles, and Hugh Ewing.** When William Tecumseh Sherman's father died, "Cump" Sherman was taken into the home of Senator Thomas Ewing, a wealthy and powerful friend of the family. When Sherman married Thomas Ewing's daughter Ellen, her brothers Tom Jr., Charles, and Hugh, who were also Sherman's stepbrothers, became his brothers-in-law. All three Ewings became Union generals.

7. **Senator John Sherman of Ohio performed valuable political service.** He was an organizer of the Republican Party and served in the House of Representatives until he moved to the Senate in 1860, replacing Salmon P. Chase. He was a moderate who backed Andrew Johnson in the impeachment crisis. He served as secretary of the treasury for Rutherford B. Hayes and as secretary of state for William McKinley. His most lasting legacy was the Sherman Antitrust Act of 1890.

8. **Compromiser John Crittenden's sons fought on different sides.** It seems almost poetic justice that the two sons of the great compromiser should chose different sides of the war. Thomas L. Crittenden rose rapidly in the Union's western army but the defeat at Chickamauga destroyed his reputation. Brother George was a

major general in gray who also saw his career destroyed when he faced charges that he was drunk while leading his troops at the Confederate defeat at Mill Springs, Kentucky. To make it unanimous, their cousin Thomas T. Crittenden became a Union general only to see his career shattered when General Forrest captured his command.

9. **The combined "Tribe of Dan" and "Tribe of John" produced seventeen union soldiers (including the fathers) and six generals.** Daniel McCook was a major who was killed trying to catch Morgan's Raiders in Ohio. His brother John was an army surgeon. Dan had ten sons in the army, four of whom were generals. John had five sons in the army including two generals.

10. **The unsuccessful suitor was Ambrose Powell Hill.** Hill lost out to McClellan in the quest for the hand of Ellen Marcy. When war came, Hill seemed to attack McClellan-led troops with a special fury. McClellan's men would shout, "Lord, Ellen, why didn't you marry him!"

SECTION VI

THE LEADERS

O nly a handful of the war's early leaders were still highly regarded late in the war. The Confederates had an initial edge with Robert E. Lee, the two Johnstons, and P. G. T. Beauregard. None of the Union's ultimate leaders who would win the war were anywhere near the top at the start. Ulysses Grant began the war as colonel of the Twenty-First Illinois, William Sherman returned to the army as a

The equestrian statue of Maj. Gen. John Reynolds stands in front of City Hall in Philadelphia. A native son who rose to command a Union Army corps and fell defending his native state at Gettysburg on July 1, 1863, Reynolds was typical of the professional soldiers produced by the U.S. Military Academy at West Point, New York. North or South, they stepped forward to do what they felt was their duty. Many, like John Reynolds, paid for that service with their lives. *Photo by the author*

colonel commanding a brigade at First Bull Run, Phil Sheridan was only a first lieutenant, and George Thomas was a major in the Second Cavalry but, partly because he was a Virginian, promotion was slow. Some of the early leaders were tried and found wanting. Others simply had the bad luck to command troops not yet fully trained or battle hardened. But as the war progressed, men of talent surfaced and won battles. The leadership on both sides improved dramatically.

QUIZ 1
Stonewall and Old Blinky

Everybody knows Stonewall but how about Old Blinky? Say "Stonewall" and most Americans know you're talking about Confederate Maj. Gen. Thomas J. Jackson. But Stonewall wasn't the only Civil War general with a colorful nickname. Let's see how many generals you can identify by the names that their soldiers, their friends, or the newspapers called them.

1. They called him "Old Brains." Name him.
2. Who was called "Old Stars"?
3. This man's soldiers affectionately called him "Uncle Billy." He was?
4. A much respected corps commander, he was called "Uncle John." Name him.
5. Two Union generals were called "Bull." Name both.
6. Behind his back, his soldiers called him "Old Blinky." He was?
7. His name wasn't Richard, but he earned the nickname "Fighting Dick." Name him.
8. His nickname was "Prince John" and he looked the part. He was?
9. This general in gray was called "Grumble." Name him.
10. One in gray and one in blue, both men were called "Baldy." Name them.

QUIZ 2
Keeping up with the Joneses

The American Civil War featured men with a dizzying array of common Anglo-Saxon names. It's no small job to separate all of the Smith, Joneses,

Johnsons, Johnstons, and so on. Let's see how you do with these characters named Jones.

- First, here's a Jones who did not seem to be a Jones. A Marylander, he was born a Jones but dropped the name about the time he graduated from West Point in 1837. He served the Confederacy well until a severe head wound at Gaines's Mill forced him out of action. Name him!

- Now, match this list of nine men named Jones to their brief biographies.

Joneses
1. Catesby ap Roger Jones
2. David Rumph Jones
3. George Washington Jones
4. Hilary Pollard Jones
5. John Beauchamp Jones
6. John Marshall Jones
7. John Robert Jones
8. Samuel Jones
9. William Edmondson Jones

Biographies
A. A former magazine editor, he became a Confederate War Department clerk and penned a famous diary.
B. West Point, class of '48, he was an able cavalry commander but had a much-publicized feud with his commanding officer, Jeb Stuart. He was killed at Piedmont, Virginia, on June 5, 1864.
C. This Virginia-born Tennessean was named to the Peace Conference in 1861 but remained at home to work for secession. He was an important member of the Confederate Congress.
D. He started as a captain in the Stonewall Brigade and rose to brigade command, but he was cashiered when he left the field at Chancellorsville claiming he had an ulcerated leg.

E. This member of the West Point class of 1846 served well under James Longstreet until forced out of action after Antietam. He died of heart disease in 1863.

F. He once replaced his near namesake in brigade command. This West Pointer, class of '41, was wounded at Gettysburg and Mine Run and killed while leading the Stonewall Brigade in the Wilderness.

G. He served throughout the war as an artillery leader, but Stonewall Jackson had a poor opinion of him and opposed his promotion.

H. When Franklin Buchanan was wounded, he took command of CSS *Virginia* (*Merrimack*) and directed its fight against USS *Monitor*. Later, he commanded the naval foundry at Selma, Alabama.

I. He was the Confederate artillery general best known as a defender of Charleston in 1864.

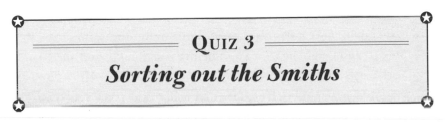

Quiz 3
Sorting out the Smiths

A great many Joneses fought in the war but even more Smiths did. Let's see if you can sort them out.

The Smiths

1. Andrew Jackson Smith
2. Caleb Blood Smith
3. Charles Ferguson Smith
4. Edmund Kirby Smith
5. Gerrit Smith
6. Green Clay Smith
7. Gustavus Woodson Smith
8. William "Extra Billy" Smith
9. William Farrar Smith
10. William Sooy Smith

Biographies

A. A member of West Point's class of '42, this troublesome Vermonter was called Baldy despite having a full head of hair. He commanded VI Corps at Fredericksburg, but his too-public criticisms of Ambrose Burnside led the Senate to refuse to confirm his appointment as major general. Later, he designed the cracker line, which fed Union troops at Chattanooga after Chickamauga. Grant brought him east and made him a major general but relieved him of command when he quarreled with George Meade over Cold Harbor and with Winfield Scott Hancock over Petersburg.

B. This Boston native rose to legal and political prominence in Indiana and served in Congress from 1843 to 1849 as a Whig. He moved to the Republican Party and seconded Lincoln's nomination in 1860. He was Lincoln's first secretary of the interior but resigned in 1863 because of ill health and died the following year.

C. A member of West Point's class of '42 from Kentucky, he served in Mexico and taught at West Point before resigning to become New York City's street commissioner. He joined the Confederates as a major general and briefly led the Army of Northern Virginia after Joseph Johnston was wounded at Fair Oaks/Seven Pines. However, Jefferson Davis realized he was not suited to command the army and quickly brought in Robert E. Lee to take his place. Smith resigned after being passed over for promotion and later led the Georgia militia during Sherman's March to the Sea.

D. A member of West Point's class of '38 from Pennsylvania, this capable officer rose to command the right wing of the Union's XVI Corps. He was very highly regarded, and the apex of his career was his defeat of Nathan Bedford Forrest at Tupelo.

E. At age sixty-four, this former Virginia congressman and governor joined up and led troops from Bull Run to Gettysburg before moving back to the Virginia governor's mansion. He was wounded four times and rose to the rank of major general.

F. A member of West Point's class of '45 from Florida, he received a serious wound at First Bull Run. Afterward he commanded

Confederate troops in eastern Kentucky and won the battle of Richmond, Kentucky. Later, he commanded the Trans-Mississippi when that area was virtually cut off from the rest of the Confederacy.

G. From Ohio, he was in West Point's class of 1856. He fought in West Virginia and at Shiloh under Don Carlos Buell. He commanded the cavalry when Sherman launched his campaign for Meridian. Forrest thoroughly trounced him, leading to his exit from the war.

H. He was from Pennsylvania and attended West Point, class of '25. He was a Mexican War hero who served as commandant of cadets at West Point. He was promoted to major general for his part in taking Fort Donelson but injured his leg shortly afterward and died of an infection.

I. A Kentucky lawyer and legislator who served in the Mexican War, he had early success against John Hunt Morgan at Lebanon, and his exploits in Tennessee won him a star. His military shortcomings, however, quickly became evident. The military was looking for a convenient way to dump him when he solved the problem by moving to Congress. In 1870, he was the Prohibition Party's presidential candidate.

J. This wealthy New Yorker was a dedicated abolitionist and, although he denied it the rest of his life, one of the Secret Six who aided John Brown in his Harpers Ferry raid. He sat in Congress as an Independent and later became a Republican. A moderate on Reconstruction, he signed the papers that freed Jefferson Davis.

QUIZ 4
Western Generals

While the eastern armies, both Union and Confederate, received more attention and are better known today, the armies of the West produced many interesting and capable leaders. Let's see how many of these men you can identify from the descriptions below.

Their Deeds

1. This Tennessee militia officer commanded troops from Belmont to Nashville, missing only the Chattanooga Campaign. John Hood blamed him for letting John Schofield escape at Spring Hill.

2. A carpenter by trade, he entered the army as a private in the engineers during the Mexican War. Later, he served as an army officer and commanded a Missouri regiment. He was a favorite of Sherman's and ended the war as a corps commander.

3. He was the driving force behind the creation of the Lightning Brigade, which was mounted and armed with Spencer carbines. Under his leadership, the brigade did great service at Hoover's Gap and Chickamauga.

4. As a congressman from "Egypt" (southern Illinois), he was pro-slavery, but when war came he joined the Union Army and became one of the best of the political generals. After the war, he returned to Congress as a Radical Republican.

5. This West Pointer left the army to teach at Cumberland University, but when war came, he joined the Confederates as an artillery officer. He rose to corps command when Leonidas Polk was killed and fought through the Atlanta and Tennessee Campaigns, ending the war in North Carolina. His men called him "Old Straight."

6. Early in the war he served in staff positions but moved to field command for Grant's Overland Campaign. He went west in 1864 and won a victory over Forrest, chased Hood after Nashville, and captured Selma, Alabama. Part of his command captured Jefferson Davis.

7. "Old Reliable" was one of the best-known officers in the old army. His text on infantry tactics was the standard. He was capable in battle but feuded with Braxton Bragg and later with Hood. Sherman forced him out of Savannah, and he served under Johnston in North Carolina.

8. This Vermont-born West Pointer led an Ohio regiment early in the war and rose to corps command as the war ended. His finest hour may have been in the Round Forest at Stone's River.

9. His prewar career included stints as a doctor, Mexican War veteran, Mississippi State legislator, U.S. marshal in Washington Territory, territorial delegate to Congress, and member of the Confederate Territorial Congress. He led troops from Pensacola to Shiloh and on to Chickamauga. Wounded at Jonesboro, he did not return to the army until late in the war.

10. This Georgia native graduated from West Point in 1859 and rose rapidly to become one of the Confederacy's best cavalry leaders. He is best known for his aggressive but unsuccessful effort to hinder Sherman during his March to the Sea Campaign.

The Generals

A. James Patton Anderson
B. Benjamin Franklin Cheatham
C. William Joseph Hardee
D. William Babcock Hazen
E. John Alexander Logan
F. Joseph Anthony Mower
G. Alexander Peter Stewart
H. Joseph Wheeler
I. John Thomas Wilder
J. James Harrison Wilson

Quiz 5
Political Generals of the South

Like the Union, the Confederacy did not have enough professional soldiers to go around and had to use civilians, often politicians, to lead troops. Like the Union, they achieved greatly mixed results. Let's see if you can match these "political generals" with their prewar biographies.

The Generals
1. John C. Breckenridge
2. Thomas R. R. Cobb
3. John B. Floyd
4. Hiram Granbury
5. Wade Hampton
6. Thomas Hindman
7. Gideon Pillow
8. Roger A. Pryor
9. William "Extra Billy" Smith
10. Richard Taylor
11. Robert Toombs
12. Zebulon Vance

Their Biographies
A. Educated in New Jersey, he was a lieutenant in the First Mississippi in Mexico. Later, he became a lawyer and was about to start his second term in Congress when his state seceded.
B. Educated at the University of Nashville, he was a lawyer and partner of James K. Polk's. He was a twice-wounded major general in the Mexican War. He was considered a political moderate before his state seceded.
C. Educated at Centre College and Transylvania, he fought in the Mexican War and served in the Kentucky legislature and in Congress before becoming vice president.
D. After a year at the University of North Carolina, he studied law and entered politics, serving in the legislature and Congress. He opposed secession.
E. He studied at Edinburgh, in France, and at Harvard and Yale before becoming a plantation owner in Louisiana. Initially a Whig,

he became a Democrat and a member of the Secession Convention, where he voted for secession.

F. After graduation from South Carolina College, he was a planter and lawyer in Arkansas. He served in the legislature before becoming secretary of war under Buchanan.

G. Educated at Hampden-Sydney College, he studied law at the University of Virginia. He became a newspaper publisher and was sent to Greece to investigate claims by American citizens. He was serving Virginia as a congressman when the war began.

H. He was educated at the University of Georgia and Union College. He practiced law and served in the Georgia legislature, the Congress, and the U.S. Senate. Initially a Whig, he reluctantly switched to the Democratic Party.

I. Educated at the University of Georgia, he practiced law and wrote extensively on the law and slavery. He played a major role in the Georgia secession convention and was a member of the Confederate Congress.

J. A third-generation aristocrat, he ran some of the largest plantations in the South and dabbled in politics. While supporting the South's right to withdraw from the Union, he doubted the soundness of slavery and the wisdom of secession.

K. A lawyer, he also ran a stagecoach line, which provided him with a colorful nickname. He was a Virginia legislator, congressman, and governor before moving to California. He returned to Virginia in 1852 and served in Congress from 1853 until the war started.

L. He was involved in local politics in Waco, Texas. When the war began, he raised a company called the Waco Guards and was its first commander.

QUIZ 6
Political Generals of the North

Not enough West Pointers were available to lead the Union Army so the Lincoln administration turned to civilians, some with military experience and some without. Often, these new generals were politicians. At best, results were mixed. Let's see if you can match these politicians-turned-soldiers with their prewar biographies.

The Generals
1. Nathaniel Prentiss Banks
2. Francis Preston Blair Jr.
3. Benjamin Franklin Butler
4. Neal Dow
5. Thomas Ewing Jr.
6. John Alexander "Black Jack" Logan
7. John Alexander McClernand
8. John McAuley Palmer
9. Alfred Howe Terry
10. James Samuel Wadsworth

Their Biographies
A. Born to the political scene, he graduated from Princeton and studied law at Transylvania. In 1848 he helped form the Missouri Free Soil Party and edited *The Barn Burner*. He was serving in Congress when the war began.
B. Raised a Quaker, he became a successful businessman, but he was a reformer at heart and led the fight for temperance in Maine.
C. A lawyer from "Egypt" in southern Illinois, he fought in the Mexican War and served in the state legislature and the House of Representatives. Many feared he would support the Confederacy,

but when Bull Run was fought, the congressman marched to the battle with a Michigan regiment.

D. This New Hampshire–born general was a successful lawyer and politician in Massachusetts who served in both houses of the legislature. In the 1860 Democratic national convention, he supported Jefferson Davis for president and walked out with the Southerners, splitting the convention.

E. This wealthy New Yorker graduated from both Yale and Harvard. Initially a Free Soil Democrat, he became a Republican and a member of the Washington Peace Conference in 1861.

F. This Yale graduate was a lawyer and clerk of the courts in New Haven. He was active in the state militia before the war.

G. Kentucky born, he became a lawyer and state legislator in Chicago, switching from the Democratic Party to the Republican Party. He was a member of the 1861 Washington Peace Conference.

H. Another Kentucky-born lawyer who moved to Illinois, he served in the Illinois legislature. Later he also served in Congress, where he was a Douglas supporter and a moderate.

I. This Massachusetts "bobbin boy" rose from humble beginnings to become the speaker of the Massachusetts House, a congressman, and the governor before moving on to major general.

J. At age nineteen he was secretary to President Zachary Taylor. Later he went to college and law school and practiced with two other future generals. In 1861, he was appointed first chief justice of the Kansas Supreme Court.

Quiz 7
Rebels with Yankee Roots

When war came, many men had hard choices to make. When George Thomas remained loyal to the old flag, it was said his family in Virginia turned his picture to the wall and never spoke of him again. Likewise, many Confederates had strong personal and emotional ties to the free states. See if you can match up this list of Rebels with Northern roots.

Yankee Roots

1. This Pennsylvania native graduated from West Point, sixth of fifty-two in the class of 1841. He served ably in Mexico and was a captain when the war began. He sided with his adopted state, Alabama, and the South made excellent use of his ordnance background.

2. His family originated in New England but moved to Georgia to escape economic hard times after the War of 1812. The son, born in Augusta, was educated at Cheshire Academy in Connecticut and appointed to the Military Academy from New York. But he saw himself as a Georgian and resigned his commission to fight for the Confederacy and became one of its leading cavalrymen.

3. Born in Windsor, New York, he came from an old Connecticut family. On a trip to Maryland and Virginia, he fell in love with the Shenandoah Valley and founded Mossy Creek Academy near Staunton. His hobby was land surveying and mapmaking, skills that Stonewall Jackson used to good effect.

4. A Bostonian and a Harvard man, he became a successful lawyer in Arkansas and won a huge court case for the Creek Indians. He sided with the South, served as a brigadier general commanding the Indian Territory, and led an Indian brigade at Pea Ridge.

5. Hard to believe that the ranking general in the Confederate army was a West Pointer from Hackensack, New Jersey. His contribution was considerable but primarily administrative.

6. The Yankee family had lived in Litchfield, Connecticut, for generations, but his father moved the family to St. Augustine, Florida. The West Pointer was one of the heroes of First Manassas but is best remembered for commanding in the West.

7. This Ohio-born Quaker graduated from West Point in 1840 but resigned after service in Mexico to teach in Kentucky and

Tennessee. He became a major general commanding in both the eastern and western theaters.

8. A New York–born and Columbia-educated lawyer and merchant, he was wiped out by the War of 1812 and moved to New Orleans. He was a senator when the Civil War began.

9. Another New Jersey–born West Pointer, class of 1843, he served in Mexico. He married into a prominent Mississippi family and owned a plantation there.

10. This West Point graduate, class of 1837, from Pennsylvania refused a federal colonelcy to fight for his wife's Virginia.

The Men

A. Samuel Cooper

B. Samuel Gibbs French

C. Josiah Gorgas

D. Jedediah Hotchkiss

E. Bushrod Rust Johnson

F. John C. Pemberton

G. Albert Pike

H. John Slidell

I. Edmund Kirby Smith

J. Joseph Wheeler

QUIZ 8
Beast Butler

No Civil War figure was more colorful or controversial than Benjamin Franklin Butler, the man Southerners came to call the Beast or Spoons. Already a successful businessman, lawyer, and politician when the war began, he quickly became a major general in Lincoln's army and was seemingly always in the middle of some action or dispute. Let's see what you know of this talented and complex man's early life.

1. When Benjamin Butler was born in Deerfield, New Hampshire, on November 5, 1818, what was his father busy doing?
2. To what did his impoverished mother turn to support her family?
3. Despite the family's limited means, young Ben received a good education, first at a prep school and later at a college. Name them.
4. Ben Butler wanted to be educated elsewhere. What was his first choice of schools?
5. What did he do to restore his health after he finished college?
6. The practice of law usually required three years of study at the time. How long did it take Butler to get his license?
7. While clerking, Butler turned to another profession to sustain himself. What was it?
8. Ben Butler's marriage was unusual owing to his bride's occupation. What was it?
9. Butler's initial law clients were highly unusual also. Who were they?
10. In 1860, state senator Butler was a delegate to the Democratic National Convention in Charleston. Who did he support?
11. When war came, what political position did he use to gain power?
12. What trump card did Butler play to ensure Gov. John Andrew would not block his move?

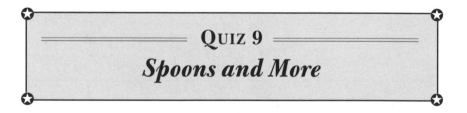

QUIZ 9
Spoons and More

So much about Ben Butler, from his comic-opera appearance to his shady business dealings to his military defeats, tempts us to treat him like a buffoon. To do so would miss the man. Though a poor field general, he made an immense impact on the war. Let's test your knowledge.

1. On his way to Washington, Butler learned that the Sixth Massachusetts had been attacked in Baltimore. How did he respond?

2. Butler soon tired of his assigned role and launched a new venture on his own. Where did he go?

3. Where did the War Department send Butler next in hopes of keeping him out of trouble?

4. While in his new position, Butler made a legal ruling that had a huge impact on the war in general and the slaves in particular. What was it?

5. A small but unsuccessful action near Fort Monroe tarnished Butler's image. What was it?

6. Next, Butler joined with the navy to capture an important doorway to the Confederacy. Name it.

7. His next campaign was also a joint naval-military venture with New Orleans as the target. What remote island was used as a staging area?

8. The New Orleans venture required Butler to cooperate with two high-ranking naval officers. He got along well with one but clashed with the other. Name them and identify the one with whom he engaged in a battle of egos, not ideas.

9. A public execution caused the local citizens to hate Butler. Who was executed, where, and why?

10. Butler's addition to a famous statue enraged the city. What was it?

11. Aristocrats in New Orleans despised Butler, but he established a domestic program that helped sway some of the poor. What did he do?

12. What other public works projects did he launch that improved the city?

13. Butler's brother, Andrew, was also operating out of New Orleans. What was his role?

14. Did Ben Butler really steal silver spoons?

15. Butler was replaced, in part, because of a lack of military ability. What general relieved him?

QUIZ 10
The Old Snappin' Turtle

George Gordon Meade seemed the complete package: a West Pointer and engineer, unquestionably brave, and with a good performance record. When he beat Robert E. Lee in the greatest single battle of the war, his status as a national hero seemed assured, but his career languished and faded. Let's look at his fascinating and eventful life.

1. Despite his foreign birth, he could have run for president. Why?
2. After service in the Second Seminole and Mexican Wars, the government put him to work constructing a certain type of building. Name it.
3. What was his rank at the outbreak of the Civil War?
4. In what battle was he wounded?
5. What distinction did his division win at Fredericksburg?
6. Meade found himself in a "losing majority" when he took what position in a council of war at Chancellorsville?
7. When Joe Hooker resigned, who did the Lincoln government consider making commander of the Army of the Potomac before turning to Meade?
8. Before arriving on the Gettysburg battlefield, where did Meade plan to move his army?
9. After Gettysburg, what message did Meade send that enraged Lincoln?
10. What offer did Meade make to Grant when he arrived to take overall command?

Quiz 11
The Boy Generals

When the war began, generals were old graybeards, such as Winfield Scott, David Twiggs, and John Wool. By war's end, generals in their twenties were far from uncommon. Let's look at some of the younger fellows.

1. This Confederate cavalry general received his wreath at age twenty-five. His father, older brother, and cousin were also Confederate generals. Name him.
2. This engineer started as a captain in the Eleventh Illinois, was a brigadier general at age twenty-eight, and was commanding a corps under Sherman when he died of the effects of multiple wounds. He was?
3. A North Carolinian and West Point graduate, he was a Confederate brigadier at age twenty-five and a major general at age twenty-seven. He was one of the South's youngest generals before dying at Cedar Creek. Name him.
4. He was the youngest Civil War general and to this day the youngest ever to achieve that rank in the U.S. Army. He was?
5. He jumped from captain to brigadier general at the age of twenty-six, but he wore his star only five days before being mortally wounded. Name him.
6. This dashing cavalryman established the youth trend early when he became a brigadier at twenty-eight and a major general at twenty-nine. He was?
7. They could not keep this staff captain out of the battles so the Union Army made him a brigadier at age twenty-three and a major general at twenty-five. Name him.

8. A North Carolina cavalryman became the youngest Confederate general when he received his wreath in 1865 at age twenty-three. He was?

9. Another North Carolinian became a brigadier at age twenty-five and a major general at age twenty-six. Some reports said Lee favored him as a possible replacement. Name him.

10. Named for the most famous Southern statesman, this baby-faced soldier left the University of Alabama to enlist as a private. He was a colonel at age twenty-two and a brigadier at age twenty-four. Who was he?

11. He started with the Harvard regiment and received his star in July 1864 at age twenty-four despite numerous crippling wounds. Name him.

12. This well-known and valuable member of Longstreet's staff had his shot at command late in the war when he became a brigadier general at age twenty-six.

Quiz 12
The Rock

Virginian George Henry Thomas was one of the Union's top generals. His epic defense of Snodgrass Hill probably saved the Army of the Cumberland and won him the title of the Rock of Chickamauga. Though the man moved slowly and deliberately, both personally and militarily, he never lost a battle. Let's look at his remarkable career.

1. When only fifteen years old, he played a heroic role in a famous civic upheaval. What was that event?

2. He tried his hand at an apprenticeship in a profession before accepting an appointment to West Point. What profession?

3. In his thirty-four years in the military he was only wounded once. What enemy wounded him?

4. While an instructor at West Point, the cadets called him Old Slow Trot. Why?

5. He was promoted to major in a new cavalry unit that Jeff Davis created. What unit?

6. What was his wife's hometown?

7. Where did he win his first Civil War battle?

8. Commanding the Union's center, he helped cobble together a defensive line, stopped a Confederate attack, and probably saved the army at what Tennessee battle?

9. When Thomas replaced William Rosecrans at Chattanooga, who made the call?

10. When Thomas's troops routed Bragg at Missionary Ridge, why was Grant upset?

11. What problem, created by nature, delayed Thomas's attack at Nashville?

12. What high position did Thomas refuse after the war?

Answers

1. Stonewall and Old Blinky

1. **Old Brains was Union Maj. Gen. Henry Wagner Halleck.** The accolade was based primarily on his West Point class standing—third in 1839—and his prewar writing; however, he proved far too cautious in the field. He performed better as chief of staff but was not up to the job of general in chief. Some have termed him "a first-class clerk."

2. **Union Maj. Gen. Ormsby MacKnight Mitchel was called Old Stars.** He was a noted astronomer. The Kentucky-born West Pointer, class of 1829, taught astronomy at Cincinnati College and helped found the Naval and Harvard Observatories. He commanded X Corps in Tennessee and Alabama but clashed with Don Carlos Buell. He was reassigned to the Carolina and Georgia coast, where he died of yellow fever in 1862.

3. **Union Maj. Gen. William Tecumseh Sherman's men called him Uncle Billy.** Although he could be a harsh disciplinarian, his men seemed to identify with him. Perhaps all the world loves a winner. The title of "uncle" was common then, often applied to any older man regardless of actual relationship.

4. **Union Maj. Gen. John Sedgwick was called Uncle John.** He commanded the large and famous VI Corps, whose men loved him. He died at Spottsylvania, shot dead by a sniper right after he supposedly told his men that the Confederates couldn't hit an elephant from that distance.

5. **Maj. Gen. Edwin Vose Sumner and Maj. Gen. William Nelson were both called Bull.** Sumner earned the nickname for his booming voice—the bull of the woods or "Old Bull Head." Nelson received his for his size, standing six foot four and weighing more than three hundred pounds. Neither man survived the war. Sumner died of natural causes in New York, and Union Brig. Gen. Jefferson Columbus Davis shot Nelson dead in Louisville, Kentucky, in 1862 during a dispute.

6. **Old Blinky was Union Maj. Gen. William Henry French.** The men noted his habit of rapidly blinking when he talked. He took command of III Corp at Gettysburg when Daniel Sickles was wounded. When the corps was disbanded he dropped from major general of volunteers to a lieutenant colonel in the regular army.

7. **Fighting Dick was Union Maj. Gen. Israel Bush Richardson.** Friends called him that rather than the more formal Israel, and he earned the "fighting" part of his nickname in the Mexican War. A native Vermonter, he had left the army and was farming in Michigan when the war began. He was wounded at Antietam and died there a month and a half later.

8. **Prince John was Confederate Maj. Gen. John Bankhead Magruder.** The nickname came from his courtly manner, acting ability, and reputation for lavish entertainment. He put his theatrical skills to good use at Yorktown and convinced Union forces that he had a huge force. However, he fell out of favor with General Lee and was packed off to the West, where he commanded in Texas and performed good service.

9. **Confederate Brig. Gen. William Edmonson Jones was Grumble.** He had a reputation as a hard man to get along with, and in that respect, he had a great deal of company. His most famous quarrel was with Jeb Stuart, who court-martialed him for disrespect. Grumble Jones was killed in the Shenandoah Valley in 1864.

10. **The generals called Baldy were Confederate Maj. Gen. Richard Stoddert Ewell and Union Maj. Gen. William Farrar Smith.** Ewell had lost most of his hair by the time of the war. Smith gained his nickname at West Point when fellow cadets thought his light blond hair made him look bald, but Civil War pictures show him with a full head of darker hair. Ewell was highly regarded early in the war and replaced Stonewall Jackson after his death; however, he performed badly at Gettysburg and was eased out of corps command. Smith is best known for designing the famous "cracker line" that supplied the besieged Union army at Chattanooga. He later commanded XVIII Corps in Virginia.

2. Keeping up with the Joneses

Answer to initial "non-Jones" question: Arnold Elzey Jones. He dropped the Jones name in favor of his middle name, that of his paternal grandmother's family. Maybe he did it to distance himself from all of these other Joneses. After West Point, he had a long career in the artillery. He won a battlefield appointment as brigadier general at First Bull Run. He was slightly wounded at Port Republic and more seriously so at Gaines's Mill. He spent the balance of the war in more administrative duties.

1. **(H) Catesby ap Roger Jones** was the executive officer on CSS *Virginia* (*Merrimack*) and was in command during its most famous battle. He played a major role in converting the damaged *Merrimack* into the South's first ironclad warship. He later commanded at Drewry's Bluff. Incidentally, *ap* being Welch for "son of," Catesby was the son of Maj. Gen. Roger Jones.

2. **(E) David Rumph Jones** was the member of the famous West Point class of 1846 who died of heart disease in 1863. He was the nephew of Zachary Taylor and a cousin of Jefferson Davis. After Antietam his health broke down and George Pickett succeeded him in division command. Had he lived, we might talk today of Jones's charge at Gettysburg.

3. **(C) George Washington Jones** was the politician appointed to the Peace Conference but continued working toward war. He had served in the U.S. Congress from 1843 to 1859 and then in the Confederate Congress. After the war he received a pardon from his old friend and political ally Andrew Johnson.

4. **(G) Hilary Pollard Jones** was the artillerist who, among many others, ran afoul of the demanding and cantankerous Stonewall. A teacher before the war, he rose from lieutenant to colonel and fought from the Seven Days battles to Appomattox. He is best remembered for Jackson's trying to block his promotion, which Lee's artillery chief, William Pendleton, had recommended.

5. **(A) John Beauchamp Jones** is the author of the well-known *A Rebel War Clerk's Diary at the Confederate States Capital*. A newspaperman before the war, he was rabidly partisan and pleasantly gossipy. His two-volume diary is a treasure trove of people, events, problems, and gossip.

6. **(F) John Marshall Jones** once replaced John Robert Jones but died leading the Stonewall Brigade in the Wilderness. A West Point graduate, class of 1841, he had received a severe leg wound on Culp's Hill at Gettysburg on the second day and a head wound at Mine Run.

7. **(D)** When **John Robert Jones** gave his excuse of an ulcerated leg, he was viewed as a coward, relieved of command, and never given another. To add insult to injury, when the Yankees later captured him, the Confederates refused to exchange him and let him live out the war in chilly Fort Warren in Boston Harbor.

8. **(I) Samuel Jones** graduated from the U.S. Military Academy in '41 as an artillery officer and taught at the academy. In the Civil War, he fought at Bull Run, in West Virginia, in the West, and on the south Atlantic coast. While defending Charleston Harbor, he began to keep Union prisoners "under the guns" as human shields.

9. **(B) William Edmondson Jones** was known as "Grumble," apparently a well-deserved moniker. He was a West Pointer, class of 1848, and saw considerable service with the Mounted Rifles, which was basically mounted infantry. He left the army before the war and joined the Confederacy as a captain, rising to brigadier general and commanding the Laurel Brigade. His feud with Stuart resulted in his court-martial. He was killed leading forces at the Battle of Piedmont.

3. Sorting out the Smiths

1. **(D) Andrew Jackson Smith**, the general who defeated Forrest at Tupelo, was one of the Union's best division commanders. The Pennsylvania native and West Pointer, class of 1838, had extensive

experience with the Second Dragoons fighting Indians and in Mexico. He was Halleck's chief of staff and a brigadier general in the Vicksburg and Red River Campaigns. He received a brevet to major general for the Battle of Nashville before reverting to his regular army rank of lieutenant colonel. He retired as a colonel and was postmaster in St. Louis.

2. **(B) Caleb Blood Smith**—how's that for a colorful name?—was Lincoln's first secretary of the interior. A former Whig he had opposed the extension of slavery and the Mexican War while he served in Congress. He seconded the nomination of Lincoln at the 1860 Republican Convention. When ill health forced his resignation on January 8, 1863, John Usher, another Indiana lawyer, replaced him in the Lincoln cabinet.

3. **(H)** If **Charles Ferguson Smith** had had political connections, he might have become the great general of the West. Smith had been superintendent of cadets at West Point when Grant and Sherman were plebes. It was Smith, not Grant, who pressed for unconditional surrender at the Union council of war at Fort Donelson. His untimely death deprived the Union of one of its best officers. He was a solid military man and a hard fighter.

4. **(F) Edmund Kirby Smith** was the Confederate general who ran the Trans-Mississippi Department at the end of the war. A Floridian and a West Point graduate, class of 1845, he was a major in the Second Cavalry when the war started. He was Joe Johnston's chief of staff, seriously wounded at First Bull Run, and cooperated with Bragg on the 1862 Kentucky Campaign. When Vicksburg and Port Hudson fell, he found himself cut off from the rest of the Confederacy and ran civilian and military affairs on his own. Under his command, the department defeated Nathaniel Banks on the Red River and Fred Steele in Arkansas, but Sterling Price's raid on Missouri was a failure. After the war, he became a college professor.

5. **(J) Gerrit Smith** was the Syracuse millionaire who financially backed John Brown and then retreated to an asylum to escape the law. He later had a change of heart and posted bail for Jeff Davis.

He was a generous benefactor of good causes, but sometimes such actions can get complicated. He continued to deny involvement in John Brown's raid, but the evidence says otherwise.

6. **(I)** Although **Green Clay Smith** garnered only 9,522 votes in his 1876 presidential bid, the total was probably less a reflection of his own unpopularity than the people's lack of enthusiasm for the Prohibitionists' cause. A Kentuckian with Mexican War experience, he rose to brigadier general but never lived up to his perceived potential. His election to Congress solved the problem. He was later the territorial governor of Montana, a Baptist preacher, and a presidential candidate.

7. **(C)** **Gustavus Woodson Smith** was a talented engineer but an ordinary general at best. He probably should have stayed in New York, where he was the street commissioner, and dealt with the potholes. A Kentucky-born West Pointer, class of 1842, he briefly commanded the Confederate Army of Northern Virginia; however, Jefferson Davis realized Smith did not have the capacity for the job and replaced him with Lee. Later, when bypassed for promotion, he resigned and headed the Georgia militia. At Griswoldville, he tried to block Sherman on his March to the Sea Campaign but was easily defeated.

8. **(E)** **William "Extra Billy" Smith** received his colorful nickname when he ran a stage line and found some creative ways to bring in extra revenue. He was a surprisingly good field officer given his age—sixty-four at the start of the war—and lack of previous training. He fought from First Bull Run to Gettysburg before returning to the governor's chair for the balance of the war.

9. **(A)** After Fredericksburg **William Farrar Smith** teamed with William Franklin to try to get Burnside replaced. Consequently Congress refused to confirm Smith as a major general. He partially redeemed himself with his design of the cracker line at Chattanooga. He commanded a corps at Bermuda Hundred, but after reinforcing the Army of the Potomac at Cold Harbor, he engaged in another dispute, this time with Meade. His excessive

caution at Petersburg, plus his close relationship with George McClellan, then the Democrats' presidential candidate, led to his being relieved of command.

10. **(G)** Perhaps **William Sooy Smith** was lucky. His tangle with Forrest wrecked his career, but more than one Yankee who tangled with Forrest had ended up dead. The Ohio West Pointer, class of 1856, rose to become Grant's cavalry chief, but when he tried to support Sherman in his Meridian Campaign and Forrest embarrassed him, Smith left the army shortly thereafter.

4. Western Generals

1. **(B) Benjamin Franklin Cheatham**, a colorful character, took part in the Mexican War and the gold rush. He was a very effective corps commander. He fought in all of the major campaigns except at Chattanooga and ended the war in North Carolina under Joe Johnston.

2. **(F)** The rise of **Joseph Anthony Mower** from private soldier to corps command was one of the period's most spectacular. He remained in the army after the war. His finest hour was at the Battle of Bentonville, North Carolina, where he almost trapped Joe Johnston's army.

3. **(I) John Thomas Wilder**, a New York native, was a visionary who saw the importance of moving men quickly from place to place and delivering maximum firepower. He advanced his own money to buy repeating rifles for his brigade and managed to get them all mounted. He resigned before the end of the war and became an important industrialist in Tennessee.

4. **(E) John Alexander "Black Jack" Logan** earned the right to lead the Army of the Tennessee, but when James McPherson was killed, Sherman gave the job to Oliver O. Howard, a West Pointer. Logan led the Army of the Tennessee in the Grand Review of the Armies in Washington after the war because Howard had been detached to run the Freedmen's Bureau. In battle, Logan inspired his men with

his presence at the front. It was said that he was worth five thousand reinforcements.

5. **(G)** After Hood resigned, **Alexander Peter Stewart** took what was left of the army and went to North Carolina to fight under Johnston. After the war he was an educator and businessman.

6. **(J)** After **James Harrison Wilson** played an important role in Grant's Overland Campaign and in the Shenandoah Valley, he went west, where he became a star of the first order. He left the army after the war but returned to command volunteers in both the Spanish-American War and the Boxer Rebellion.

7. **(C)** **William Joseph Hardee**'s war service never seemed to quite come up to the level of his prewar reputation, but he was still a competent officer, especially at corps command level.

8. **(D)** **William Babcock Hazen** was only two years out of West Point when the war started, and he moved up steadily. His troops captured Fort McAllister, opening the door to Savannah for Sherman.

9. **(A)** **James Patton Anderson** had an adventure-packed lifetime. His service to the Confederacy was valuable, but his wound near Atlanta effectively ended his military career.

10. **(H)** **Joseph Wheeler**, a.k.a. "Fighting Joe," was an Alabama congressman after the war and returned to the U.S. Army for the Spanish-American War, seeing duty in Puerto Rico and the Philippines. He is one of the few Confederates buried in Arlington National Cemetery.

5. Political Generals of the South

1. **(C)** **John C. Breckenridge** turned out to be a surprisingly able general. The high point of his field career was his victory at New Market, Virginia. At the end of the war, he was secretary of war.

2. **(I)** The brother of Howell Cobb, **Thomas R. R. Cobb** proved to be a capable general but was killed defending the sunken road at Fredericksburg.

3. **(F) John B. Floyd** left the cabinet amid accusations of financial improprieties and shipping military stores to the South in case of war. He commanded at Fort Donelson and tried to break out but lost his nerve. Then he and a few others escaped, leaving the rest to be captured. That move ended his military career.

4. **(L) Hiram Granbury** rose steadily from captain to brigadier general and led a brigade in Patrick Cleburne's division. Granbury was one of five Confederate generals, including Cleburne, killed in Hood's ill-advised attack at Franklin, Tennessee.

5. **(J)** The ultimate Southern aristocrat, **Wade Hampton** became one of the South's top generals, succeeding Jeb Stuart when Stuart was killed. He was later a governor and a senator, and his statue stands on the Capitol grounds in Columbia.

6. **(A)** Though barely five feet tall, **Thomas Hindman** was a fighter but not always a smart one. A wound in the face at Kennesaw Mountain almost blinded him. After the war, he was murdered in Arkansas.

7. **(B)** At best, **Gideon Pillow** was controversial and suspect. After he abandoned Fort Donelson he was relieved of command. He returned briefly at Stone's River but reportedly hid behind a tree rather than leading his men.

8. **(G)** Red-hot secessionist **Roger A. Pryor** rose to division command, but he was squeezed out because Virginia had too many generals. He finished the war as a sort of freelance scout. Later in life, he was a justice of the New York Supreme Court.

9. **(K)** Although much older than sixty, **William "Extra Billy" Smith** proved a capable brigadier and fought through the Gettysburg Campaign before resigning to become governor. After the war, he served in the state legislature until he was past the age of eighty.

10. **(E) Richard Taylor** was son of President Zachary Taylor and brother-in-law to Jeff Davis, and he proved an able general under Jackson in Virginia. Later in the West, he defeated Banks in the Red River Campaign.

11. **(H) Robert Toombs** wanted to be the Confederacy's president but had to settle for secretary of state. He resigned that non-job and became a brigadier general. His finest moment was holding off Burnside's attempt to cross the bridge at Antietam. He detested the professionals and said that the Confederacy "died of West Point."

12. **(D) Zebulon Vance** was colonel of the Twenty-Sixth North Carolina and led it ably at New Bern and in the Seven Days battles. Then he was elected governor and became a major thorn in the side of Jeff Davis because of his prickly states-right positions.

6. Political Generals of the North

1. **(I) Nathaniel Prentiss Banks** was always ready to fight but usually ended up being beaten. After being roundly defeated in the East, he went west and Port Hudson fell into his hands after Grant captured Vicksburg. For Port Hudson, he won the Thanks of Congress. Later, he made a botch of the Red River Campaign and was moved out of field command.

2. **(A) Francis Preston Blair Jr.** The Blairs had been a force in American politics since the age of Andrew Jackson. Blair's first service to the war was to keep Missouri from seceding. He commanded the XVII Corps under Sherman and was widely recognized as a competent field commander.

3. **(D) Benjamin Franklin "the Beast" Butler,** known as the most hated Union general in the South, was aggressive and had an inventive mind, but he proved inept in leading troops. Lincoln finally dumped him after his failure at Fort Fisher. However, Butler did play a role in the relief of Washington in 1861, the capture of Hatteras Inlet, the capture and occupation of New Orleans and eastern Louisiana, and the concept of treating escaped slaves as contraband of war.

4. **(B)** Twice wounded at Port Hudson, **Neal Dow** was captured and sent to Libby Prison, where the Confederates refused to exchange

him because of his abolitionist views. He was finally exchanged for Robert E. Lee's son, William Henry Fitzhugh "Rooney" Lee.

5. **(J)** Son of an Ohio senator, **Thomas Ewing Jr.** had two brothers who were generals, as well as his brother-in-law William T. Sherman. He is best remembered for his Order No. 11, which depopulated four Missouri counties in an unsuccessful effort to stop guerrilla activity. He won a brevet for Pilot Knob.

6. **(C)** Early in the war **John Alexander "Black Jack" Logan** promised his recruits that, if it ever became a war to end slavery, he'd lead them home. After the Emancipation Proclamation, however, he told them that "things had changed." Indeed, they had and so had Logan. He eventually became a Republican Radical. He probably deserved the chance to lead the Army of the Tennessee when McPherson was killed at Atlanta, but the job went to Oliver O. Howard. That oversight bothered Logan, and he blamed the slight on West Point bias.

7. **(H)** **John Alexander McClernand**'s main value to the Union was as a recruiter, but he wanted military fame and was a thorn in the side of Grant and Sherman. Eventually, he was frozen out. McClernand used his friendship with Lincoln to angle for an independent command. Lincoln considered him brave and competent but too ambitious.

8. **(G)** **John McAuley Palmer** rose to major general and corps command under Sherman. However, he became embroiled in a dispute with John Schofield over rank and asked to be relieved while the army was before Atlanta. He spent the rest of the war in Kentucky. After the war he was governor of Illinois and a senator.

9. **(F)** One of the best of the nonprofessionals, **Alfred Howe Terry** led the army force that captured Fort Fisher in 1865 and won the Thanks of the Congress. He remained in the regular army and won fame as an Indian fighter. He was George Custer's superior officer when Custer was killed at Little Bighorn.

10. **(E)** After an unsuccessful run for governor of New York in 1862, **James Samuel Wadsworth** returned to the army and became a good

division commander. He was killed in the Battle of the Wilderness. He could have stayed at home and lived in comfort, but he considered it his duty and honor to serve his country.

7. Rebels with Yankee Roots

1. **(C)** Faced with staggering shortages of almost everything, **Josiah Gorgas** used his Yankee creativity and put his department into good condition by 1863. On his own initiative, he organized a fleet of blockade-runners to bring in materials unavailable in Dixie. He was promoted to brigadier general and chief of ordnance. After the war, he was in the iron business in Alabama, vice chancellor of the University of the South at Sewanee, Tennessee, and president of the University of Alabama.

2. **(J) Joseph Wheeler** graduated from West Point an undistinguished nineteenth of twenty-two in 1859. He joined the Southern army as a first lieutenant but caught Bragg's eye. Soon he was heading the cavalry of the Army of the Tennessee. After the war he was a congressman from Alabama and returned to the army to lead troops in the Spanish-American War. He is one of a small handful of Confederates buried in Arlington National Cemetery.

3. **(D) Jedediah Hotchkiss**'s maps of the valley gave Stonewall Jackson the edge he needed in his brilliant campaign in 1862. Hotchkiss continued as cartographer for the Confederate II Corps and kept detailed journals of military activity, a boon to historians. He continued surveying and mapmaking after the war and was a charter member of the National Geographic Society.

4. **(G)** A huge bear of a man, **Albert Pike** was a Mexican War veteran and internationally known writer and poet. He greatly aided the South in bringing the Oklahoma Indians into the war on the Confederate side, but they proved of little value. Later, he broke with the South and resigned. After the war, he lived in Washington and Memphis and was a recognized legal scholar.

5. **(A)** Having married a woman from Virginia, **Samuel Cooper** cast his lot with the South. As the first appointed full general of the Confederacy, he outranked even the Johnstons, Beauregard, and Lee. His administrative ability was valuable to the South, and his preservation of some Confederate records has been a boon to historians. After the war he farmed near Alexandria, Virginia, but lived in desperate financial conditions.

6. **(I)** After early success in the East, **Edmund Kirby Smith** commanded in eastern Tennessee and cooperated with Bragg on the Kentucky invasion that ended at Perryville. Unable to work with Bragg, he was transferred to the Trans-Mississippi, where he found Dick Taylor impossible to work with as well. After the war he was a teacher at the University of the South at Sewanee, Tennessee, and the last surviving full general of the Confederacy when he died.

7. **(E) Bushrod Rust Johnson** saw service at Fort Donelson, Shiloh, Perryville, Murfreesboro, Chickamauga, Knoxville, Drewry's Bluff, Petersburg, and Sayler's Creek, where Lee relieved him from duty. After the war he returned to the University of Nashville as chancellor.

8. **(H)** Appointed Confederate minister to France, **John Slidell** and James Mason were captured and later released in the famous *Trent* Affair. His mission to France did not bear fruit. After the war he remained in France. He lived out his days in England.

9. **(B) Samuel Gibbs French**'s most prominent service was in Johnston's failed attempt to relieve Vicksburg, the Atlanta Campaign, and Hood's Franklin and Nashville Campaigns. After the war he returned to his plantation.

10. **(F) John C. Pemberton** commanded at Charleston but was unpopular. Davis moved him to Mississippi to protect Vicksburg. When he surrendered it on July 4, 1863, many accused him of treason. After he returned in a prisoner exchange, he resigned his commission as major general and offered to serve as a private. Davis instead appointed him lieutenant colonel of artillery. He

served out the remainder of the war at Richmond. He farmed in
Virginia after the war.

8. Beast Butler

1. **The elder Butler was dying.** Capt. John Butler recruited and
   commanded a cavalry company in the War of 1812, but was forced
   from the army by a broken leg that did not properly heal. Then he
   became a privateer, first for the United States and later for Simón
   Bolívar. He contracted yellow fever on the island of St. Kitts and
   died from it.

2. **His mother ran a boardinghouse.** Initially she moved in with
   relatives, but when a prominent clergyman offered her the chance
   to manage a boardinghouse in Lowell, Massachusetts, she took it.
   Butler obviously had enterprising parents.

3. **Butler attended Exeter Academy and Waterville College.** Exeter in
   New Hampshire is now known as Phillips Exeter, and Waterville in
   Maine is now Colby University. In both places, young Butler earned
   academic notice and a reputation for fighting and bucking the system.

4. **He would have preferred West Point.** He applied to Congressman
   Caleb Cushing for an appointment, but the family lacked influence
   and the appointment went to another boy. Butler never forgot the
   slight, which probably contributed to his antipathy for West
   Pointers and men of wealth and influence.

5. **To restore his health, he went to sea.** He had always been sickly,
   and at age twenty he weighed only ninety-seven pounds. After a
   four-month cruise his health was restored, and he was ready to take
   on the world.

6. **Butler completed his law training in two years rather than the
   traditional three.** Butler felt he was ready after only two years and
   applied to a local judge. Annoyed by this pushy young man, the
   judge made him sit through a case and then quizzed him on the
   finer points. Never intimidated, Butler answered his questions and
   told him he had ruled incorrectly in the case. After hearing Butler

out and reviewing the law, the judge reversed himself. He gave Butler the chance to take the test, which, of course, he passed.

7. **He supported himself by teaching.** In Dracut, Massachusetts, he took on a class of mostly boys who had been expelled. His heavy-handed method of teaching and thrashings resulted in a high drop out rate, but eventually he was successful.

8. **He married an actress.** Sarah Hildreth was the daughter of a Dracut doctor and a successful young actress. She was two years older than Ben and reportedly a great beauty, but somehow the marriage clicked and was successful. Beauty and the Beast!

9. **Butler's first law clients were poor young factory girls**. They turned to the young lawyer when they felt unfairly treated by the mill owners of Lowell, and Butler fought the system on their behalf, leading the fight in court and politics for a ten-hour workday. Ben Butler, champion of the working girl!

10. **He supported Stephen Douglas and then Jefferson Davis in the 1860 Democratic National Convention.** He went to the convention as a Douglas supporter but switched to Davis in the mistaken belief that he was a moderate Unionist. He voted for Davis more than fifty times. Certainly his support proved a great irony since Davis later wanted to hang him.

11. **Butler used his position as brigadier general of the state militia.** Simon Cameron called on Massachusetts for troops, Butler persuaded his old friend to ask for a full brigade with a brigadier general and staff. Butler planned to be that general.

12. **His trump card was money.** Butler knew that Governor Andrew would be concerned about the cost of sending the troops, so he arranged a $50,000 loan to the state and presented it to Andrew. The job was Butler's.

9. Spoons and More

1. **He bypassed troubled Baltimore by going to Annapolis.** He obtained a railroad ferry and sailed to the Maryland capital city,

allowing troops from the north to bypass Baltimore. Then he
opened a railroad route to Washington. Maryland governor Tom
Hicks was incensed, but the deed was already done. Butler and his
brigade were assigned to guard the route.

2. **On his own hook, Butler moved into Baltimore.** Tired of guarding
railroads, he noted that still hostile Baltimore was a part of his
department. Feigning a move toward Harpers Ferry, he went to
Baltimore by rail, marched his men up Federal Hill in a blinding
thunderstorm, and entrenched. The next morning, Baltimore's
rebellious citizens awoke to find themselves under his guns. The
secessionists were trumped and Baltimore was in Union hands to
stay.

3. **To keep him out of trouble, he was sent to Fort Monroe in
Hampton, Virginia.** Since the state had already seceded, it seemed
that he could not get into much trouble there. They
underestimated him.

4. **He declared slaves to be "contraband of war" and refused to
return them to their owners.** The North, especially the
Republicans, loved the ruling. The South screamed, and
slaveholders found themselves arguing for protection under the
Constitution that they claimed they had abandoned. Butler's legal
opinion solved problems for the Union. It now had a logical reason
not to return runaway slaves and could take their labor away from
the Confederates and put it to work for the Union. It also nudged
Lincoln a step closer to emancipation.

5. **His reputation was tarnished by the Battle of Big Bethel.** It was
not much of a battle. Massachusetts Brig. Ebenezer Pierce tried a
complex pincer movement, and his force of 3,500 was not up to it.
Butler, who never took the field, blamed Pierce. Shortly after,
Butler received his second star. The boy who was disappointed
when he failed to get into West Point became a major general well
before most West Pointers did.

6. **He helped to capture Hatteras Inlet, North Carolina.** Cooperating
with Flag Officer Silas Stringham, the combined force captured

Forts Clark and Hatteras, closing the door to blockade-running and opening the door for Burnside's successful 1862 North Carolina Campaign. In order to get credit, Butler hustled back to Washington to give the report, even commandeering a train so he could arrive first with the good news.

7. **The jumping-off place for the Battle of New Orleans was Ship Island, Mississippi.** This remote island, fifteen miles off Biloxi, was an ideal base of operations against either New Orleans or Mobile. However, it offered little but discomfort to those living on it.

8. **Butler worked with David Farragut and David Dixon Porter, clashing with the latter.** Farragut was in overall commend and Porter commanded the mortar boats. Porter, Farragut's younger foster brother, was as ambitious and vain as Butler was, and it was almost a given that they would dislike each other. Both wanted credit for success and did not want to share it with anyone.

9. **He hanged a gambler named William Mumford.** He was hanged on the roof of the U.S. Mint for tearing down an American flag and desecrating it. Mumford was, briefly, a local hero, but he was rash in wearing a shred of the flag as a boutonniere. Union soldiers spotted him and Butler made good his threat to hang the man who did it. Later, Butler aided Mumford's widow and orphaned children.

10. **He added a Jackson quote to Andrew Jackson's equestrian statue in Jackson Square.** He had "The Union Must and Shall Be Preserved" carved in the base of the statue. Jackson spoke the words when causing South Carolina to back down during the nullification crisis. Having a Southern hero's words used against them was a bitter pill for the Confederates.

11. **He fed the poor.** When Maj. Gen. Mansfield Lovell and his Confederate troops evacuated the city, he took much of the food with him. Prices rose and the poor were starving. Butler launched a public works project to put them to work and imported food for them. He paid for it by confiscating the property of the rich and imposing a special tax on them.

12. **He made inroads in sanitation and yellow fever quarantine.** He flushed drainage ditches to reduce disease and quarantined arriving ships during fever season. Even his enemies had to admit that the city had never been healthier.

13. **His brother apparently served as a bag man!** If you wanted something from the general you first crossed his brother's palm with silver. Confiscated property was sold for a song. Evidence indicated that some civilians with passes from the Butlers were smuggling goods to the Confederates. Seeming to see no conflict between good administration and personal gain, the Butler brothers were getting rich.

14. **He didn't really steal silver spoons.** He took over the former house of Maj. Gen. David Twiggs and found the general's sword and a box of silverware. He sent the sword to Lincoln and put the silverware to use. A woman who had been living in the house claimed both, but Butler denied her claim, leading to the accusation. Later, when he confiscated silver from another man, the charge was renewed.

15. **Butler was replaced by Nathaniel Banks.** One inept Massachusetts politician replaced another. Butler went back to Washington and was given command of the Army of the James, which he got bottled up at Bermuda Hundred on the Virginia peninsula. Then he failed to capture Fort Fisher in Wilmington, North Carolina. With Lincoln's reelection in 1864, the president no longer needed him, and he was sacked.

10. The Old Snappin' Turtle

1. **His parents were U.S. citizens.** He was born in Cadiz, Spain. His father was a businessman who traveled abroad frequently and for long periods. The question of "native birth" as a qualification for the presidency had not been tested at the time, and some believed that Meade would *not* have been considered eligible.

2. **Meade was assigned to build lighthouses.** Meade left the army for six years and worked as a surveyor. However, he returned in 1842 as

an engineer and worked on lighthouses along the Atlantic coast and the Great Lakes. He was in Michigan when the Civil War began.

3. **At the outbreak of the war he was still a captain.** When he returned to the army, he was a second lieutenant of engineers and his original commission was in the artillery. He won a brevet to first lieutenant in Mexico, but by 1861 he was only a captain.

4. **He was wounded at the Battle of Glendale.** It was one of the Seven Days battles, with George McClellan changing base from the York to the James, and in the process was driven from the gates of Richmond. Meade's wounds were severe, but he was back at Second Bull Run, this time in command of a division. Not bad for a man who had almost no experience in commanding troops.

5. **At Fredericksburg, his division briefly broke through the Confederate line.** Attacking Stonewall Jackson at Hamilton's Crossing, Meade's division with help from Brig. Gen. John Gibbon punched through, but Jackson brought up reserves and was able to push Meade back to his original position. It was one of the few Union bright spots in a disastrous battle. Had Meade been reinforced at the right moment, the battle might have gone differently.

6. **At Chancellorsville, he wanted to continue the battle.** Meade, Oliver Howard, and John Reynolds all wanted to continue. Darius Couch and Daniel Sickles voted to retreat. Hooker and his chief of staff, Daniel Butterfield, trumped them and gave orders to recross the Rappahannock. So much for asking the guidance of your subordinates!

7. **Lincoln's first choice was John Reynolds.** When Reynolds heard the rumors, he dashed to Washington and told Lincoln he would not accept the job unless some of the usual restrictions on the commander were removed. Some also think that Reynolds was bypassed in favor of Meade because the politicians believed that Meade's foreign birth would prevent him from seeking the presidency. In either case, Meade received the job, and Reynolds

was killed on the first day of the Battle of Gettysburg. The government seemed to want a Pennsylvanian. Lincoln said, "Every rooster fights best on his own dung hill." If a politician said such a thing today, all Pennsylvania would take offense and he would be forced to apologize.

8. **Meade wanted to take a position at Pipe Creek in Maryland.** That defense line, by the way, is the same position where Longstreet tried to convince Lee to position his troops. When the battle opened, Meade sent Winfield Hancock ahead to take command and pick the position. When Meade arrived around midnight, he approved of Hancock's choice and decided to stay.

9. **Lincoln was annoyed by Meade's message: "The enemy has been driven from our soil!"** Lincoln asked, "When will they realize that it is *all* our soil?" Meade, his army in shambles from the victory, was ready to let Lee return to Virginia unmolested. Lincoln pressed him for a pursuit. The VI Corps, largest in the army, had come up late on the second day and was only lightly engaged. Lee had the swollen Potomac River behind him and was short of ammunition, but Meade gave him a two-day head start and failed to deliver the fatal blow. Had he done so, Meade—not Grant—might have emerged as the great hero of the war.

10. **Meade offered to step down as commander of the Army of the Potomac.** He expected Grant to want the job. Instead, Grant kept him on but went along with the army, thereby greatly reducing Meade's role and the glory of any victories. Meade was, at heart, a good man. He avoided the cliques and cabals so common in the army. He could be charming when he chose, but he could also be prickly. His nickname of Snappin' Turtle reflected his short temper. Meade looked down on volunteers, distrusted politicians, and battled with newspaper reporters. Small wonder his career stalled. The darkest day of his life came when Grant moved up to the War Department and Sherman took the top army job. Meade died of pneumonia seven years after the war at age fifty-six. They said he never fully recovered from his war wounds.

11. The Boy Generals

1. **"Rooney" Lee was a general at age twenty-five.** William Henry Fitzhugh Lee was a Harvard graduate and an army officer at the outbreak of the war. He won his general's wreath in September 1862 at age twenty-five. Recovering from a wound received at Brandy Station, Lee was captured and involved in threats and counter threats to hang imprisoned officers as reprisals. He was not exchanged until March 1864. He was given a division and made a major general at age twenty-six. Ironically, he became a general before his West Point–trained older brother, who served early in the war in staff positions.

2. **Thomas Ransom was a corps commander at age twenty-eight.** The Norwich graduate joined the Eleventh Illinois as a captain and commanded the regiment seven months later. In November 1862 he won his star at age twenty-eight. He was commanding a corps at age twenty-nine, but he had been wounded four times and never properly recovered before returning to action. He died near Rome, Georgia, on October 29, 1864, of the effects of those wounds.

3. **Stephen Dodson Ramseur was a major general at twenty-seven.** A West Pointer, class of 1860, he went with his home state as an artillery officer. He was a brigadier general at age twenty-five and a major general at twenty-seven, one of the youngest in the Confederate army. He went with Jubal Early on his raid on Washington and in the Shenandoah Valley. At Cedar Creek, he received a mortal wound and was captured, dying among Northern friends. Only three days earlier, Ramseur had learned that his wife had given birth to a baby girl.

4. **Galusha Pennypacker was the youngest of all.** He started as a quartermaster sergeant in the Ninth Pennsylvania, but despite his youth, by August 1864 he was a colonel of the Ninety-Seventh Pennsylvania. In the closing months of the war, he moved quickly to brigade command. At Fort Fisher he led the attack that took the fort, receiving his seventh wound in eight months. He received his

brigadier's star on January 15, 1865, before his twenty-first birthday. After the war, he returned to the army as colonel of the Sixteenth Infantry. By the way, there was one other younger general before him but his commission was of a more political nature. The Continental Congress made the Marquis de Lafayette a major general at nineteen, sight unseen.

5.   **Elon Farnsworth had a short career as a general.** No doubt Farnsworth was a talented young man, but he owed his rapid promotion to his uncle John Farnsworth, who organized and led the Eighth Illinois Cavalry and later returned to Congress. Maj. Gen. Alfred Pleasonton, Elon's superior, bartered young Farnsworth's promotion with the congressman in exchange for his help in obtaining another division. At Gettysburg, Farnsworth was ordered to charge Confederate positions south of Little Round Top after Pickett's defeat. He thought it unwise and died in the attack with five bullet wounds to the chest. Any one of them would have killed him.

6.   **Jeb Stuart was one of the earliest promoted to general during the war.** James Ewell Brown Stuart was already a veteran of Indian fighting and Bleeding Kansas when he joined the Confederates. On September 24, 1861, he became a brigadier general at age twenty-eight. Less than a year later, he was a major general. Can you imagine what the fifty-year-old captains and majors were saying about that? But war creates opportunity, and by later standards, Stuart would have been considered almost elderly.

7.   **George Armstrong Custer went from captain to brigadier general.** West Point-trained officers were much in demand, even those who finished last in their class. Early in the war, Custer was on the staffs of George McClellan and Alfred Pleasonton. He showed a strong desire to lead and a willingness to get into the action, so Pleasonton accommodated him by making him a brigadier general at age twenty-four. His Michigan regiment had the highest casualties of any cavalry regiment in the war. His performance at Gettysburg, Yellow Tavern, Cedar Creek, and the Appomattox Campaign made

Pleasonton look like a genius. By the time the war ended, Custer was a twenty-six-year-old major general. And, as a footnote, Custer was a distant cousin of Galusha Pennypacker's.

8. **William Paul Roberts was youngest Confederate general.** He enlisted in the Nineteenth North Carolina Infantry, but it was converted to the Second North Carolina Cavalry. Working his way up, he held all but two ranks from third lieutenant to colonel, and took over the brigade when James Dearing was transferred. His tiny brigade was decimated at Five Forks and surrendered at Appomattox. After the war, he was a legislator and state auditor.

9. **Some thought Robert Hoke was Lee's preference to succeed him.** He was a graduate of the Kentucky Military Institute and fought at Big Bethel and was captured at New Bern, North Carolina. He fought with the Army of Northern Virginia from the Seven Days battles to Chancellorsville, where he was wounded. He returned to North Carolina, where he unsuccessfully tried to retake New Bern but did recapture Plymouth. Back in Virginia, he led his division at Bermuda Hundred and Cold Harbor. He returned to North Carolina and was with Joe Johnston when he surrendered. Lee was initially impressed with him but probably came to see that Hoke sometimes had difficulty cooperating with others.

10. **John Caldwell Calhoun Sanders was a colonel at age twenty-two.** He marched away with the Eleventh Alabama, having been elected captain of his company. Initially part of Johnston's army in the Shenandoah Valley, Sanders saw action from the Peninsula Campaign to Petersburg. He was wounded at Frayser's Farm and, more severely, at Gettysburg. He was only twenty-two when he became colonel of his regiment. He commanded the brigade at Cold Harbor and Petersburg but lost his life at Globe Tavern in the fight for the Weldon Railroad in August 1864.

11. **William Francis Bartlett was a young general from Harvard.** A captain in the Twentieth Massachusetts "Harvard" Regiment, he fought at Ball's Bluff and lost a leg at Yorktown. His return to action required him to lead his regiment mounted, which made

him a target. He took command of a nine-month regiment and fought at Port Hudson, where he was wounded twice more. Mustered out, he raised another regiment and led it in the Overland Campaign and was wounded in the Wilderness. After Cold Harbor he received his general's star at age twenty-four. He received his fifth wound and was captured at the Battle of the Crater. After the war, he set aside his disabilities to reach out to Southerners.

12. **Gilbert Moxley Sorrel moved from staff to infantry general.**
Moxley Sorrel was from a wealthy Savannah family and served as a volunteer aide at Fort Pulaski. He joined Longstreet's staff as a captain, rising to lieutenant colonel. Sorrel's direction of a flanking movement in the Wilderness drew attention and won him a chance to command. He became a brigadier general at age twenty-six and was wounded at Petersburg and again at Hatcher's Run, where he received a serious chest wound that ended his war service. After the war, he was in business in Savannah and authored a fine book of recollections.

12. The Rock

1. **As a boy he was caught up in Nat Turner's Rebellion.** The 1831 slave revolt in Southampton County, Virginia, drove the Thomas family from their home. Young George was only fifteen and his father was dead, but he helped his mother lead the younger children to safety. At one point they had to abandon their wagon and take to the woods, chased by some of the rebellious slaves.

2. **He started to study for the law.** His uncle was a local clerk of the courts and young George became his assistant with an eye toward becoming a lawyer. However, he became restless and decided to try the army. It was a fortunate choice. It's hard to say what kind of lawyer he might have become, but he certainly was a great general.

3. **He was wounded by Comanche Indians.** In 1860, while fighting Indians on the Texas plains, he narrowly escaped death when an

arrow glanced off his chin and lodged in his chest. He pulled it out himself, had the wound dressed, and immediately returned to action. He saw a great deal of action in the Seminole War in Florida, at Monterrey and Buena Vista in the Mexican War, on the Texas plains, and in the Civil War, but that one arrow caused his only wound in combat.

4. **He was called Slow Trot because of his concern for West Point horses.** As cavalry instructor, he was concerned for the health and safety of the horse herd at the academy and issued orders against galloping the aging nags. Needless to say, this command did not sit well with the young cadets, who liked nothing better than to race off at breakneck speed. Thomas's work at the academy caught the eye of his boss, Superintendent Robert E. Lee.

5. **He was commissioned major in the Second Cavalry.** As secretary of war, Davis created the new unit and staffed it with a who's who of future Confederate generals, including Albert Sidney Johnston, Robert E. Lee, William Hardee, Earl Van Dorn, and Jeb Stuart. The sectional favoritism was obvious, but Davis's actions were probably not related to a future test of arms between North and South.

6. **His wife was from Troy, New York.** In 1852, a year after taking his new assignment at the academy, he married Frances Kellogg, the cousin of a cadet. Troy is about a hundred miles up the Hudson from West Point. Having a Yankee wife probably played a role in his decision to remain loyal to the Union. A number of Northern officers with wives from the South sided with the Confederacy. Of course, men paid a price for going against their home states. Some Confederate officers cursed Thomas, and Jeb Stuart even threatened to hang him. At least some members of Thomas's family were upset by his decision, reportedly turning his picture toward the wall and no longer speaking of him. Some accounts dispute this story and maintain that some family members stayed in touch with him.

7. **His first victory was at Logan's Cross Roads, Kentucky.** The battle is also known as Mill Springs and Fishing Creek. Thomas

commanded a division in Don Carlos Buell's Army of the Ohio and came up against Confederates under George Crittenden and Felix Zollicoffer. A newspaper editor turned general, Zollicoffer had managed to move his men out of the position he was supposed to be guarding, the Cumberland Gap. He compounded his problems by riding up to the Fourth Kentucky and ordering its colonel, Speed Fry, to stop firing on his own men. Trouble was, the Fourth Kentucky was a Union regiment, and its men shot and killed the near-sighted Zollicoffer. The sides were about even, but Thomas handled his green troops better than Crittenden did and caused the Confederates to retreat and abandon most of their supplies and equipment.

8. **Thomas helped save the army at Stones River.** At the end of 1862, William Rosecrans moved out of Nashville to attack Bragg at Murfreesboro. Both sides adopted the same plan—to attack the enemy at dawn. The Confederates started earlier and drove back the weakened Federals' right almost to the Nashville Pike, their escape route. By late afternoon, Union commanders had put together a line of artillery that stopped the Confederate drive. Thomas played a major part in the effort.

9. **Ulysses Grant selected Thomas for Army of the Cumberland command.** After Chickamauga, Lincoln sent Grant to Chattanooga to assess the situation. He had the power to leave Rosecrans in command or to name Thomas to replace him. Grant decided on Thomas although he was not especially fond of either man. Grant's bad feelings may have stemmed from the period after Shiloh when, during the advance on Corinth, Grant was made second in command with no real duties while Thomas commanded Grant's former units. Grant could be vindictive.

10. **Grant wanted that honor for Sherman.** Thomas had orders to attack the first line of rifle pits at the bottom of the ridge and stop there. After a brief halt the men, seemingly on their own, began to attack up the steep ridge toward the line at the crest four hundred feet above them. Thomas was with Grant a distance away and

watched the surprising attack that drove Bragg's men from the ridge and back to Dalton, Georgia. With the fighting at Chattanooga over, Grant was given command of all Union armies. Sherman replaced him in command of the western army, which would capture Atlanta the following year. But all was not well. Both Grant and Sherman may have suspected that Thomas was behind the "spontaneous" attack.

11. **At Nashville, Thomas was stopped by ice.** Sherman headed for Savannah and sent Thomas back to Nashville to deal with Hood. After Schofield defeated Hood at Franklin, Tennessee, he joined Thomas. Hood followed and made camp outside Nashville. Grant and Lincoln pressed Thomas to attack, but given an ice storm and other factors, he was not ready. Grant sent Maj. Gen. John Logan to Nashville with the power to replace Thomas. Logan took his time getting there, probably to give Thomas time to move. Finally, the ice storm ended. Thomas attacked and won the most complete victory of the war, sending Hood reeling out of the war and all the way back to Mississippi.

12. **Thomas turned down a chance to be commanding general of the army.** President Andrew Johnson offered him the job when Grant moved up to become secretary of war. This period saw open political warfare between the president and Congress. Thomas realized the job would put him in a sensitive political position so he declined. He was given command of the Department of the Pacific with headquarters at the Presidio in San Francisco. After suffering a stroke, he died there in 1870 at age fifty-three.

SECTION VII

NEARING THE END

B y the fall of 1864, the Union clearly had the upper hand. In a hard and costly campaign, Ulysses Grant had pushed Lee's army into an entrenched line that stretched from Richmond to Petersburg. William Sherman's western army captured Atlanta and was ready to

The agrarian South performed wonders in improvising and manufacturing, but it could not supply itself for a long war. It had to rely heavily on bringing supplies through the blockade. Slowly, the Union Navy tightened the blockade and combined forces captured key ports. The massive earthen Fort Fisher at the mouth of the Cape Fear River in North Carolina, shown here, kept Wilmington open until January 15, 1965. When the fort fell to a combined army and navy attack, it virtually guaranteed the abandonment of Richmond and Petersburg and the end of the war. Seventy-seven days after Fort Fisher surrendered, General Lee was forced to abandon both cities. *Photo by the author*

march toward Savannah. In the Shenandoah, Phil Sheridan had smashed Jubal Early's army and put the valley out of operation as a base of supplies. Most important, Northern morale was lifted and Abraham Lincoln would be reelected president. Bloody work remained, but victory was at hand.

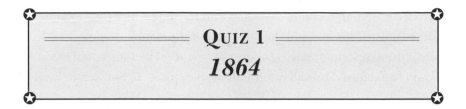

QUIZ 1
1864

In the last full year of the Civil War the North finally took the upper hand but at the cost of thousands of casualties. Let's review some of the momentous events of that pivotal year.

1. In February, Congress passed a law about military rank that impacted only one man. Who was he and what was the law?
2. On February 9, Abraham Lincoln sat for photos, one of which would be the most duplicated picture of him. How was it used?
3. On February 9, Col. Thomas E. Rose led 109 Union officers on a daring adventure. What was it?
4. On February 17, the Confederate submarine CSS *H. C. Hunley* sank the USS *Housatonic*, a historic first. Where did the *Hunley* go after sinking the *Housatonic*?
5. In early March, a thirteen-year-old Virginia boy named William Littlepage found papers on a dead Union officer that touched off a controversy. Who was the officer and what did the papers say?
6. In the Battle of the Wilderness, the Union lost one of its most successful political generals. This graduate of both Yale and Harvard read law in Daniel Webster's office. After an unsuccessful run for governor in New York in 1862, he returned to the army to lead a division in the V Corps. Who was he?
7. In his Red River Campaign, Nathanial Banks left the protection of his gunboats to march on a road away from the river. Why?
8. As a result of the Battle of Pleasant Hill, Louisiana, on April 9, 1864, a rare phenomenon took place involving both armies. What was it?
9. In October, little Phil Sheridan made his famous ride from Winchester to the Cedar Creek battlefield to rally his men and lead them to victory. What was the name of the famous horse he rode?

10. As 1864 ended, Benjamin Butler and David Dixon Porter led an attack on Fort Fisher in an attempt to close the blockade-runner port of Wilmington, North Carolina. In what gimmick did Butler invest a good deal of his time and trust?

QUIZ 2
U.S. Colored Troops

From the start of the Civil War, black leaders were urging the Lincoln government to allow their people join the fight. They had to wait two years, until the Emancipation Proclamation was signed, but they finally had a chance and made the most of it. Let's see what you know about the U.S. Colored Troops (USCT).

1. How many black soldiers enlisted? (A) 142,200. (B) 186,000. (C) 205,300. (D) 238,000.
2. While the Fifty-Fourth Massachusetts "Glory" Regiment was the best-known black regiment, which one was the first?
3. What famous black abolitionist had two sons in the Fifty-Fourth Massachusetts?
4. One of John Brown's Secret Six backers commanded a black regiment. Name him and the regiment.
5. Confederates launched an attack from west of the Mississippi to take pressure off besieged Vicksburg. USCT troops, although lacking training, stopped it. Name the battle.
6. When Robert Gould Shaw was killed leading the Fifty-Fourth Massachusetts at Fort Wagner, who succeeded him in command?
7. Most USCT officers were white, but by the end of the war a few blacks held officer rank including two who were majors. Name them.

8. Who was the veteran general who led the board that screened officer candidates for the USCT?

9. Twenty-nine members of the USCT won Medals of Honor, and fourteen of the men won them in the same battle. Name it.

10. True or false: Black soldiers were paid the same as white soldiers.

11. Approximately how many black soldiers died during the war? (A) 26,000. (B) 30,500. (C) 36,000. (D) 40,000.

12. Did the early units designated by state keep those designations?

QUIZ 3
Cedar Creek

Jubal Early was a pesky and persistent antagonist. After throwing a major scare into "Old Abe Lincoln" outside Washington, he had been chased back into the Shenandoah Valley, but he simply would not go away. Despite major defeats at Winchester and Fisher Hill, he hung on, looking for his chance. He found it at Cedar Creek. Let's test your knowledge of this important 1864 battle.

1. The Confederate plan of attack was the brainchild of a Georgia lawyer turned general. Who was he?

2. An event occurred prior to the battle that infuriated the Confederates. What was it?

3. When the fighting started, Phil Sheridan was away from the army. Where had he gone and where was he when the battle started?

4. Who commanded the Union Army on the morning of the attack?

5. One Union corps had started to depart for Petersburg when a rumor that Longstreet was reinforcing Early caused it to return. Which corps was it?

6. The Confederates had a different name for the battle. What was it?

7. Who commanded the first Union unit to be struck?

8. Once the first Union troops were surprised and routed, why was it so difficult for the others to mount a defense?

9. The VI Corps, farther from the initial assault than the others, broke camp and moved into a line of battle before they were struck. Which division commander is generally given credit for breaking the Confederates' momentum?

10. When Jubal Early's army reached the north side of Middletown, what did he do?

11. At what time did Phil Sheridan reach his troops?

12. What aspect of the Federals' counterattack broke the back of the Confederates?

13. Two promising young officers—one a Confederate infantry division commander and the other a Union cavalry brigade commander—died in the battle. Name them.

14. What happened in the center of Strasburg that completed the Confederate panic and rout?

QUIZ 4
Columbia Burning

General Sherman's army occupied Columbia, South Carolina, on February 17, 1864. President Lincoln quipped that Sherman had been flirting with Augusta and was embracing Columbia but had his eye on Charlotte. That embrace came at a high cost. Despite assurances to the mayor that his city was as safe as it would have been in the hands of his own army, a huge piece of Columbia lay in ashes the next morning. Let's test our knowledge of that cataclysmic event.

1. Before entering the city, Union troops passed a prisoner of war site on a bluff above the Saluda River west of Columbia. Name it.

2. Some South Carolinians had sent a valuable commodity to the city for safekeeping. Its presence contributed to the disaster. What was it?

3. What other commodity was stacked high in the streets of Columbia?

4. The burning of Columbia was a man-made event, but nature provided another major component. Name it.

5. Why were the Union sentries ineffective?

6. Which Union general was responsible for the city?

7. Who did Sherman blame for the fires?

8. Who did both sides blame for the fires?

9. What large religious facility was destroyed?

10. Approximately what percentage of the city was destroyed?

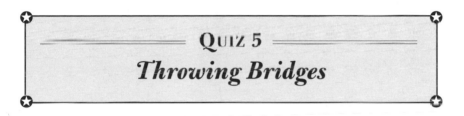

QUIZ 5
Throwing Bridges

Moving armies across broad and deep rivers was a challenge for Civil War generals. Their solution was the pontoon bridge. Engineers "threw" bridges across many rivers, and they were an important part of many major battles and campaigns. Let's see what we know about them.

1. True or false: The Civil War was the first war in which American armies used pontoon bridges.

2. Who invented pontoon bridges? (A) The British Army. (B) The ancient Greeks. (C) The Persians. (D) The Chinese.

3. On what river was the longest pontoon bridge of the war built?

4. George McClellan rejected the lighter inflatable and "Russian"-type pontoons in favor of the heavier "French" style. Why?

5. The greatest pontoon failure of the war occurred when pontoons arrived at Fredericksburg six days late. What engineer officer was relieved of duty in that incident?

6. Individual pontoon trains could span streams seven hundred to a thousand feet wide. About how long was a pontoon train on the march?

7. When bridges were in place, how far apart were the pontoons?

8. What was the name of the supporting beams that carried the bridge from boat to boat?

9. What was the name of the flooring?

10. Why were bands not allowed to play while marching across pontoon bridges?

11. When Grant moved his army from Cold Harbor to Petersburg, from what point on the James River did the pontoon bridge start?

12. What Connecticut general handled that assignment?

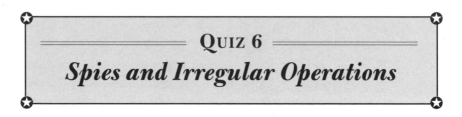

Quiz 6
Spies and Irregular Operations

The Civil War offered plenty of opportunities for brave men and women to play heroic roles away from the main stage of battles and campaigns. Many risked and sometimes lost their lives in the dark worlds of espionage and special operations. See if you can match the adventures with the adventurers.

Spies and Adventurers

1. James J. Andrews
2. John Yates Beall
3. Belle Boyd
4. James Dunwoody Bulloch
5. William B. Cushing
6. Sara Emma Edmonds
7. Rose O'Neal Greenhow
8. John W. Headley

9. Allan Pinkerton
10. Jacob Thompson
11. Bennett H. Young

The Adventures

A. He receives high marks for gathering information for the Union but a failing grade for his ability to analyze it, reporting extra Rebels by the thousands to an already jittery Maj. Gen. George McClellan.

B. He led a party of rebel soldiers out of Canada to St. Albans, Vermont, to terrorize the town and rob the banks of more than $200,000. He also touched off an international incident.

C. Teddy Roosevelt's beloved uncle worked behind the scenes in Great Britain to secure ships for the Confederacy.

D. His bold plot to seize a Union warship on Lake Erie and use it to free Confederates on Johnson's Island almost worked.

E. He led a party of Union sailors up the Roanoke River and sank the ram *Albemarle*, causing the Confederates to abandon Plymouth, North Carolina.

F. She is credited with providing the Confederates the information they needed to win the first battle of Manassas/Bull Run. She continued spying even while locked up in the Old Capitol Prison.

G. He led a team of Confederate officers who tried to burn down New York City in November 1864.

H. She enlisted as a man, and her ability to pass as either a man or a woman later made her an effective Union spy.

I. This former congressman and cabinet officer directed Confederate operations from Canada.

J. In an attempt to disrupt the Confederate railroad from Atlanta to Chattanooga, he led a spectacular but unsuccessful Union raid.

K. She spied for Stonewall Jackson and Turner Ashby from her father's hotel in Front Royal. Ashby was so pleased with her work that he made her an honorary captain.

QUIZ 7
The Medal of Honor

It is looked upon today as the ultimate recognition for military bravery, but the Medal of Honor was a work in progress during the Civil War. Some 1,522 were bestowed, with most won fairly but others awarded on more questionable grounds. Let's look at some who won the honor.

1. Who created the award?
2. The brother of a famous general won two of them. Name him.
3. The first two colonels of a famous regiment were winners. Name the regiment.
4. One woman won the award. Who was she?
5. He was later a member of Grant's staff and one of his biographers, but at Chickamauga he was one of the heroes of the retreat, holding an important position and buying valuable time. Name him.
6. The sergeant major of the Fourth U.S. Colored Troops won the medal for action at Chaffin's Farm. He was?
7. After President Lincoln's death, twenty-nine men won the medal for a special service. It was?
8. The highest-ranking Union general to win the medal received it for service as a major in the Battle of Wilson's Creek, Missouri. He was?
9. The commander of the Philadelphia brigade won the medal for his leadership in turning back Pickett's Charge at Gettysburg. Name him.
10. This Pennsylvania-born regular won his medal for leading his brigade in an attack at Jonesboro, Georgia, during the Atlanta Campaign. He was?

11. All 864 members of a Maine regiment were awarded the medal for remaining in service for four extra days. Name the regiment.

12. This D.C.-born Ohio lawyer and Harvard graduate won his medal in the Battle of Atlanta. Name him.

QUIZ 8
"Damn the Torpedoes!"

The North eyed Mobile, Alabama, the South's second-largest port, from the beginning of the war but made no effort to take it until August 1864. Natural and man-made defenses combined to pose major problems for the attacking army and naval forces under Rear Adm. David Farragut and Maj. Gen. Gordon Granger. Let's test your knowledge of this important battle.

1. Twin forts guarded the Gulf of Mexico entrance to Mobile Bay. Name them.

2. A second major entrance to the bay lay to the west. Name it and the fort that guarded it.

3. Farragut had four monitors in his attack fleet. Two of them were of a new design. What set them apart from the originals?

4. What formation did Farragut select for his attack?

5. What position did Admiral Farragut select for directing the battle?

6. What near disaster beset the fleet as the lead ship drew even with Fort Morgan?

7. What major Union disaster occurred in front of Fort Morgan?

8. Why did the torpedo field fail to stop the attack?

9. Once inside the bay, the Union fleet faced another major obstacle. What was it?

10. Who commanded the CSS *Tennessee*?

11. What was the Achilles' heel of the CSS *Tennessee*?

12. What was the fate of the three forts?

QUIZ 9
Fort Fisher, 1864

By the winter of 1864–1865, Wilmington, North Carolina, was the most important major port open to blockade-runners, and at the mouth of the Cape Fear River, Fort Fisher—the largest earthen fort in the Confederacy—held that door open. In December, the Union made its first attempt at taking the fort. Test your knowledge of this unsuccessful venture.

1. Name the Lincoln cabinet member who lobbied hard for an expedition against Fort Fisher.
2. Name the ill-starred Confederate general who oversaw the design and construction of the fort.
3. Name the Confederate colonel who commanded the fort.
4. Two men with towering egos led the Union's army and naval forces. Name them.
5. Who had General Grant selected to lead the expedition?
6. The Union Army commander had a secret plan to destroy the fort. What was it?
7. The navy commander decided to steal the army's thunder. What happened when he did?
8. What high-ranking Confederate general was sent to Wilmington to coordinate defenses?
9. General Lee detached a division from his army to reinforce Wilmington. Who led it?
10. How many ships of line did the navy bring against the fort? (A) Twenty-nine. (B) Forty-two. (C) Sixty-four. (D) Eighty-one.
11. Name the two Union division commanders in the attacking force.
12. What did the fort commander do when the ships ceased firing?
13. What impact did this tactic have on Benjamin Butler?
14. What happened to the Union brigade of N. Martin Curtis?
15. What happened to Butler?

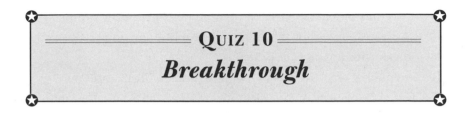

Quiz 10
Breakthrough

As the winter of 1864–1865 ended, a war-weary nation braced for a final convulsion that might bring peace. In the Richmond/Petersburg entrenchments, Robert E. Lee knew he could not hang on much longer. Test your knowledge of the events that marked the beginning of the end.

1. The final Confederate offensive came on March 25 when Confederate troops attacked this fort in the Union's Petersburg line. Name the fort.
2. The Union launched its offensive when this officer returned from the Shenandoah Valley. Name him.
3. The Union objective was to cut one road and the final rail line running into Petersburg from the south and west. Name them.
4. Petersburg became untenable when the Union forces won a battle at a distinctive country crossroads. Name the place/battle.
5. The general commanding the Union offensive faulted an infantry corps commander for poor performance and sacked him. Name the corps commander.
6. When General Grant received word of the Union victory, what did he order his other corps commanders to do?
7. Which Union corps, commanded by a Connecticut general, was first to break through the Petersburg lines?
8. As the breakthrough developed, a Confederate corps commander rode into marauding Yankees who shot him dead. Who was he?
9. What Confederate general replaced the dead corps commander?
10. This twenty-six-year-old Union major general, a store clerk when the war began, won a bloody victory when his division smashed a Confederate line at Sutherland Station. Name him.

11. A valiant Confederate defense at these two forts finally stopped the Union steamroller for the night and gave Lee time to execute an orderly withdrawal. Name the forts.

12. Lee's initial objective was to retreat to a small village forty miles west of Petersburg on the Richmond & Danville Railroad. Name the place.

QUIZ 11
The Last Ditch

When Grant's spring 1865 campaign broke the Confederate lines at Petersburg, the Davis government was forced to flee. Robert E. Lee began a planned retreat but it would lead to Appomattox Court House and the end of the war. Let's see what you know about this final campaign.

1. When Lee's retreating army reached Amelia Court House, he lost a day looking for something. What was it?

2. Retreat plans called for troops to move west from three cities and towns. Name them.

3. A sizable contingent also came from a fourth location, which was unanticipated when the plan was drafted. Name it.

4. The earliest engagement of the retreat came April 3 when Union cavalry attacked Confederates retreating from that fourth location. Name the location of this battle.

5. Lee's route along the Richmond & Danville Railroad was blocked when Union cavalry under Ranald Mackenzie and, later, infantry under George Crook cut off his path. At what Virginia town did they block the way?

6. The Confederate army ran into disaster on April 6 when a segment of the army was trapped between Union cavalry and the VI Corps. Name the place.

7. Longstreet almost lost the race to this important crossing of the Appomattox River, but he sent Tom Rosser ahead to thwart a federal raiding party. Name the bridge.

8. When Confederate Brig. Gen. James Dearing was mortally wounded in the action he gained a dubious distinction. What was it?

9. On April 7, the Union found the Confederates at this location and a sharp fight developed. The entrenched Southerners gave the Union a sharp repulse before turning west toward Appomattox Court House. Name the skirmish.

10. On the march to Appomattox, Fitzhugh Lee warned his uncle Robert that the Union cavalry was sprinting ahead to cut them off. How did he know?

11. At Appomattox, when Lee tried to punch through the Union cavalry, what did he find that caused him to change his mind?

12. The home of Wilmer McLean was borrowed for the surrender conference. Where did McLean live before he moved to Appomattox?

QUIZ 12
The End of the Road

The great epic war that began in Charleston Harbor finally ended in a tiny Virginia village. Thinned by hard campaigning, battle losses, and desertion, Robert E. Lee's army could no longer resist. Let's test your knowledge of the actual surrender at Appomattox Court House.

1. What did Lee say he would rather do than ride out and meet with Grant?

2. The surrender took place on a holiday. What day was it?

3. Who arrived at the McLean house first, Lee or Grant?

4. The two generals had met once during the Mexican War. One remembered but the other had no recollection. Who had the better memory?

5. Only one Confederate officer accompanied Lee to the McLean house. Name him.

6. The yard of the McLean house quickly filled with Union soldiers. A lone Confederate stood with them. Who was he?

7. Some paintings show Grant and Lee seated at a small table. Others show them seated at separate small tables. Which is correct?

8. When introduced to Grant's staff members, some thought Lee stiffened when he met Lt. Col. Ely Parker. Why?

9. Lee expressed his satisfaction with Grant's surrender terms with a short comment. What was it?

10. Lee asked for one additional item that Grant happily added. What was it?

11. While the surrender terms were being copied, Lee chatted with a member of Grant's staff, a friend from the old army. Name him.

12. In one more housekeeping item Grant provided provisions for hungry Confederate soldiers. How many rations did the quartermasters send?

13. How many men were in the room for the surrender?

14. Grant made one final gesture as Lee departed. What was it?

15. Wilmer McLean later filed a claim against the U.S. government. For what was he seeking restitution?

ANSWERS

1. 1864

1. **The law restored the rank of lieutenant general for Ulysses Grant as he became commanding general of the U.S. Army.** Winfield Scott held the rank but on a brevet or honorary basis. The last and only other man who previously held the rank on a permanent basis was George Washington. The Confederates, meanwhile, used the rank to designate corps commanders. Eighteen men held the rank.

2. **Lincoln's photo is on U.S. money.** You may well have one of those photos in your pocket as one of the portraits was later used, and is still in use, on the five-dollar bill. Of course, an even better known and much more widely circulated likeness of our sixteenth president is on the penny. For a man widely regarded as homely at best, his likeness has been re-created in many places and many forms.

3. **Colonel Rose led a prison escape.** Col. Thomas E. Rose, a Pennsylvania engineer, led a successful tunneling effort and 109 officers broke free of Libby Prison in Richmond. Two drowned; 48, including Rose, were recaptured; and 59 made it back to Union lines. The operation almost fizzled at the start when Col. Abel Streight was given the honor of being one of the first men through the tunnel. He was a man of great girth and got stuck halfway. It took a good deal of pushing and shoving to get him through. He went to the home of Union spy Elizabeth Van Lew, who hid him until he could be smuggled out. The army put out a story that he had reached Union lines, so the Confederates stopped looking for him, and Streight managed to get safely home.

4. **The *Hunley* went to the bottom.** It, too, sank off Charleston. During tests and its single action, the experiment killed thirty-three Confederate sailors. After the action, the lookouts thought they saw a blue light indicating that it was okay, but it never returned to port. In recent years, the *Hunley* made headlines once again when

it was found and recovered. Tests on why it sank were inconclusive. We can only conjecture on why it sank.

5. **Col. Ulric Dahlgren's papers, supposedly a speech, outlined orders to kill Jefferson Davis and his cabinet if his raiding party reached Richmond.** The Union denied the authenticity of the papers and pointed out that Dahlgren's name was misspelled on them. Survivors of the raid denied that they had been given any such order. Southerners, however, continued to believe the story and were outraged. One of the raid's main goals was to free Union prisoners of war held in and around Richmond.

6. **Political Gen. James Samuel Wadsworth was killed in the Wilderness.** He was a Free Soil Democrat who became a Republican and a delegate to the 1861 Peace Conference that attempted to head off the Civil War. He proved a capable general, especially in the first day fighting at Gettysburg, but was mortally wounded at the Battle of the Wilderness. Born to great wealth, he was noted for his philanthropy.

7. **Banks probably left the ships so he wouldn't have to share the glory of a victory with the navy.** In the Battle of Mansfield/Sabine Cross Roads, Banks ran into a small but very aggressive force under Dick Taylor and suffered a stinging defeat. He retreated to Pleasant Hill but not before losing much of his wagon train and supplies.

8. **After Pleasant Hill, both armies retreated.** Dick Taylor's Confederates were repulsed, but Banks had had enough, left the field too, and began his retreat to the Mississippi. He finally caught up with Porter and his ships at Alexandria on the Red River only to discover that low water had stranded Porter's fleet. Some brilliant engineering work by Col. Joseph Bailey saved the day as he partially dammed the river and floated the ships to safety.

9. **Sheridan's horse was named Rienzi.** Sheridan had obtained him near Rienzi, Mississippi, but renamed him Winchester after his famous ride. After Rienzi/Winchester's death, he was stuffed and put on display at Governor's Island, New York. By the time Sheridan reached his army, the retreat that began in the fields near

Belle Grove Plantation had reached the north side of Middletown. However, Jubal Early's thus-far successful army had paused to catch its breath, blocked by the Union VI Corps. Sheridan used the time to bring calm and to build a new line of battle with cavalry at each end. When he attacked, George Custer's cavalry on the Union right flanked the Confederates, and a new rout was on, with the Confederates in flight and the Union now in pursuit. Union forces chased the defeated Confederates past the starting point and all the way into and through Strasburg. The Shenandoah was back in the Union.

10. **Butler planned to explode a powder ship.** The ever-inventive Butler loaded USS *Louisiana* with two hundred tons of gunpowder and planned to ground it near the fort and blow it up. He hoped the fort would be heavily damaged or destroyed, too. Many, including Lincoln, doubted his plan would work but let him try anyway. One of the doubters was Porter. When weather delayed Butler's transports and spoiled the timing of the attack, Porter decided to explode the hulk before Butler arrived. The explosion did almost no damage to the fort. Butler sent his men ashore but aborted the attack and went back to Virginia. It would be his final failure before he was dumped.

2. U.S. Colored Troops

1. **(B) 186,000 black soldiers served.** As is so often the case, different sources give different numbers. Some sources say 178,000 while others, probably unrealistically, go as high as 300,000. Add in as many as 19,000 black sailors who served in the Union Navy, and you have a remarkable contribution. Whatever the final number, the largest portion—144,000 men—came from slave states and the vast majority of them were former slaves.

2. **The first black regiment was the First South Carolina.** Some units are hard to date because they were started before the Lincoln government formally authorized recruiting. Benjamin Butler in

Louisiana recruited three regiments of Louisiana Native Guards and Nathaniel Banks expanded it to his Corps d'Afrique. The Fifty-Fourth Massachusetts was unusual in that it was the first regiment of volunteers who were primarily free blacks from the North.

3. **Frederick Douglass's sons served.** His sons Lewis and Charles left their home at Anacostia in the District of Columbia and went to Massachusetts to enlist. Lewis became the regimental sergeant major and was wounded in the attack on Fort Wagner. Charles transferred to the Fifth Massachusetts Cavalry and became his company's first sergeant. A third son, Frederick Jr., served as a recruiter for the Fifty-Fourth but did not enlist.

4. **Thomas Wentworth Higginson led the First South Carolina.** This Massachusetts abolitionist minister became a captain in the Fifty-First Massachusetts (a white regiment) before becoming colonel of the First South Carolina, which Brig. Gen. Rufus Saxton had raised in the Sea Islands. He led the regiment on the Carolina coast and in Florida before being forced out by a wound. His book *Army Life in a Black Regiment* is one of the best accounts of the black soldiers in the war. Incidentally, some of his critics claimed that he wrote altogether too much.

5. **Black troops won respect defending Milliken's Bend.** Confederates of Maj. Gen. James G. Walker's Greyhound Division attempted to break Grant's supply line on the west bank of the Mississippi south of Vicksburg. He encountered the Corps d'Afrique Brigade under Col. Herman Lieb. Although lacking in training and poorly armed, the black troops fought well and, with the help of Union gunboats in the river, drove off the Confederates. Many saw the victory as proof that black troops could and would fight.

6. **Robert Gould Shaw's successor was Edward Needles "Ned" Hallowell.** He came from an abolitionist family in Philadelphia and served as a lieutenant in the Twentieth Massachusetts, the "Harvard" Regiment, until appointed a major in the Fifty-Fourth. He received three wounds in the attack on Fort Wagner. After his recovery he

assumed command as a colonel and led the Fifty-Fourth for the rest of the war through battles in South Carolina and Florida. He was typical of the young and idealistic aristocrats who led the black troops.

7. **The Negro majors were Martin Delaney and Francis Dumas.** Delaney, born a free black in Virginia, was a doctor, writer, and the editor of the black-run *North Star* abolitionist newspaper. He had been admitted to Harvard Medical School but was forced out by prejudice. Dumas, pronounced Du-Ma, was a Creole—part French and part black—from New Orleans. He was a successful sugar planter who owned slaves. He became a captain and freed any of his slaves who would join his regiment. He could speak five languages and impressed Benjamin Butler. The USCT eventually featured many black captains and lieutenants plus thirteen black chaplains and eight black surgeons.

8. **The head of the screening board was Silas Casey.** He was a lieutenant colonel in his mid-fifties when the war began. He commanded a division at Seven Pines but was moved to duty in the Washington defenses. Casey had high praise for the officers he was approving for duty with the black units, saying that they were at least the equal of leaders in established units. Best known as the author of a standard infantry tactics book, Casey wrote a companion piece for black troops.

9. **The Medals of Honor were earned at New Market Heights.** Also known as Chaffin's Farm and Laurel Hill, Fort Harrison and Fort Gilmer. Grant wanted to apply pressure to Lee to keep him from sending aid to Jubal Early in the Shenandoah Valley. In the close, hand-to-hand fighting USCT members seized a number of Confederate flags. Armies placed great value on flags then, and capturing one was an automatic ticket to the medal.

10. **False. Promised pay equity did not, initially, happen.** Despite promises to the contrary, Union paymasters initially paid black soldiers $10 per month rather than the $13 paid to white privates. This arrangement was based on a pay scale established for black

civilians who did labor or other jobs for the Union Army. Some black units refused the lower pay, and some of them were threatened with disciplinary action for their refusal. Finally, justice was done but not without a fight.

11. **(D) 40,000 black soldiers died in service.** As with white troops, 30,000 of the deaths—or three-quarters—were from disease. The remainder—10,000 battle deaths and mortal wounds—is lower than that for white troops but black troops were engaged for a shorter period. In addition, some Union generals were reluctant to use black troops for anything but garrison, guard duty, and labor. Sherman is on record as favoring using black troops for building entrenchments because they worked better than white troops did and he wanted to save the whites for the actual fighting.

12. **Most units were renumbered, but a few retained their state numbers.** Those units manned primarily by former slaves were re-designated as USCT regiments. However, four units—the Fifth Massachusetts Cavalry, the Fifty-Fourth and Fifty-Fifth Massachusetts Infantry, and the Twenty-Ninth Connecticut Infantry—were treated as conventional volunteer units and not transferred to the USCT. Those units comprised mostly free blacks who had been living in the North.

3. Cedar Creek

1. **The plan of the Cedar Creek attack came from John B. Gordon.** He climbed to the signal station on top of "Three Top," or Massanutten Mountain, where he could see the entire Union position. With the help of mapmaker Capt. Jed Hotchkiss he developed a plan to bring Early's troops into position on the east flank of the Cedar Creek line. The Union did not expect an attack from that direction because traversing it was difficult.

2. **Confederates were upset because of the "Burning."** Union soldiers spread out across the valley and methodically burned every barn and mill, killed or confiscated farm animals, and destroyed

the crops in the fields and the crops in storehouses, stripping the valley of all sustenance from Staunton to Strasburg. The Confederates saw this operation as an attack on innocent women, children, and the elderly and thirsted for revenge.

3. **Sheridan had been away at Washington and Winchester.** Little Phil had been summoned to the capital for a strategy conference. On his way back to the army, he spent the night in Winchester. Rising early, he headed south as the sounds of battle grew louder.

4. **In Sheridan's absence, Horatio Wright was in command.** The Clinton, Connecticut, native turned the VI Corps over to Brig. Gen. James Ricketts. Wright was wounded in the face as he impetuously led a counterattack; however, it did not knock him out of the battle.

5. **The VI Corps had started to leave, but it had been recalled.** It was lucky for the Union that the corps had not departed because it played a large role in stopping the rout. The Confederates had received reinforcements—Maj. Gen. Joseph Kershaw's division from Longstreet's corps. These troops from South Carolina, Mississippi, and Georgia were a vital part of the assault.

6. **Confederates called the battle Belle Grove.** The Belle Grove Plantation was a short distance behind Union lines and served as army headquarters. Heavy fighting occurred around the elegant manor house.

7. **First Union troops attacked were commanded by Col. Joseph Thoburn under Gen. George Crook's command.** Colonel Thoburn's First Division of Crook's Army of West Virginia took the initial assault at 5 a.m. in the fog. Crook's command is often called the VIII Corps but this name is not technically correct. Crook received some criticism for allowing such a large force to be so close to him without his knowledge; however, Crook was not the only one taken by surprise that morning.

8. **Union troops could not hold because they were flanked.** Once Crook's troops gave way, Brig. Gen. William Emory's XIX Corps found Confederates on their flank and rear. That made their

position indefensible so they had to pull back. While a few of
Crook's units fought bravely, notably Col. Thomas Wildes's
brigade, his force was mainly routed in great confusion. Emory's
retreat was more orderly.

9. **Brig. Gen. George Getty's Second Division of the VI Corps is
credited with finally stopping the attack.** From a position in the
town cemetery west of Middletown, he fought off successive attacks
by each of the four Confederate divisions. Early thought he was
fighting the entire VI Corps. When Early brought up all his
artillery and blasted away, the division was forced to retreat, but
Getty had bought precious time.

10. **North of Middletown, Gen. Early called a halt.** He knew he had
already won a great victory, but his troops were tired and somewhat
disorganized. Besides, he could see the Union line forming about
two miles north of Middletown. And the Union cavalry was present
again, the same group that had defeated him so often before.
Gordon and others urged him to attack immediately, but he said
they had earned plenty of glory for one day.

11. **Phil Sheridan arrived about 10:30 a.m.** The effect was electrifying.
He was greeted with cheers from the men and a hug from Custer.
He immediately went to work completing the new line that Wright
had started. Then he galloped the length of it as the men cheered.
The fight would be different now.

12. **The big difference was the presence of the cavalry.** Sheridan put
Custer's division on his right and Brig. Gen. Wesley Merritt's on
the left. The fighting was intense for about an hour before
Gordon's men gave way and Custer's troopers made a move for the
Confederate rear. The rout was on, and this time the men in gray
and butternut were doing the running.

13. **Two valuable generals killed were Stephen Dodson Ramseur and
Charles Russell Lowell Jr.** Ramseur of North Carolina, a member
of the West Point class of 1860, was mortally wounded in the Union
counterattack. The previous day he had learned of the birth of his
daughter. Lowell took first honors at Harvard and proved equally

adept at soldiering. The Boston blue blood had a dozen horses shot out from under him prior to receiving a mortal wound during the Union counterattack at Cedar Creek.

14. **In Strasburg, a bridge collapse proved a Confederate disaster.** The narrow bridge near Spangler's Mill on the Valley Pike collapsed. Artillery and wagons piled up behind it and were abandoned as the men fled. The Union thus recaptured all of its artillery, most of its wagons, and a fair share of the guns and wagons from Early's army. Early's career was in ruins. The Confederates would never launch another offensive in the Shenandoah Valley.

4. Columbia Burning

1. **Sherman's men saw Camp Sorghum.** It was another example of an open field with no shelter other than what the prisoners could improvise. Those Union troops who saw it were said to have become quite angry. Their reaction was not an encouraging sign for the citizens of Columbia. After seeing the camp, one battery commander lobbed a few shells into the not-yet-completed state Capitol Building.

2. **Whiskey held for safe keeping created problems.** It was of growing importance in the South. The price had risen to $25 per gallon from a prewar price of 25 cents a gallon. With food in short supply, the Confederate government had placed restrictions on distilling. Columbia was seen as a safe storage place. Once Union troops arrived, it wasn't.

3. **Cotton, bales and bales of it, was piled up in the middle of the streets.** The people had put it there to keep it out of Union hands. It turned out to be the wrong thing in the wrong place at the wrong time. The bales became tinder for an upcoming disaster.

4. **Another complication was a high wind.** Sherman planned to destroy some public buildings but put it off until the gale-force wind died down. But all the ingredients for a disaster were in place and a single spark would be enough to ignite it. That night saw plenty of sparks.

5. **Union guards were ineffective because they were drunk.** Oddly enough regulations did not prohibit drinking while on duty, only drunkenness, and every unit that came into the city to replace the drunks proceeded to get roaring drunk themselves. No sooner did the sentries change than the replacements were well on the way to shaking off sobriety.

6. **Oliver O. Howard was responsible for the city.** Howard commanded the Army of the Tennessee. The troops in the city were part of Jack Logan's XV Corps. Both Sherman and Howard were tired and had gone to bed. Authority then seemed to be in the hands of Logan and Maj. Gen. Charles Woods, who were slow to react to the men's drunkenness and looting. When the fires flared up, the Union commanders sprang into action, but by that time it was probably too late.

7. **Sherman blamed retreating Confederates.** Sherman claimed that Hampton's retreating cavalry set fire to the cotton, and Howard supported him. It's possible that the Confederates could have done so in a few examples, but they almost certainly did not cause all of the fires.

8. **Everyone seemed to blame drunken Negroes.** Certainly drunken Negroes were in the crowd, as well as many drunken escaped Union prisoners and drunken soldiers and civilians; however, the Union soldiers did the bulk of the damage. The Negroes were a handy scapegoat for all.

9. **The Ursuline Convent was burned.** Guards had been posted to protect the nuns and their students, but they could not stop the fire. They did, however, lead the nuns to safety at South Carolina College, now the University of South Carolina.

10. **About a third of the city burned.** An estimated 458 buildings were burned although some estimates are even higher. The main area of devastation ran thirteen blocks north to south and five blocks wide in some places. A separate fire on Gervais Street in the Red Light district seems to have arisen out of a dispute over business matters.

5. Throwing Bridges

1. **False. The United States started to develop pontoons for the Mexican War.** Winfield Scott assigned Capt. George Cullum of the Corps of Engineers to the job, and he went high tech, using three inflatable 20-foot rubber tubes in each wood frame unit. Each tube had a brass valve and was inflated using a bellows. However, they were time consuming to produce, and when they finally arrived in Mexico, the war was all but won.

2. **(D) The Chinese were first to use pontoon bridges.** The first recorded use was 2,600 years ago in China. Persian king Xerxes used one to cross the Dardanelles and attack ancient Greece. The bridge worked fine, but poor old Xerxes lost the war.

3. **The longest pontoon bridge was on the Ohio River.** When Grant moved from Cairo, Illinois, to Paducah, Kentucky, he had his engineers build a bridge across the Ohio to consolidate his supply line into Illinois. The elaborate span used several barges and had a swing section in the center to allow ships to pass. It was variously reported at 3,600 feet, 3,960 feet, and 5,000 feet long, but even 3,600 feet was the record for the war.

4. **McClellan opted for heavier pontoons because they would be safer in a retreat.** He called the other two types "untested" and felt that the French style would be more likely to hold up to an army retreating in panic. He was probably right, but it is interesting to note that the "Young Napoleon" based much of his planning on the possibility of failure rather than the opportunity for success.

5. **Engineer Daniel Woodbury took the blame for the late delivery of pontoons to Fredericksburg.** Many hands were dirty in that mess. James Duane, George McClellan's chief engineer, ignored an order from McClellan to bring the pontoons to Washington. Commanding general Henry Halleck gave a vague order and never told Ambrose Burnside, whose men were waiting for the bridges, that they would be late. Burnside did not follow up and then launched an attack anyway after he had lost the advantage of

surprise. Woodbury was sent to take a new command on the Florida coast and died of yellow fever there.

6. **A pontoon train on the march was nearly a mile long for a 450- to 1,000-foot-long bridge.** The train consisted of 34 pontoon wagons, 22 wagons hauling decking, 4 tool wagons, 2 forge wagons, and 368 horses and mules. The Army of the Potomac had ten to fifteen such trains, usually traveling with either division or corps headquarters.

7. **Pontoons were placed twenty feet apart.** Pontoons were put into the water upstream from the bridge and floated or rowed into position. When they were in the right place, the men dropped an anchor. A trained company of engineers could put a bridge in place in a surprisingly short period.

8. **Supporting beams were called balks.** These timbers were five inches square and twenty-seven feet long. They ran from the outside of one pontoon to the outside wall of the next and were lashed into place. It took four men to carry them. In transit, they traveled on the same wagon as the pontoons. The builders also lashed side rails, of the same size, into place on top of the decking on both sides.

9. **The decking was called chess.** The planks were thirteen feet long and tapered on both ends to allow for lashing the chess to the balk and the side rails on top. Sometimes, dirt or pine boughs were put on top of the chess to muffle the sound of the wheels.

10. **Men marching in step can cause rhythmic shaking that can destroy a bridge.** Soldiers marching in step can create a rhythmic bouncing called resonant frequency. That movement can dangerously shake any bridge, especially a pontoon structure. Engineering officers controlled the traffic on all pontoon bridges and had to educate the civilian colonels about such restrictions.

11. **The James River bridge started at Wilcox Landing.** Disengaging in the presence of the enemy is a delicate move. Everything has to go right, and if the army disengaging shows its hand, the troops remaining in the enemy's presence can be in big trouble. The movement to the James went almost perfectly, but at Petersburg the

battle went badly. Rather than quickly taking the city, Grant had to settle into a long siege.

12. **The bridge to the south side of the James River was handled by Henry Benham.** A highly regarded engineer who was first in the West Point class of 1837, Benham had command of troops in South Carolina and was badly defeated in the Battle of Secessionville. It cost him his rank of brigadier general of volunteers, and he reverted to engineering duty with the Army of the Potomac as a lieutenant colonel. Back in his natural element, he performed well. Building a superb bridge from Wilcox Landing to City Point reestablished his reputation and won him promotion to colonel in the regular army.

6. Spies and Irregular Operations

1. **(J) The Georgia railroad raider was James Andrews.** He was a man of mystery, possibly born in Finland and a former Russian army officer although other reports say otherwise. He led twenty-two Ohio soldiers on the famous locomotive raid and chase. After an eighty-seven-mile run, the Union men fled but were all captured. Andrews and seven others were hanged and the rest sent to prisons. When finally exchanged, the survivors became the first to receive the new Medal of Honor.

2. **(D) John Yates Beall seized a ship on Lake Michigan.** This Virginia officer put together a team to seize the USS *Michigan* on Lake Erie and use it to free the Confederate prisoners on Johnson's Island. They seized a lake steamer, the *Philo Parsons*, but the plan unraveled when their man onshore was arrested as a spy. Beall was later captured near the Canadian border and hanged on Governors Island, New York.

3. **(K) Belle Boyd aided Stonewall Jackson at Front Royal.** She used her father's Front Royal hotel to gather information and keep Jackson and Ashby informed. She was betrayed to the Union by a lover and held in the Old Capitol Prison. Later, in ill health, she

sailed for Europe, but her blockade-runner was captured. She promptly fell in love with the leader of the prize crew who allowed her to escape. After the war, she enjoyed a career on the stage.

4. **(C) James Dunwoody Bulloch secured ships for the Confederacy.** The half brother of Teddy Roosevelt's mother, Bulloch was a U.S. Navy officer when the war began. He refused to hand over his ship to the Confederates and delivered it to the North before resigning and joining the South. Sent to Europe, he skirted English and French Admiralty law to obtain the CSS *Alabama*, CSS *Florida*, and other valuable ships for the Confederacy.

5. **(E) William B. Cushing destroyed the Albemarle.** He was one of the great daredevils of the war. He led two small boats up the Roanoke River and sank the dreaded Confederate ram *Albemarle*. Only Cushing and one other man of his fifteen-man party escaped capture or death. He performed equally valuable service at New River and Fort Fisher. He was the younger brother of Alonzo Cushing, who died directing his artillery battery at the high-water mark at Gettysburg.

6. **(H) Sarah Emma Edmonds could pass for a man or different women, white or black.** She was born in Canada and passed as a man before the war. Her first attempt to enlist as a man failed when she flunked the physical because she was too short. Later accepted, she served as a hospital steward before volunteering to do spy duty. She excelled because in disguise she could pass for either a man or a woman, white or black. In Kentucky in 1863 she came down with malaria and deserted because she feared her secret would be discovered. After the war she had her desertion removed from her record and was the only female member of the Union veterans' organization, Grand Army of the Republic.

7. **(F) Rose O'Neal Greenhow was a Washington spy.** She used her Washington social and political contacts to gather information for the Confederates. Some credit her with giving P. G. T. Beauregard and Joe Johnston sufficient advance warning of Irvin McDowell's advance to allow them to unite and defeat Union forces at First

266

Manassas/Bull Run. Imprisoned, first in her home and later in the Old Capital Prison, she continued to spy. The Union sent her to Richmond, and the Confederates sent her to Europe to build sympathy for their cause. On her return, she drowned off Cape Fear, weighted down by the English gold she had sewn into her clothing.

8. **(G) John W. Headley's target was New York.** One of John Hunt Morgan's Raiders, Headley led a party of Confederate officers down from Canada to burn New York City. They were unaware that a double agent had sold them out and that detectives were shadowing them. They managed to set fires in nineteen hotels and Barnum's Museum, but little damage was done. One member of the team, Robert C. Kennedy, was captured and hanged at Fort Lafayette in New York Harbor.

9. **(A) Allan Pinkerton found too many Confederates.** He virtually invented the detective business, but his work for McClellan only fed the general's paranoia of being outnumbered by the Confederates. After the war, his agency was highly successful, especially at strike breaking. Some claim that the term "fink," describing one who informs, was originally "pink" as in Pinkerton detective.

10. **(I) The Confederates' man in Canada was Jacob Thompson.** He was a Mississippi secessionist but briefly served as a member of James Buchanan's cabinet. He directed various raids and spying operations from Canada. At the end of the war he fled to England, where former Confederate officials accused him of taking rebel funds for his own. The charge probably had merit. He was a wealthy man after the war thanks to as much as $300,000 in Confederate gold that found its way into his pocket.

11. **(B) Bennett H. Young robbed banks in Vermont.** Another of Morgan's Raiders, he led the raid on St. Albans, Vermont. Most of his group escaped back across the Canadian border. A posse chased them into Canada and captured them there, but Canadian officials seized them. Later, when the Canadians released them, it touched off American outrage and official protests. After the war,

Young wrote a book on his war adventures but not a word on St. Albans. He still feared prosecution for bank robbery.

7. The Medal of Honor

1. **George Washington created the award.** Washington saw a need for such a medal and created the Badge of Military Merit in 1782. It fell into disuse, but during the Mexican War, it was revived as the Medal of Merit. In December 1861 Lincoln approved a Navy Medal of Valor that was later adopted by the Army, too.

2. **Thomas Custer won two of them.** After serving three years in the ranks of the Twenty-First Ohio Infantry, Tom Custer enlisted as a lieutenant in the Sixth Michigan Cavalry. He quickly transferred to his famous brother's staff. In April 1865, he won his first medal for capturing an enemy flag at Namozine Church. Later in the month, he jumped his horse into the enemy works at Sayler's Creek, captured two more stands of colors, had his horse shot out from under him, and received a wound. He stayed in the army as a captain (brevet lt. colonel) and was killed with his brother at Little Bighorn.

3. **The first two colonels of the Twentieth Maine won them.** West Pointer Adelbert Ames, the regiment's first commander, won his medal for service at First Bull Run before he commanded the Twentieth Maine. Joshua Chamberlain won his medal for his famous defense of Little Round Top on the second day at Gettysburg.

4. **The only woman to win one was Dr. Mary Edwards Walker.** Flamboyant and controversial, she was a women's rights advocate and—horror of all horrors—she wore bloomers. Unable to obtain an appointment as an army surgeon, she volunteered in the Patent Office Hospital in Washington. George Thomas appointed her assistant surgeon of the Fifty-Second Ohio, but she was captured and exchanged. After that experience, she was kept out of the field. She was awarded the medal in June 1865, but the army changed the

rules in 1917 and asked her to return the medal. She refused and wore it every day. Long after her death, President Jimmy Carter restored her medal status.

5. **Horace Porter won his medal at Chickamauga.** A class of 1860 West Pointer, he served in ordnance and rose to the rank of lieutenant colonel. At Chickamauga, he rallied enough men to allow wagons and artillery to escape. He caught Grant's eye, and the general added Porter to his staff. His book, *Campaigning with Grant,* is still widely read.

6. **Negro sergeant major Christian Fleetwood was a winner.** Born free in Baltimore, he was a newspaper editor, musician, and member of the American Colonization Society before the war. At Chaffin's Farm near Richmond, he led a section of his regiment, the Fourth USCT, in a charge. When the color bearer went down, he seized the national colors and continued. Forced to fall back, he used the colors to rally his men and continue the fight. Every officer in the regiment signed a petition asking that he become an officer. Secretary of War Edwin Stanton rejected it, not crossing the color line. After the war, Fleetwood was a major in the District of Columbia militia.

7. **The members of the Honor Guard for Lincoln's body were awarded medals.** The 1917 review board decided that the medal should not be awarded for noncombat duties, so those medals were also revoked.

8. **John Schofield was the highest-ranking winner.** Wilson's Creek was nominally a Confederate victory, but the audacity of Schofield's commander Nathan Lyon, who lost his life there, helped keep Missouri in the Union. Schofield rose rapidly in rank and commanded the Department of Missouri, where both sides complained bitterly about his partisanship toward the other. Later, he won the Battle of Franklin, Tennessee, and commanded troops in North Carolina cooperating with Sherman. He went on to become commanding general of the army.

9. **Alexander Webb won his medal for turning back Pickett's Charge.** He was one of those valuable young West Pointers (class of 1855)

who moved from staff work to command the Philadelphia brigade. That position put him in the crosshairs of Pickett's Charge, where he won his Medal of Honor. A later report of the battle by II Corps staff officer Frank Haskell cast doubt on the bravery of the brigade and resulted in something of a feud. After the war, he spent more than three decades as president of the City College of New York.

10. **Absalom Baird played a key role near Atlanta.** A West Pointer from the class of 1849, he commanded a brigade in Sherman's army when he led his successful attack at Jonesborough, the battle that forced John Hood to evacuate Atlanta. Baird remained in the army after the war and retired a brigadier general.

11. **The Twenty-Seventh Maine received 864 medals.** A nine-month regiment, the men were in the Washington defenses and due for discharge when the Gettysburg Campaign was fought. Desperate for manpower, the men were offered medals if they would stay on until the crisis past. More than three hundred members of the regiment volunteered and remained four extra days. Because no reliable list was available, the entire unit was issued medals. This matter later came to light when a barrel loaded with Medals of Honor was found in the attic of a Maine farmhouse. The 1917 review invalidated these awards, too.

12. **Harvard lawyer Manning Force was among the winners.** He prepared for West Point but switched to Harvard and the law. The advent of the war allowed him a second chance at a military career and he made the most of it, rising from major to brigadier general and division commander. He fought in the western army from Fort Donelson through Sherman's Carolina Campaign.

8. "Damn the Torpedoes!"

1. **Fort Gaines and Fort Morgan guarded Mobile Bay.** Fort Morgan was the larger structure on Mobile Point to the east and directly on the shipping channel. Fort Gaines to the west was on Dauphin Island. The bay entrance is about thirty miles from the city.

2. **Fort Powell at Grant's Pass guards the other entrance.** A less formidable work than Gaines and Morgan, it defended the bay from an incursion from Mississippi Sound.

3. **Farragut had two new monitors with twin turrets.** The originals had one revolving turret. The new ships were USS *Winnebago* and USS *Chickasaw*. The other ships were conventional monitors, USS *Tecumseh* and USS *Manhattan*.

4. **Ships would enter two by two.** Weaker ships were tied to the more powerful ones and they entered in a line of double ships. The monitors, anchored off Sand Island, swung inside the formation to place themselves between Fort Morgan and the wooden ships.

5. **Farragut had himself lashed to the rigging.** He climbed to a position directly below the mainmast platform with his telescope, and a lieutenant tied him in place so he could not fall. From that exposed position he directed the battle.

6. **The battle started to go badly when the USS *Brooklyn* stopped and started to reverse.** Fearing he would end up in front of the monitors and seeing the "torpedo" or mine fields dead ahead, Capt. James Alden panicked. Farragut's famed command to Alden—"Damn the torpedoes, full speed ahead!"—might not have been his exact words, but they certainly catch the spirit of his order.

7. **The sinking of the monitor *Tecumseh* was the Union's main loss.** The ship struck a torpedo and went down. Only 21 members of the 113-man crew escaped. Among those who drowned was Capt. Tunis A. M. Craven.

8. **Many of the torpedoes were damaged by marine worms.** As the ships passed over the torpedoes, crew members reported hearing the torpedoes' primers snapping, but they did not explode. A later inspection showed a buildup of marine worms on the mechanisms that apparently rendered them impotent.

9. **Inside the bay, the Union fleet faced the Confederate ironclad *Tennessee*.** Farragut delayed his attack until the monitors arrived because he did not want to fight the *Tennessee* with wooden ships only. In the fight that followed, his instincts would prove right.

10. **Franklin Buchanan was aboard the *Tennessee*.** James D. Johnston was the captain, but Adm. Franklin Buchanan, famed as the captain of the *Virginia* (*Merrimack*), was in overall command and had his flag on the *Tennessee*. He emerged from the battle a prisoner of war with a broken leg.

11. **The *Tennessee*'s major problem was a lack of power.** The Confederates built great ironclads but lacked the capacity to provide them with equally powerful engines. Union firepower made little impact on its sides, but with its steering and gun ports damaged and its stack shot away, the *Tennessee* was forced to surrender.

12. **With the fleet in the bay, Powell was evacuated and Morgan and Gaines surrendered.** Powell lacked guns on the bay side and was doomed when Union ships entered the bay. Gaines surrendered when its officers saw nothing more to be done, but Morgan took a battering before it gave in. While the city of Mobile would not fall until early April, blockading was finished there, and Farragut's victory largely negated the city's value.

9. Fort Fisher, 1864

1. **Gideon Welles wanted Fort Fisher taken.** The secretary of the navy understood the blockade-runners' importance as the lifeline to General Lee's army, and he knew that only a combined army and navy force could capture the fort and close Wilmington.

2. **William H. C. Whiting designed and built Fort Fisher.** A graduate of Georgetown, where he set academic records, and West Point, where he finished first in his class, Whiting was a brilliant engineer. He commanded a division under Lee in Virginia, but Lee was dissatisfied and shunted him off to North Carolina.

3. **William Lamb was the colonel commanding the fort.** He was a publisher in Norfolk, Virginia, at the outbreak of the war and rose from captain to colonel while commanding coast artillery batteries and eventually Fort Fisher. Lamb supervised some of the fort's construction.

4. **Maj. Gen. Benjamin Butler and Adm. David Dixon Porter commanded the joint attacking force.** In a war filled with towering egos, these men stood out. The mixture almost guaranteed competition and failure. Grant and Sherman worked well with Porter at Vicksburg, but most of the time he clashed with other generals. Butler, a politician turned general, was equally a glory seeker with no desire to share credit with anyone.

5. **Grant selected Maj. Gen. Godfrey Weitzel to lead the effort.** Second in his West Point class of 1855, he was the chief engineer for Butler's Army of the James before being promoted to command the all-Negro XXV Corps. But Butler could not resist going along on the expedition, thus relegating the more competent Weitzel to the number two spot.

6. **Butler planned to use a powder ship.** Butler was convinced that a ship loaded with explosives could level the fort and stun the garrison. The navy scoffed but Butler got his way. The men stripped the blockader *Louisiana* to look like a blockade-runner and packed it with explosives and fuses.

7. **The powder ship plan fizzled.** While Butler was still at Hilton Head, Porter hijacked the *Louisiana*, set it adrift toward the fort, and exploded it. As Porter had predicted, it did little damage. The garrison hardly noticed. The ship did not get close enough.

8. **Braxton Bragg was sent to save the day.** He was always a favorite of President Davis's, but by that time Bragg had few other friends. One Southern newspaper stated it plainly: "General Bragg has been sent to Wilmington. Good-bye, Wilmington." Bragg was militarily competent but had little ability to get along with people.

9. **Lee sent troops under Robert Hoke.** His division consisted of troops from North Carolina, South Carolina, and Georgia, or the brigades of Brig. Gen. Thomas Clingman, Brig. Gen. Johnson Hagood, and Brig. Gen. Alfred Colquitt. Earlier in the year, Hoke's division had been in North Carolina but was sent to reinforce Beauregard at Petersburg.

10. **(C) The Union naval force consisted of sixty-four fighting ships.** They ranged in size from the huge fifty-gun USS *Colorado* to the tiny *Fort Donelson* with one. It was the largest combined army and navy operation until World War II.

11. **Brig. Gen. Adelbert Ames and Brig. Gen. Charles Paine commanded the divisions in the attacking force.** Ames was a West Pointer and the first colonel of the Twentieth Maine. He was married to General Butler's daughter. Paine, a Boston lawyer, rose to brigadier general and led black troops in the battle.

12. **When naval gunfire ended, Colonel Lamb ordered his troops out of the bomb-proof areas to fire on the attackers.** Colonel Lamb assumed that the Union force was about to assault the fort and rushed his troops into position to defend.

13. **This tactic convinced Butler to end the campaign.** He could see that the massive naval bombardment had accomplished almost nothing. Deteriorating weather and the fear of being caught between the fort and an attacking force from Wilmington also figured into his decision.

14. **N. Martin Curtis's brigade was stranded on the beach for two days.** Reluctant to break off the attack, Curtis was the last to return to the landing zone and by that time windswept seas prevented his returning to the ships. After two days they were pulled off, much to the disgust of the Fort Fisher officers who thought that Bragg should have captured them.

15. **Butler was sacked.** With Lincoln reelected, the administration no longer needed him. And with his sad record of inept field command, Grant was only too glad to be rid of him. A week later the fort fell to a new Union attack.

10. Breakthrough

1. **Lee's last attack was at Fort Stedman.** Troops under Maj. Gen. John Gordon attacked the fort and briefly held it, but a Union counterattack and artillery fire pinned them down. The

Confederates lost 3,500 men in the gamble, including about 1,900 prisoners.

2. **The spring offensive began when Phil Sheridan returned.** Fresh from crushing Jubal Early and laying waste to the great valley of Virginia, he was ready to stretch the Confederate lines to the breaking point.

3. **Sheridan's job was to cut the Boydton Plank Road and the Southside Railroad.** They were Lee's last links to supplies from the south and west. Without them he could not remain in the Petersburg lines.

4. **Petersburg was doomed when Sheridan took Five Forks.** Maj. Gen. Thomas Rosser was hosting Maj. Gen. George Pickett and Maj. Gen. Fitzhugh Lee at a shad bake two miles away when Sheridan struck. Union forces captured more than half of the ten thousand Confederate troops. It's doubtful if the Union attack could have been stopped even if all three officers had been there, but their absence sure looked bad.

5. **Sheridan sacked corps commander Gouverneur K. Warren.** The fiery Sheridan accused him of not being aggressive enough. Warren was a skilled engineer but not a distinguished leader of infantry. Fourteen years after the war he was cleared of the charges, but his career was ruined.

6. **Grant ordered the rest of his troops to attack all along the line.** He wanted to keep the Confederates pinned down so they could not send reinforcements to Pickett. He also hoped that some weak point in the line might crack. It did.

7. **The initial breakthrough was made by the VI Corps under Horatio Wright.** The Connecticut native had already matured plans for rushing a point in his front where a swamp created a weak point in the Confederate line. His predawn attack broke through the line.

8. **Ambrose Powell Hill was killed in the confused fighting.** He commanded the portion of the line where the VI Corps broke through. Riding to the scene of the action with only one other

man, he encountered two soldiers from the 138th Pennsylvania who shot him dead.

9. **Corps command went to Henry Heth.** Lee placed him in command of the scattered remnants of Hill's III Corps, but by that time it was hardly more than a division.

10. **Twenty-six-year-old Maj. Gen. Nelson Appleton Miles won a battle at Sutherland Station.** He would go on to win both fame and criticism as Jeff Davis's jailer and, after the war, as an Indian fighter.

11. **Fort Gregg and Fort Whitworth slowed the Union attack.** The Union finally took the positions, but the Confederate defenders bought time for the first of Longstreet's Corps to arrive from Richmond.

12. **Lee's retreat plan took him to Amelia Court House.** Lee had ordered supplies to be waiting there. The Confederates hoped to either set up a new capital in Lynchburg or unite with Joe Johnston in North Carolina, but the race would end at Appomattox Court House.

11. The Last Ditch

1. **Lee was trying to find rations at Amelia Court House.** He had ordered them, but they were not there. He spent the day scouring the countryside for food for his hungry men, a delay he later termed "fatal."

2. **Confederate troops were retreating from Richmond, Petersburg, and Chester.** Chester is midway between the two and north and west of Bermuda Hundred. All three columns were to converge on Amelia Court House.

3. **There were also units retreating from Five Forks.** The Confederates were forced to extend their lines south and west. When Sheridan broke through there, those troops also joined the retreat.

4. **The first rear guard action came at Namozine Creek or Namozine Church.** Custer jumped the Confederate cavalry screen there but met a bloody repulse when infantry under Bushrod Johnson came to the cavalry's aid.

5. **Union cavalry and infantry blocked the retreat at Jetersville.** This important maneuver cut Lee off from using the railroad for moving supplies and troops. When the V Corps came and dug in, Lee had to find another way west.

6. **On April 6, cavalry and the VI Corps trapped Confederate units at Sayler's Creek.** Between seven thousand and eight thousand men—or almost a third of Lee's army—were captured. Among them were Generals Richard Ewell, Joseph Kershaw, Custis Lee, Dudley Du Bose, Eppa Hunton, and Montgomery Corse.

7. **Longstreet almost lost his race for High Bridge.** Rosser stopped a Union attempt to take the railroad bridge over Appomattox Gorge. Lee was sidestepping the Union forces at Jetersville to reach the South Side Railroad at Farmville.

8. **James Dearing was the last Confederate general killed in the war.** The Virginian attended the Military Academy, class of '62, but resigned when Virginia seceded. He rose from lieutenant to brigadier general. He died at Lynchburg a few days after the surrender. Some are reluctant to list him as the last general killed because the Confederate congress had not acted on his appointment.

9. **Union pursuers suffered a sharp repulse at Cumberland Church.** Confederate infantry dug in and stopped the Union advance north and west of Farmville before continuing their retreat. It would be the last successful fight for the Army of Northern Virginia.

10. **Fitz Lee realized that the Union Cavalry was riding around them because the cavalry was not behind them.** Fitz Lee, riding two miles behind Longstreet and two miles ahead of the Union II Corps, recognized what was happening and warned his uncle, Robert E. Lee.

11. **When Lee tried to punch through at Appomattox he found Union infantry.** When Lee saw that Maj. Gen. Edward Ord and the Army of the James had joined Sheridan's cavalry he knew the fight was done.

12. **Wilmer McLean's previous address was Manassas, Virginia.** After the First Battle of Bull Run, fought partly on his property, McLean

sought a quieter place away from the war. Four years later, it would end in his new parlor. Another of those great ironies!

12. The End of the Road

1. **Lee said he'd rather "die a thousand deaths."** Most people would probably prefer surrender to dying even one death, but Lee probably meant it. Still, his iron self-discipline and sense of duty carried him through what must have been the worst day of his life.

2. **The surrender took place on Palm Sunday.** Many of the men saw a significance to it, a rebirth after being close to violent death for so long. But some Southerners cursed and wept, angry that the end had come.

3. **Lee arrived first.** Grant was a distance away and kept Lee waiting for about a half hour before he reached the McLean house. When he arrived, Grant was muddy from the field. Lee was decked out in his best uniform for the occasion. The contrast must have been striking.

4. **Grant had the better memory.** Captain Lee of the engineers was the son of a famous Revolutionary War hero, as well as a man of distinction in his own right. Grant was simply a face in the crowd. Lee was aware they had met but said he could not recall a single feature of Grant's.

5. **The only officer with Lee was Lt. Col. Charles Marshall.** A valuable member of Lee's tiny staff, he was great-grand nephew of Chief Justice John Marshall and the uncle of Gen. George Marshall of World War II. He was educated at the University of Virginia and had taught at the University of Indiana before practicing law in Baltimore. Lee had planned to also take along his military secretary, Walter Taylor, but Taylor declined.

6. **The lone Rebel on the front lawn was Sgt. George W. Tucker.** A daredevil courier, he rode to the surrender with Lee, Marshall, and their Union escort, Lt. Col. Orville Babcock, who was also Grant's aide-de-camp. Tucker's job was to hold the horses, but it must have

been an uncomfortable assignment. Tucker, by the way, was the same man riding with A. P. Hill the morning he was killed at Petersburg.

7. **Grant and Lee were seated at two small tables.** Louis Guillaume's romanticized painting of the surrender shows the two generals seated together. It is inaccurate, as are many of the paintings of the scene.

8. **Lee may have thought Ely was a black man.** Parker was a full-blooded Seneca Indian and sachem of his tribe. A lawyer and engineer, he served Grant faithfully and well during the war. It was his hand that copied the official form of the surrender documents.

9. **Lee commented, "This will have a happy effect on my army."** Lee seemed relieved that his army would be paroled and not held prisoner. His men would all be on the way home in a few days.

10. **Lee asked for horses.** He pointed out that in the Confederate army, cavalrymen and some artillerists had brought their own horses. He realized that the men would need these animals when spring crops were planted.

11. **Lee chatted with Brig. Gen. Seth Williams.** A West Pointer from Maine, he had extensive experience in the adjutant general's department. McClellan brought him onto his staff, and he remained on the staff of the Army of the Potomac until the end of the war.

12. **Lee was sent twenty-five thousand rations.** Lee could not know the exact number of men he had left. He lost a large chunk of his command at Sayler's Creek and many more from straggling and desertion. The supplies provided to the Confederates may have come from the railroad cars that Sheridan and Custer captured at Appomattox Station.

13. **History is not precisely certain how many men were in the room.** Lee and Marshall were the only Confederates. Grant was there with much of his staff plus field commanders Sheridan and Ord. Custer, present in many of the paintings, was not there; indeed, he had been told to stay away. The best guess is that somewhere between

fifteen and twenty people were present. Some fanciful paintings show political figures who were not within a hundred miles of the place.

14. **On parting, Grant saluted Lee.** Grant stepped into the yard as Lee was mounting his horse and lifted his hat in salute. The other Union officers present followed his example. The lifting of the hat was a common form of salute then.

15. **McLean put in a claim for stolen and destroyed furniture.** Everybody wanted a souvenir and some attempted to buy tables, chairs, and other items. When McLean refused, a wild scramble followed, with his belongings going out the door and couches shredded. Even bricks disappeared. Union soldiers kidnapped Lula McLean's rag doll, naming it the Silent Witness, and threw it about. The doll finally found its way back to the McLean house in 1992. The museum gift shop does a brisk business in replicas.

SECTION VIII

ONE NATION

The American nation was saved but at what cost? The price in human life and property was enormous. Much was left unresolved. A century would pass before the issue of the freedmen's rights would even begin to be addressed. But we would, once again, stand as one nation and take our place on the world stage as a powerful force for good. In two world wars and the Cold War, we would rescue the old world from totalitarian powers. A splintered America could not have done that. A hundred and fifty years later, we still ponder the meaning of this period, but without passing through this crucible, could we have become the America of today?

Despite the bitterness of the conflict, Americans are one people, joined by optimism and the desire for a fair opportunity to profit from our own efforts. Generals often had a hard time keeping the soldiers from working out their own cease-fire arrangements and swapping tobacco, coffee, newspapers, and gossip. This statue, *Moment of Mercy* by Terry Jones, is based on an incident at the Battle of Fredericksburg. Union attacks met a bloody repulse and Union wounded and dead were scattered in front of the Confederate position behind a stone wall. Unable to bear the piteous cries of the wounded, Sgt. Richard Rowland Kirkland gained permission to take water to the wounded. He knew he was taking a huge risk, but both sides held their fire. Sadly, the brave Kirkland, later a lieutenant, was killed in the Battle of Chickamauga. The statue is on the grounds of the National Civil War Museum in Harrisburg, Pennsylvania. *Photo by the author*

QUIZ 1
"Now He Belongs to the Ages"

At the apex of his fame and glory, Abraham Lincoln was struck down by an assassin's bullet. The nation was outraged and Southern leaders feared repercussions. In the hours following the attack, a remarkable drama played out in a boardinghouse across from Ford's Theatre in Washington.

1. On the day he was assassinated, Lincoln's first appointment was with a politician who had a direct tie to John Wilkes Booth. Who was he?

2. One couple invited to join the Lincolns at the theater that night begged off and were on a train heading for New York when Booth struck. Who were they?

3. The other man in the theater box was wounded trying to stop Booth. Who was he, and who was his date?

4. Who was the police officer assigned to guard the president that night?

5. The first doctor to reach the stricken president was a young army surgeon. What was his name?

6. A young man was brought in to record testimony and events. He was?

7. When Lincoln died, who made the famous statement, "Now he belongs to the Ages"?

8. What general commanded the honor guard that took the president's body to the White House?

9. Who performed the autopsy and where?

10. Where did the president's body lie in state?

11. A second coffin was on the funeral train. Why?

12. How many miles did the train cover on the trip to Springfield?

Quiz 2
War's Long Shadow

Wars cast long shadows. Many who served as young men went on to have long and productive lives and to father children who would make an impact on the world themselves. For others, the postwar period brought bitter disappointment. Let's see what you know about these people.

1. On the Antietam battlefield near Burnside's bridge stands an elaborate monument to a commissary sergeant of the Twenty-Third Ohio who coolly served hot coffee and food to his regiment while they were under fire. Who was he and where did he go after the war?

2. This young Massachusetts captain reportedly gave Lincoln some sound if impolitic advice while the president was under fire during Jubal Early's 1864 raid on Washington. Who was he and what was his postwar career?

3. With American military employment out of the question for former Confederates, some took their experience and talents abroad. This Floridian former "boy soldier" of the Seminole War, Mexican War hero, and Confederate general took his military career to Egypt. Name him.

4. This Massachusetts-born member of the Twenty-Fourth Wisconsin rose from adjutant to lieutenant colonel and won the Medal of Honor. He stayed in the army and rose to brigadier general in the Spanish-American War, but he is best remembered as the father of an even more famous military son. He was?

5. This Confederate colonel was a great-grandson of Revolutionary War hero Hugh Mercer, and he had two brothers who commanded Virginia regiments. He did not survive the war, but his bloodline did and his namesake grandson was one of the best-known generals of World War II. Name the grandfather.

6. The highest-ranking American general killed by enemy fire in World War II was the son and namesake of a Kentucky West Pointer who served the Confederacy in the West. When he died, he was the longest-surviving Confederate general above the rank of brigadier. He was?

7. He was a Union officer from Michigan who won the Medal of Honor at Fair Oaks and later led a black regiment. He stayed in the army and led U.S. troops in Cuba, but he was so heavy he could not mount a horse and had to ride in a buggy that sagged in the middle from his great weight. Name him.

8. This diminutive Georgia-born West Pointer led Confederate cavalry in the West. After the war, he represented Alabama in Congress. In the Spanish-American War, he donned Union blue as a general and is one of the few Confederates to be buried in Arlington National Cemetery. He was?

9. This young Pennsylvania-born engineering officer returned to the family business after the war and built the Brooklyn Bridge. Name him.

10. This Boston crockery clerk took to soldiering and was a twenty-six-year-old general. With three wounds, a Medal of Honor, and division and corps command on his résumé, many had high expectations of him, but his harsh treatment of Jefferson Davis and deceitful dealings with a famous Indian chief tarnished his record. He was?

QUIZ 3
Captured Chieftain

As the Civil War ended, Lee's army was in retreat and the civil government of the Confederacy in flight. The federal government posted a $100,000 reward for the capture of Jeff Davis. Let's see what you know about the events that followed.

1. What article of clothing was Davis wearing when he was captured that led some to claim he was disguised as a woman?
2. In what state was Davis captured?
3. In what "prison" in a city near the site where he was captured was Davis first held?
4. What government facility was he eventually moved to and held until his release?
5. What Union general was his jailer?
6. What controversial step did that jailer order that evoked sympathy for Davis?
7. What was the name of the Union Army doctor who treated Davis, became his friend, and eventually wrote a book about Davis's confinement?
8. What pet did Davis have during his confinement?
9. What prominent Northern editor demanded a speedy trial for Davis?
10. To what crime did the federal government try to tie Davis?
11. What Supreme Court decision made a military court trial of Davis impossible?
12. What two prominent Northerners posted $100,000 bond for Davis's release?

Quiz 4
The Civil War and the Presidency

Between 1856 and 1900, fifteen Civil War generals or other officers ran for president or vice president on both major and minor tickets. See if you can match them up.

The Candidates

1. The Republican presidential candidate in 1880 was a Union major general. His finest hour was at Chickamauga, where he helped Maj. Gen. George Thomas organize and hold his line.

2. The Democrats ran him for president in 1864, hoping his popularity with the soldiers would defeat Lincoln.

3. He never commanded troops but held the rank of general when he was wartime governor of Tennessee.

4. He ran for president on the Prohibition Ticket in 1880. In the army, he is best remembered for being confined a long stretch in the South's Libby Prison.

5. He commanded a corps under Sherman and was the vice-presidential candidate for the Democrats in 1868.

6. Military success led him to head the Republican ticket in 1868 and 1872.

7. This Confederate general ran for vice president in 1856 and for president in 1860.

8. He enlisted as a private and ended a major. The Republican Party ran him for the White House in 1896 and 1900.

9. This superb Union corps commander was the Democratic presidential candidate in 1880.

10. An Ohio brigadier general was the Republican standard bearer in the centennial year election.

11. This Kentuckian was a general, a congressman, territorial governor of Montana, and Prohibition candidate for president in 1876.

12. This famous if unsuccessful Union general was the first Republican to run for president.

13. One of the Union's most controversial generals was the Greenback candidate for president in 1884.

14. This Union brevet brigadier from a famous Southern family ran for president twice. He won once and lost once, although he lost the popular vote both times.

15. This Kentucky-born Illinois politician and corps commander ran for president in 1896 as the candidate of a wing of the Democratic Party.

The Men

A. Francis Preston Blair Jr.

B. John Cabell Breckenridge

C. Benjamin Franklin Butler

D. Neal Dow

E. John Charles Frémont

F. James Abram Garfield

G. Ulysses Simpson Grant

H. Winfield Scott Hancock

I. Benjamin Harrison

J. Rutherford Birchard Hayes

K. Andrew Johnson

L. George Brinton McClellan

M. William McKinley

N. John McAuley Palmer

O. Green Clay Smith

ANSWERS

1. "Now He Belongs to the Ages"

1. **Lincoln's appointment was with Senator John P. Hale.** Lincoln had recently appointed the New Hampshire senator the minister to Spain. Hale's daughter Lucy was engaged to John Wilkes Booth. Some questioned that relationship, but when Booth was killed he was carrying a picture of Lucy Hale.

2. **On the train were General and Mrs. Grant.** Grant attended a cabinet meeting that day that dealt with Reconstruction policy. He declined the theater invitation because he and Julia had promised to visit their children in New York. Others, including Mr. and Mrs. Edwin Stanton, were later invited. Stanton lectured Lincoln about the danger of public appearances.

3. **The couple with the Lincolns was Maj. Henry Rathbone and Clara Harris.** Booth slashed Rathbone on the arm. Major Rathbone of the Twelfth Infantry was the stepson of New York senator Ira Harris and Clara was the senator's daughter. They married, but the marriage ended tragically. Rathbone was appointed U.S. counsel to Hanover, Germany, where he murdered Clara and spent his final years in a German hospital for the insane.

4. **John Parker was the policeman assigned to guard the president.** He had the reputation of being less than reliable. He was assigned to guard the box door, but he moved to the audience to get a better view of the play. At intermission, he joined Lincoln's driver and a footman at a local saloon for a drink. However, some have speculated that Lincoln himself may have told Parker to go and enjoy the play because a later hearing exonerated him from blame. Despite repeated warnings about his safety, Lincoln took the position that if assassins wanted to kill him they would probably succeed. Sadly, he was right.

5. **Dr. Charles Augustus Leale was the first doctor to reach Lincoln.** The twenty-three-year-old was quickly joined by Dr. Charles Sabin

Taft. Leale almost immediately pronounced the wound mortal. He used his finger to break up a blood clot and probably extended Lincoln's life by several hours. He then performed mouth-to-mouth resuscitation on him and restored his breathing. Doctors Leale and Taft accompanied Lincoln to the back bedroom on the ground floor of the Petersen house and remained with him. At least a half dozen other doctors were there that night at various times. Young Leale remained to the end, holding the president's hand to reassure him should he be conscious enough to be aware of his presence. It was Leale who pronounced him dead.

6. **Cpl. James Tanner came to take notes.** He had lost both legs at Second Bull Run. When officials asked the theater crowd for a man who could take shorthand, Tanner, who lived next door to the Petersen house, volunteered. He recorded testimony of witnesses and made his own notes of the comings and goings and comments being made. History owes him a debt of gratitude.

7. **Edwin Stanton uttered the famous quote.** Interestingly, Tanner heard it differently. He recorded it as "He belongs to the Angels now." It seems likely that Tanner's version is incorrect. It hardly sounds like the gruff and businesslike secretary. Popular reports say that Stanton also stopped the clock in the room. Mary had visited about a half hour before the death but was in the front parlor when the end came. Son Robert leaned his head on the shoulder of Senator Charles Sumner and sobbed. The nation was plunged into mourning.

8. **Christopher Columbus Augur commanded the honor guard.** As commanding officer of the Washington defenses, he rushed to the scene, took over the security of the site, and began the investigation into what had happened. Augur, a New Yorker, was a West Point graduate from the class of 1843. He was severely wounded at Cedar Mountain while leading a division and was second in command at Port Hudson. He was the longest-serving corps commander because he commanded the Washington defenses until the end of the war.

9. **Army Assistant Surgeons Joseph Janvier Woodward and Edward Curtis performed the autopsy at the White House.** Also present were Surgeon General Joseph Barnes; Lincoln's family physician, Dr. Robert King Stone; three more army surgeons; Quartermaster Gen. Daniel Rucker; and Lincoln's friend, Orville Browning. It was a cranial autopsy only. The skull was opened, the brain removed, and the bullet found. Dr. Curtis marveled at the little black mass, no bigger than the end of his finger, that changed history. The autopsy was done in a guest bedroom in the northwest corner of the second floor, now the presidential dining room.

10. **The president's body was to lie in state in the East Room of the White House. Because of the crowds, it was moved to the Capitol Rotunda.** However, it does not end there. The presidential train heading for Springfield, Illinois, followed a route that took it through many of the major population centers of the North. In some cases the train rolled through small towns at a normal clip. At others, it slowed so that the locals could salute their fallen leader. In the major centers, it stopped, and the coffin was unloaded so that the huge crowds could pay their respects. VIPs, naturally, received special treatment, but most of America wanted to share in the moment.

11. **The second coffin contained the remains of Willie Lincoln.** William Wallace Lincoln, the president's third son, died of typhoid fever at age eleven in 1862 in the White House. The Lincolns had always planned to take him home with them. Now he traveled with his dead father. They would, initially, occupy a temporary tomb before being permanently interred at Oak Ridge Cemetery in Springfield. Eventually, all the Lincolns—save one—would be reunited there. The eldest son and the last survivor of the clan, Robert, chose to be buried at Arlington National Cemetery, where he rests with his wife and daughter. His son Jack, who died young, is in the crypt with his grandparents in Springfield.

12. **The train traveled seventeen hundred miles.** That's more than double the direct distance. The train went north through

Baltimore, Philadelphia, and Trenton into New York. Then it went to Albany and west through Syracuse, Rochester, Buffalo, and Cleveland before heading south to Columbus and Indianapolis. Chicago was the last stop before Springfield. As noted previously, the train stopped at some cities, and at several Lincoln was removed for public viewing. The New York stop had 100,000 visitors and a parade with 160,000 marchers. Tiny hamlets along the way built elaborate displays. Hundreds of thousands waited by the track even in the dark and the rain to watch the train roll past.

2. War's Long Shadow

1. **Sgt. William McKinley went to the White House.** He worked his way up past coffee to become a captain and a brevet major. The elaborate coffee memorial and renaming of Mount McKinley in Alaska were part of the buildup for his run for president. The Twenty-Third Ohio produced two presidents—McKinley and Rutherford Hayes. McKinley was the last Civil War soldier to be elected president.

2. **Oliver Wendell Holmes went to the Supreme Court.** He may or may not have said, "Get down, you old fool!" to Lincoln, but his warning was something to that effect while under fire at Fort Stevens. Lincoln and his civilian party had attracted the attention of rebel sharpshooters, and one man standing nearby had been shot. Holmes went on to become one of the great Supreme Court justices, serving on the court for nearly thirty years, and was highly regarded for his writing and his clear and fair logic. He was a brave soldier, too, having received wounds in three major battles.

3. **William Wing Loring went to Egypt.** His life read like an adventure novel, with one success after another until he ran afoul of Stonewall Jackson and was shunted off into western Virginia. He finished the war with the western army. In 1869 he went to Egypt and served there for ten years helping to modernize the Egyptian Army. He rose to the rank of *fereek pasha* (major general).

4. **Arthur MacArthur Jr. sired a famous son.** He had an outstanding military career, but the exploits of his son Douglas, a general in three wars, eclipsed his accomplishments. Arthur enlisted in the Twenty-Fourth Wisconsin and fought in several major western battles. At Missionary Ridge, he carried the regimental flag and planted it on the Confederate ramparts. For this action, he was awarded the Medal of Honor. Arthur and Douglas are the only father and son winners of the nation's top military award for bravery. Arthur's exploits earned him promotions to brevet colonel. He stayed in the army, rose to the rank of major general, and served as governor general of the Philippines. That stint was cut short by disagreements with future president William Howard Taft.

5. **Col. George S. Patton of the Twenty-Second Virginia was grandfather to "Old Blood and Guts" Gen. George S. Patton Jr.** The elder Patton was a Virginia Military Institute graduate who carved out a fine war record, rising from captain to brigade command. He accompanied Jubal Early in his raid on Washington and received a severe leg wound at Third Winchester. He refused amputation and died several days later from blood loss.

6. **Simon Bolivar Buckner's son was killed on Okinawa.** The elder Buckner was a friend of Ulysses Grant's from West Point days and had the dubious honor of surrendering to him at Fort Donelson. Buckner rose to the rank of lieutenant general and performed good service but was never considered in the top tier of Confederate commanders. His friendship with Grant continued after the war, with Buckner serving as a pallbearer at Grant's funeral.

7. **William Rufus Shafter led the army in Cuba.** He had been on the retired list for three years when the Spanish-American War began and seemed an unlikely choice to head the Cuba invasion. Some suspected he was picked because he had no political ambitions. He had little to do with its eventual success. In the Civil War, he started as a lieutenant, was a prisoner of war, and led a black regiment in the Battle of Nashville.

8. **Fighting Joe Wheeler led the cavalry in the West.** He was brought back for the Spanish-American War, largely as a way to unify the country behind it. When his troops were in the thick of it, battling the Spaniards, he reportedly would exhort them to "give it to those damned Yankees!"

9. **Washington Augustus Roebling was an engineer.** He was the son of brilliant German-born engineer John Roebling. The elder Roebling had designed the Brooklyn Bridge and won the commission to build it. After his death, the son did the job. Washington Roebling had an excellent war record, having been on the staff of Gouverneur K. Warren at Gettysburg and playing an important role in the defense of Little Round Top.

10. **Nelson A. Miles went from store clerk to general.** His unnecessarily harsh handling of Jeff Davis at Fort Monroe and his later perfidy in dealing with Geronimo tarnished an otherwise brilliant career. He played a role in capturing both Chief Joseph of the Nez Percé and Geronimo but did not honor the terms of Geronimo's surrender.

3. Captured Chieftain

1. **Davis was wearing a shawl.** On the approach of the Union cavalry, Davis threw a shawl around his shoulders and ran for the horses but was captured before he could reach them. The dress story was created to make Davis appear cowardly by disguising himself as a woman.

2. **He was captured in Georgia.** The party was in southern Georgia less than fifty miles from the Florida State line. They had come a long way, but, of course, they were still a very long way away from escaping the country.

3. **His "jail" was the best hotel in Macon, Georgia.** Davis was held in high style while Washington was notified and the cavalry troopers angled to collect the reward.

4. **Davis was held at Fort Monroe.** It was America's largest fortress at Hampton Roads, Virginia. His prison was one of the casemates, or gun chambers.

5. **His jailer was fort commander Nelson Miles.** A Massachusetts farmer's son and a store clerk at the outbreak of the war, he rose from first lieutenant to major general and corps commander by age twenty-six and in his later years was army commander. The Davis family hated him.

6. **Davis was placed in irons.** Manacles were applied to his ankles. It seemed more a way to make Davis uncomfortable than to prevent his unlikely escape. However, they were removed after only five days.

7. **He received kindly treatment from Col. John Craven.** Although no friend of Davis or the Confederacy at the start, the prison doctor proved a godsend to the imprisoned politician. He came to see Davis as a person and not as the symbol of secession and the war.

8. **His prison pet was a mouse.** Davis and the mouse shared the cell and Davis fed the little creature. Dr. Craven wrote about the mouse in his book. Of course, it made Davis look more human and more compassionate.

9. **Horace Greeley urged a speedy trial.** The editor and publisher of the *New York Tribune* was something of a loose cannon who, eventually, would be found on both sides of almost every issue.

10. **Many hoped to pin the assassination of Abraham Lincoln on Davis.** With Booth dead, many in the North would gladly have hanged Davis, but no real evidence indicated that he had participated in the plot or had any knowledge of it.

11. **The *ex parte Milligan* decision ruled out further military trials.** The high court ruled in December 1866 that the government could not try civilians in military courts where civilian courts were in operation. The ruling rose from the suspension of habeas corpus in Maryland early in the war. Of course, it applied to the situation with Davis.

12. **Gerrit Smith and Horace Greeley bailed him out of jail.** Some of the $100,000 came from Cornelius Vanderbilt and others. Smith, the wealthy abolitionist, and the powerful newspaperman Greeley effectively ended the issue by gaining Davis's release. Charges were later, quietly, dropped.

4. The Civil War and the Presidency

1. **(F) James Abram Garfield.** There are open questions about his loyalty to his commanding officer, William Rosecrans, at Chickamauga and after the battle. Shortly after Chickamauga he left the army to serve in Congress. Elected the twentieth president, he was mortally wounded on his way to attend a reunion at Williams College.

2. **(L) George Brinton McClellan.** Early on it looked as if McClellan might defeat Lincoln, but Union victories at Atlanta, Cedar Creek, and Mobile lifted Northern spirits and the soldiers' vote, which McClellan supporters had counted on, went strongly to Lincoln. McClellan broke with the Democrats over the peace plank of their party platform, but it is impossible to know how he would have reacted had he been elected.

3. **(K) Andrew Johnson.** He was elected vice president in 1864 and became president on the death of Lincoln. However, Johnson reverted to his Democratic Party roots and battled the Radical Republican Congress throughout his presidency.

4. **(D) Neal Dow.** He led the temperance crusade that caused Maine to vote "dry" in 1851 and carried the national banner in 1880. Also a strong abolitionist, he was captured at Port Hudson and the Confederates were reluctant to let him go. He was eventually exchanged for one of the sons of Robert E. Lee.

5. **(A) Francis Preston Blair Jr.** The politically powerful Blair clan all returned to the Democratic Party after the Civil War.

6. **(G) Ulysses Simpson Grant.** He emerged from the war the North's greatest hero, and a grateful nation accorded him its highest honor.

His presidency was marred by scandal, and when friends tried to secure the nomination for him again in 1880, it fell through. Grant was personally honest but politically naive and allowed some supporters to use him.

7. **(B) John Cabell Breckenridge.** He was Buchanan's vice president and the candidate of the Southern Democrats against Lincoln and Douglas. He proved himself a pretty good general and later served the South as secretary of war.

8. **(M) William McKinley.** He defeated William Jennings Bryan twice for the presidency, but shortly after winning his second term anarchist Leon Czolgosz fatally shot him in 1901. McKinley was the last Civil War veteran to be president.

9. **(H) Winfield Scott Hancock.** He was considered a dull candidate, but he lost the popular vote by less than 10,000 out of more than 9 million cast. However, Garfield won the electoral vote by a convincing 214 to 155.

10. **(J) Rutherford Birchard Hayes.** This disputed election landed in the House of Representatives, where Hayes won the job but the Democrats managed to have the occupation troops removed from the South. Many believe that Samuel Tilden actually won the election, but disputed votes from Florida, South Carolina, and Louisiana clouded the issue.

11. **(O) Green Clay Smith.** Despite early success in the war, he proved a flop as a general, and the army was spared a problem when he was elected to Congress in 1863. In his 1876 presidential run, he got only 9,522 votes, proving either the unpopularity of the Prohibition Party or the unpopularity of General Smith.

12. **(E) John Charles Frémont.** The "Pathfinder" was well connected and the darling of the Radicals, but he was mediocre at best as a general. However, his strong showing against Buchanan in 1856 demonstrated that the Republicans would be a force in national politics.

13. **(C) Benjamin Franklin Butler.** The "Beast" had an active mind and a zest for combat but no talent for field leadership and a deficiency in ethics. His lone presidential run garnered only 175,370 votes.

14. **(I) Benjamin Harrison.** Though a descendant of the famous Virginia Harrisons, he had gone to Ohio to seek his fortune and cast his lot with the North. As a military leader he was unpopular with his troops for insisting on rigid discipline.

15. **(N) John McAuley Palmer.** A capable corps commander in the West, he returned to his Democratic roots after the war and headed the National Democrats, or Gold Democrats, in 1896 against McKinley and Bryan.

COMMENTS ON SOURCES

The first important point to make is that answers to Civil War questions are often as much a matter of opinion as a matter of fact. Almost every aspect of this conflict is subject to multiple interpretations. Many of the stories and traditions that have come down to us are either not entirely true or, at least, subject to question. It can be next to impossible to find facts upon which everyone will agree.

In putting these quizzes together, I have tried to stay close to the most popular views of things and to avoid extreme positions. The careful reader may well find sources that disagree with mine. Perhaps that's what makes the Civil War so endlessly fascinating.

Any researcher worth his or her salt will not present facts unless they come from multiple sources. That is my practice. Of course, the reliability of the sources must be considered. For example, I place a great deal more reliance on the work of respected scholars than on that of some unknown fellow who happens to have a website. Internet sources are very helpful, but much material out in cyberspace is also unreliable. Even the books of respected scholars are not totally free from errors. Let the reader beware!

The book that I have relied upon most in building these quizzes is *The Civil War Dictionary* by Mark Mayo Boatner III. Except for a strong West Point and army bias, it is the best single source I have found for military figures, battles, and campaigns. It is less complete for those below the rank of general officer and of persons and issues naval or political.

Another excellent source is *Who Was Who in the Civil War* by Stewart Sifakis. Often, I find people there who are not covered in Boatner's book.

I also keep a six-volume set of *Appleton's Cyclopedia of American Biography*, the 1888 edition edited by James Grant Wilson and John Fiske.

Later versions are less helpful to Civil War scholars because the biographies of lesser figures are dropped to make room for more recent ones. The 1888 set contains most of the major war figures and details of their postwar lives. Although these biographies tread lightly on areas of controversy, they are useful nonetheless.

Also valuable is *Battles and Leaders of the Civil War*. I have the four-volume 1887 set edited by Robert Underwood Johnson and Clarence Clough Buel. The books contain articles on many battles, campaigns, and leaders and are written by prominent participants. This connection guarantees familiarity but not objectivity. Sadly, many military leaders' accounts are self-serving, are aimed at claiming credit or dodging responsibilities, and are too often designed to injure enemies and praise friends. It might be said that Civil War battles happened in two parts—the shooting part and the credit/blame part. The latter included the participants' testimony before congressional committees, their speeches, and their memoirs.

My personal library contains more than 450 volumes related to the Civil War and allows me great flexibility in fact-checking. A book's index allows for a quick lookup and an equally quick review of all references to the subject. By thus cross-referencing multiple sources, I can identify points of general agreement and points of contention.

While I am reluctant to base any quiz primarily on one source, some works are so clearly superior to others on a given subject that relying heavily upon them becomes a necessity. An excellent example is Phillip M. Thienel's *Mr. Lincoln's Bridge Builders: The Right Hand of American Genius*, which is *the* authoritive work on pontoon bridges. Likewise, if you want to know everything about artillery, by far the best source is Augustus Buell's long out-of-print book *The Cannoneer*, which was published in 1890.

Another such gem is Edwin C. Fishel's *The Secret War for the Union: The Untold Story of Military Intelligence in the Civil War*. He details the birth and development of military intelligence operations in the eastern armies.

There was a time when serious students of the Civil War wanted a full set of the Official Records on their shelves, but that was no small investment. Between 1880 and 1910, the government published 128 volumes. They are still available, but they have lost much of their popularity, partly because of their size and partly because the records are now readily available on CD and the Internet. The Internet or CD versions, of course, are far easier to access and search. In either form, they are an essential resource for the serious scholar. The records contain the actual reports, orders, dispatches, and so forth, but they are entirely without annotation.

Beware the "facts" found in Civil War novels. Fiction writers commonly either are ignorant of some facts or intentionally bend them to suit their plot. A few fiction writers are highly knowledgeable of the war and very careful not to distort or exaggerate. However, unless you really know the writer is reliable, a healthy amount of skepticism is in order.

Also, beware of the enamored biographer. One trait that haunts many biographers is their tendency to fall in love with their subjects. Only by reading or consulting several sources can we come to a balanced view of any person or event.

There were many leaders in the Civil War and almost none were either all bad or all good. The best of them made mistakes and misjudgments. Many of the far less successful leaders also had their talents and their moments of productive effort.

The most important point to remember is that education is not simply the accumulation of facts. The greater adventure is to become acquainted with the men and women who played both major and minor roles in our nation's greatest struggle. Find out how they viewed their world and why they risked everything for their belief of what was best for their homeland! When these perspectives become clear, then you will understand your nation better and, perhaps, yourself.

ABOUT THE AUTHOR

Dave Smith grew up in Massachusetts, loving the rich history of the region and stories of his paternal grandfather and maternal great-grandfather, who fought in the Civil War. He joined the U.S. Marine Corps in 1950 and served in Korea before earning a degree in journalism from Boston University.

He began his career in Connecticut as a newspaper reporter, columnist, and editor before moving to business communications. He spent twenty-eight years with a major Hartford insurance company, where he managed the communications department for one of its divisions.

Since his retirement, in addition to volunteer consulting work, he has devoted considerable time to writing and lecturing on the Civil War.

He makes his home in Old Saybrook, Connecticut, with his wife, Joan.